*Women in the Field*

# Women in the Field

## AMERICA'S
## PIONEERING WOMEN NATURALISTS

### Marcia Myers Bonta

TEXAS A&M UNIVERSITY PRESS
*College Station*

Quotations in chapter 25, on Rachel Carson, are used courtesy
the following sources: Paul Brooks, *House of Life*, © 1976 by
Paul Brooks, reprinted by permission of Houghton Mifflin, Co.;
Dorothy Seif's manuscript, © 1987 by Roger Christie, reprinted
by permission of Frances Collin, Trustee; and Shirley Briggs, "A
Decade after Silent Spring," reprinted by permission of Frances
Collin, Trustee.

The paper used in this book meets the minimum requirements
of the American National Standard for Permanence of Paper for
Printed Library Materials, Z39.48-1984. Binding materials have
been chosen for durability.

∞

*Library of Congress Cataloging-in-Publication Data*
Bonta, Marcia, 1940–   .
     Women in the field : America's pioneering women naturalists /
Marcia Myers Bonta. — 1st ed.
          p.   cm.
     Includes bibliographical references and index.
       ISBN 0-89096-467-X (cloth). — ISBN 0-89096-489-0 (paper)
       1. Women naturalists — United States — Biography.   I. Title.
QH26.B66   1991
508'.092'2 — dc20
[B]                                                         90-20729
                                                                CIP

*To my husband Bruce*

for his continual support, both psychological
and financial, without which this book
would never have been written.

# Contents

Contents

# Illustrations

# *Preface*

NEARLY A DECADE AGO I was browsing through the open stacks of
Penn State's Pattee Library, searching for books about nature. As
a self-taught naturalist living on a remote Pennsylvania mountain-
top, I was eager to read about other such people who had lived or
were living similar nature-infused lives. Usually those people were
men. Certainly the major historical figures, such as John Muir, John
Burroughs, and Henry David Thoreau, were.

But then a small volume entitled *Rural Hours* caught my eye. I
pulled it from the shelf and discovered that it was a reprint of a
book published in 1854 by Susan Fenimore Cooper, the eldest child
of novelist James Fenimore Cooper. The modern introduction to the
book claimed that it had been the first synoptic nature book written
in North America and that it had been published four years before
Thoreau's *Walden.*

Why hadn't I heard of it before? I wondered. And furthermore,
how many women naturalists had there been in the days when women
were perceived as fragile beings fit only to keep house and raise children? My interest in nature had long ago extended to a study of the
history of natural history in the United States, but I had never heard
of a woman naturalist, ornithologist, entomologist, or botanist.

I read *Rural Hours* and was impressed by Cooper's knowledge
of the natural life around her home in Cooperstown, New York. I
began searching library reference sources for other women naturalists. The Belknap Press of Harvard University had recently published
the first three volumes of *Notable American Women,* which listed
a very few botanists and ornithologists. *Women's History Sources,*
edited by Andrea Hinding and Ames Sheldon Bower, was another

valuable resource. But by and large my research advanced because of serendipity. I just happened to glance at an issue of *The Auk* and catch a brief review of a book called *Beyond the Spring* about Maine ornithologist Cordelia Stanwood or to run across a reference to the life study of song sparrows by Margaret Morse Nice.

My enthusiasm for the subject made me eager to share what I knew with others. When articles of mine about some of the women appeared in national publications, I began receiving letters and telephone calls from people who knew of other women naturalists, such as Althea Sherman, Annie Trumbull Slosson, Mary Sophie Young, E. Lucy Braun, and Mary Treat. In most cases they also knew where I could find information about them.

That, of course, was crucial. Although a few women had had full biographies written about them, most had been acknowledged in obscure journals with only a brief article or two. Even the biographies were difficult to find. Many had long been out-of-print and originally published in limited editions. Almost all had to be either read on microfilm or obtained through interlibrary loans or specialist book shops. The paucity of secondary sources forced me to search for original papers in libraries, archives, and museums. Even though I turned up some papers in the twenty-eight research centers I visited from coast to coast and the several more I corresponded with, often their sources were scanty. Neither the women nor their friends and colleagues had thought their papers important enough to save. In fact, modesty was one of several traits most of the women shared. The early western botanist Kate Brandegee seemed amazed when she was asked to write her autobiography. "What does the world care for me?" she asked and refused to write more than a few paragraphs. Unlike the male naturalists, most women did not want plants and animals named for them. Botanist Kate Furbish agreed only because women were rarely honored in that way and she felt she owed it to her sex. Naturalist Annie Alexander bluntly refused saying, "You know my aversion to having things named after me."

Other similarities also existed among women naturalists. None liked housework although most did enjoy cooking for friends. They had no interest in clothes and continued to wear the same outfit years after it had gone out of style. Many had been favorite daughters of unusually enlightened fathers who themselves appreciated nature and who nurtured their daughters' interest in the subject. Others had independent mothers who provided excellent role models for their daughters. Such parents frequently encouraged their daughters to attend college soon after the doors began to open for women in the 1870s.

Of the twenty-five major women portrayed in this book, eleven never married. Five others started careers only after the early deaths of their husbands, two married in middle age after they had done the bulk of their natural history work, six married supportive males in similar fields, and only two were actively discouraged by their mates. All but two of the married women were childless.

Certainly not having children and/or a husband to care for freed the women to do as they wished with their lives, and it was obvious that several of the women had remained unmarried out of choice. None, though, disliked men; in fact, nearly all had had male mentors early in their careers. Because most women naturalists believed that the work was all that mattered, they seemed to feel little or no rivalry toward the more powerful males in their fields and were pleased and grateful for whatever help these men gave them.

The males, on the other hand, were proud of their protégées and usually acknowledged their assistance in their own work. Charles Darwin, for instance, gave New Jersey naturalist Mary Treat credit for her help in his book *Insectivorous Plants*. Konrad Lorenz claimed that not he, but ornithologist Margaret Morse Nice, had discovered the science of ethology, and John James Audubon praised the botanical drawings of Maria Martin that appeared in his *Birds of America* portfolio. Of course, the male mentors also profited from their relationships with these women naturalists who willingly allowed them to use their material, take credit for their discoveries, and receive recognition for their scientific advances.

Although some women naturalists did have professional positions, they were, by and large, field people. Sometimes, as with California naturalist Annie Alexander and New York entomologist Annie Trumbull Slosson, they even turned over their material to male professionals to write up in journals and books. For several of the women, field work led to a university, government, or museum-related job, usually at the lowest level; but perseverance and creativity, such as that shown by Texas naturalist Ellen Quillin in the founding of the Witte Museum in San Antonio, often put the women in positions of power.

Many, though, were known only in their immediate areas, such as Maine ornithologist Cordelia Stanwood, Louisiana ecologist Caroline Dormon, and Texas botanist Mary Sophie Young. In their day, however, a handful of the women were nationally, and in some cases internationally, recognized as experts in their fields. When she died, Agnes Chase was considered not only the most famous agrostologist in the world but also the best; western botanist Alice Eastwood was made Honorary President of the Eighth International Botanical

Congress in Sweden and allowed to sit in Karl Linnaeus's chair; and Colorado naturalist Martha Maxwell was the most renowned of all the exhibitors at the 1876 Centennial Exhibition in Philadelphia.

The work the women did was important. It has been overlooked in the standard chronicles of American natural history because of women's position in society during the eighteenth, nineteenth, and early twentieth centuries. Women were viewed as amateurs, even though professional men in the same field who had achieved great renown often had the same amount or even less professional training than the women. Frank and Carol Crosswhite point out in an article they wrote in *Desert Plants* that western botanist Kate Brandegee was overlooked solely because she was a woman. Like Asa Gray, the dean of American botany, she had a doctor's degree in medicine, and like him she believed in evolution and was a conservative "lumper" in her designation of plant species. Ornithologist Margaret Morse Nice, who had her master's degree in zoology, had to protest constantly that she was not a housewife, but a professional. Even so, as late as 1955 when *Life* magazine featured outstanding amateur scientists, Nice was one of their subjects.

As Margaret Rossiter has proved in her excellent book *Women Scientists in America*, women did not have the same job opportunities as men and were often shunted into low prestige positions. The wonder of it was that so many persisted in their fields and accomplished so much. They helped found major museums of natural history, collected plants and insects in obscure corners of both North and South America, and started major trends, such as Anna Comstock's Nature Study Movement and Rachel Carson's crusade against the unquestioning use of pesticides. Women naturalists also pioneered in the life studies of bird species, worked to save vital natural areas, wrote and illustrated wildflower identification books, and wrote detailed scientific treatises on such subjects as the birds of New Mexico, aphids of the world, mayflies, the ecology of a winter pond, and the mosses of Bermuda and the Bahamas.

Not only did the women work on their own but many helped each other. To a surprising degree, the women knew each other and, especially among the ornithologists and the western botanists, formed what today we would call mutual support groups. For instance, agrostologist Agnes Chase, retired but still working for the federal government at the age of eighty in Washington, D.C., and botanist Alice Eastwood, retired but still working for the California Academy of Sciences at ninety in San Francisco, showed their support for each other's perseverance in a delightful exchange of letters that acknowledged some infirmities of body but none of mind. For them not to work at their chosen jobs, even without pay, was to die; in fact, both did die within months of being forced, by illness, to give up the work that had nourished them well into their nineties.

That story and others, about the women as individuals, as field persons, as professionals, as friends is the focus of this book. Because the information on most of the women is not enough for full biographies, I decided to give each of the twenty-five women I considered most important her own life story. Others, whose contributions were less important, or where the information about them is particularly sparse, I have included in the introductory parts of each section.

As it turns out, Susan Fenimore Cooper was one of the least important of the women naturalists I eventually discovered. She devoted larger portions of her life to charitable works and to caring for her father and his literary reputation than she did to nature. Nonetheless, I am grateful to her for arousing my curiosity which has led to revising my whole vision of women's relationship to nature. Louise Bogan in her poem "Women" says that women have no wilderness in them. But she is wrong. Henry Chester Tracey was also wrong when he wrote in his book *American Naturalists* back in 1930 that "by long inheritance and habit a woman's interest is personal and indoor. It does not go out instinctively to an impersonal and a useless outdoor world."

I hope that the lives and thoughts of my women field naturalists will not only convince others that women and nature were and still are compatible, but also that the women's contributions to the study of nature were important — in fact, amazing, given the prejudices they had to contend with. Best of all, I no longer have to turn to the words of male naturalists to enrich my own love of nature. I can read what women naturalists have to say and nod in agreement. Who, indeed, could disagree with the still-living English naturalist, Miriam Rothschild, a worldwide expert on fleas, when she says, "If I had to wish one wish for my children, I would wish that they were interested in natural history, because I think there you get a spiritual well-being that you can get no other way, and what is more, life can never be long enough. . . . I think all naturalists retain a sort of keen interest in what's going on in life. It's all part of natural history."

# Acknowledgments

I WOULD LIKE TO THANK the many people who have helped me over the years with their encouragement and expertise. I am indebted to three editors — Arthur J. Mekeel, editor of *Quaker History*; Barbara Ellis, former publications director of *American Horticulturist*; and especially Mary Bowers, editor of *Bird Watcher's Digest*, who not only published several of my articles on American women ornithologists but also gave me valuable leads to other women naturalists. The readers of *Bird Watcher's Digest* were also unusually helpful, notably Norma Siebenheller of Staten Island, New York, and Philip A. DuMont of Washington, D.C.

Most writers I contacted about their special women were generous with information. These include Dr. Marianne G. Ainley of Montreal, Canada; Dr. Maxine Benson, author of the recently published *Martha Maxwell, Rocky Mountain Naturalist*; Dr. K. Elizabeth Gibbs of the Department of Entomology, University of Maine, Orono; Fred Pierce, editor of *Birds of an Iowa Dooryard*; Elise Pinckney of Charleston, South Carolina; Donald M. Rawson, former professor of history at the Northwestern State University of Louisiana at Natchitoches; the late Chandler Richmond, author of *Cordelia Stanwood, Beyond the Spring*; the late Doris Speirs, editor of *Research Is a Passion With Me*; William Campbell Steere of the New York Botanical Gardens, Bronx; Dr. Michael T. Stieber, formerly of the Hunt Institute for Botanical Studies, Pittsburgh, Pennsylvania; Dr. Milton B. Trautman of Columbus, Ohio; and Deborah Warner, author of *Graceanna Lewis*.

Others who assisted in a variety of ways were Alice Howard of Oakland, California; Evelyn Anderson of Erie, Pennsylvania; Richard and Jessie Johnson of the Caroline Dormon Nature Preserve, Saline, Louisiana; Shirley Briggs of the Rachel Carson Council, Inc., Chevy Chase, Maryland; Dorothy Seif of the Rachel Carson Homestead Association, Pittsburgh, Pennsylvania; Dr. David Wake of the Museum of Vertebrate Zoology at the University of California, Berkeley; Annetta Carter and Dr. Barbara Ertter of the University of California Herbarium, Berkeley; and George Beatty of Lemont, Pennsylvania.

Librarians and archivists were always outstandingly helpful, especially Anita L. Karg of the Hunt Institute for Botanical Studies, Pittsburgh, Pennsylvania; Carol M. Spawn of the Library of the Academy of Natural Sciences, Philadelphia, Pennsylvania; Clair Carr of the Vineland Historical and Antiquarian Society, Vineland, New Jersey; Geraldine C. Kaye of the Farlow Reference Library and Herbarium of Cryptogamic Botany, Harvard University, Cambridge, Massachusetts; Jane Gates of the Helen Crocker Russell Library, Strybing Arboretum, San Francisco, California; Dr. Jon Perry of the Gray Herbarium, Harvard University, Cambridge, Massachusetts; Alice Landauer of the Museum of Vertebrate Zoology, University of California, Berkeley; Barbara Wiseman of the Museum of Science, Boston, Massachusetts; Martha Utterback of the Library of the Daughters of the Republic of Texas, San Antonio; Lothian Lynas, formerly of the New York Botanical Gardens Library, Bronx; Muriel Sanford of the Raymond H. Fogler Library, University of Maine, Orono; Arnold D. Roggman of the Garnavillo Historical Society, Garnavillo, Iowa; Mildred G. Morgan of the American Entomological Society, Philadelphia, Pennsylvania; and Carol Wells and Mildred Lee of the Eugene P. Watson Memorial Library, Northwestern State University of Louisiana, Natchitoches.

Staff members of the following institutions were also cooperative: Williston Memorial Library Archives, Mt. Holyoke College, South Hadley, Massachusetts; State Historical Society of Iowa, Des Moines; Missouri Botanical Garden, Saint Louis; Smith College Archives, Northampton, Massachusetts; Charleston Museum and the South Carolina Historical Association, Charleston; Huntington Library, San Marino, California; Friends Historical Library of Swarthmore College, Swarthmore, Pennsylvania; Smithsonian Institution Archives, Washington, D.C.; Colorado Historical Society, Denver; Witte Museum, San Antonio, Texas; Bowdoin College Library, Brunswick, Maine; California Academy of Sciences Library, San Francisco; Bancroft Library, University of California, Berkeley; Eugene C. Barker Texas History Center, University of Texas, Austin; Department of Manuscripts and University Archives, Cornell University Libraries,

Cornell University, Ithaca, New York; and Staten Island Institute of Arts and Sciences, Staten Island, New York.

Most of my basic research was done at Pattee Library, Pennsylvania State University, State College, Pennsylvania. I had help from my husband Bruce, who was head of reference, as well as the many fine people in circulation, interlibrary loan, microforms, rare books, and the Life Science Library. Having a major research library so close was invaluable, and I applaud their open stack policy, which allowed me to find *Rural Hours* by Susan Fenimore Cooper while browsing.

Last of all, I would like to thank my three sons and husband who were always willing to encourage and edit my work.

Part I

# The Pioneers

---

Women have always been interested in natural history, but because of societal limitations, they have had to study the subject in ways that were acceptable to the thinking of their times. Thus, during the eighteenth and early nineteenth centuries, they "slipped" into natural history by way of the garden, the artist's brush, and the writer's pen.

A knowledge of gardening was a necessity for many women in eighteenth-century America since not only food but household medicines were produced in them. But some women went beyond growing and experimented in crop improvement as well. Historical records from South Carolina identify at least three prominent women gardeners — Martha Daniel Logan, Martha Laurens Ramsey, and Eliza Lucas Pinckney. Logan, who lived from 1702 until 1779, wrote THE GARDEN's KALENDAR, a standard work of gardening in upper South Carolina; Ramsey experimented with the growing and preserving of olives during that same period; and Pinckney devised a method for producing a profitable indigo crop.

Little more is known about either Ramsey or Logan, but Pinckney kept a letterbook which reveals a young woman interested not only in horticultural schemes — planting a fig orchard, experimenting with growing cotton, "Guiney" corn, ginger, and "Lucern grass" (alfalfa) — but also a woman appreciative of the natural world *around her. She took special delight in the mocking-bird, "her little darling that sweet harmonist" who inspired her to write a poem while she was lacing her stays! And she rejoiced in the beauty of a South Carolina spring. "The majestik pine imperceptable puts on a fresher green, the young mirtle joining its fragrance to that of the Jesamin of golden hue [which] perfumes all the woods and regales the rural wander[er] with its sweets; the daiseys, honesuckles, and a thousand nameless beauties of the woods. . . ."*

*Pinckney was also a lover of trees, particularly of the "oaks which we have of Various sorts [and] fine magnolia which in our moist land . . . grow to a very great height . . . the most beautiful of all trees." The Palmetto Royal, which she called "Pennento Royal," was another favorite of hers. It "bears the most noble bunch of flowers I ever saw. The main stem of the bunch is a foot and a half or two foot long with some hundreds of white flowers hanging pendant upon it!"*

*While Pinckney took refuge in the beauty of nature and the hard work of gardening, particularly after the sudden death of her husband, she never extended her interest into the study of botany as some Colonial women did. Again, early records are scanty. Only the work of Jane Colden, the so-called first American woman botanist, was adequately documented, but sometimes other women, such as Maria Drayton, appear in historical documents under "botanist."*

*Drawing was another acceptable pastime for women; some, such as Maria Martin and Lucy Say, became exceptional illustrators of natural history subjects. Martin began by painting flowers, butterflies, and moths as background for many of John James Audubon's bird portraits, but ended up doing reptiles for John Edwards Holbrook's NORTH AMERICAN HERPETOLOGY and insects copied from Thomas Say's exquisite AMERICAN ENTOMOLOGY.*

*Say followed up that volume with his book AMERICAN CONCHOLOGY, and of the sixty-eight plates, all but two were drawn by his wife Lucy. She also colored 2,450 impressions with the help of two schoolchildren, Henry Tiebout and his sister Caroline, at the utopian community of New Harmony, Indiana, where she and Say lived. Unfortunately Say died prematurely at forty-seven, and the work was never finished. Lucy wrote, shortly after his death, "My greatest desire is to be able to contribute to the continuation of the "Conchology" by drawing and engraving, and by thus devoting or appropriating a portion of my time, I shall feel that I am still forwarding the great object to which my dear husband devoted himself at the expense of health and many personal sacrifices." Despite her resolve, though, she reported to one friend that her shell collection had not grown since she had no sympathy from those around her and did not know enough to work without help. With the death of Thomas, Lucy's work in natural history had been effectively terminated, but unlike many such women, she received a singular honor anyway. She was elected the first woman member of the prestigious Academy of Natural Sciences in Philadelphia on October 26, 1841, and became a life member two months later, probably because she had presented Say's collections to the academy.*

*There was still another acceptable way in which women "slipped" into natural history during the pioneer period. They became writers. Mary Townsend, invalid sister of naturalist John Kirk Townsend, published* Life in the Insect World: or, Conversations upon Insects between an Aunt and Her Nieces *in 1844, hoping that her descriptions of the appearances and habits of insects would teach children the importance of nature study.*

*Six years later Susan Fenimore Cooper's* Rural Hours *became an overnight hit. "It is a great book — the greatest of the season," William Cullen Bryant assured his good friend James Fenimore Cooper about the second book written by his oldest daughter Susan. The first, a novel, had not been a success, but* Rural Hours, *which was based on her daily nature journal, hit a responsive chord. Henry David Thoreau mentioned Miss Cooper's book in his journal, four years before he published* Walden.

*Centered on the environs of Cooperstown, New York,* Rural Hours *was a compilation of many years of journal writing condensed into one year. Like later nature writers, Susan began her book with spring and cov-*

3

*ered many subjects still prevalent in nature writing—wildflowers, birds and the mystery of migration, the decline of animal populations, and conservation. She sometimes conducted her own botanical research; one October day, she counted the 570 seed-vessels of a mullein stalk. She speculated on bird migration, suspecting that "perhaps birds generally follow the same course, year after year, in their annual journeyings" and calling migration "a singular instinct implanted in the breast of the fowls of the air." She noted that passenger pigeons came each spring in March, passing over the valley one year in "large unbroken flocks several miles in extent." But, she added ominously, "there have not been so many here since that season." Twenty years after the founding of Cooperstown, she reported, the deer had completely disappeared and beavers had become rare in New York. Clearly foreseeing the evils of the clear-cutting forest practices of the day, she pleaded for "thinning woods and not blasting them; clearing only such ground as is marked for immediate tillage, preserving the wood on hill-tops and rough side-hills. . . ."*

*With* RURAL HOURS, *Susan Fenimore Cooper began a tradition of observational nature writing that other women took up. To do it, they had to conduct field work—in their own backyards, in nearby woods and fields, and finally far afield. Not all women in the field became writers, but certainly those first women who dared to go abroad set a precedent for the field naturalists, botanists, ornithologists, entomologists, and ecologists who followed.*

# Jane Colden

## COLONIAL BOTANIST

JANE COLDEN'S FATHER, Cadwallader Colden, believed that women were eminently suited to the study of botany because of "their natural curiosity and the pleasure they take in the beauty and variety of dress." Furthermore, most women spent too much of their time in "trifling amusements" and needed a serious pursuit like botany to keep them gainfully occupied.

His second daughter, Jane, seemed to him the best choice for training in botany because of her "natural inclination to reading and a curiosity for natural . . . history, and a sufficient capacity for attaining a competent knowledge." He taught her the Swedish botanist Linnaeus's new binomial system for naming plants, translating the Latin terms into English so she would not be deterred by a language he thought too difficult for women to learn.

Despite what might seem condescending today, Cadwallader Colden was advanced in his attitudes toward women's abilities at a time when upperclass women were generally consigned to the drawing room and occupied by such genteel pursuits as needlework, music, and sketching. Unlike most people, Colden thought women should be educated. When he and his wife moved to the New York countryside in 1719, they worked hard to educate their six children. At the time Colden, a Scottish immigrant who arrived in America in 1710, was a doctor. They settled on two thousand acres in what today is the town of Montgomery in Orange County, and there they lived on the estate they named Coldingham.

Both Colden and his wife were considered intellectuals because they believed in the virtues of raising their family in the country. Shortly after settling in Montgomery, inspired by the profusion of wild plants he found growing on his land, he began corresponding with eminent European and American botanists and collecting plants for them. Eventually his work, and that of his daughter Jane, led to the publishing of the first local flora of New York called *Plantae Collinghamiae* in 1749. In the meantime Colden became heavily involved in politics, first as a member of the Council of New York and then as surveyor general of the colony. Later, from 1761 until the outbreak of the Revolution, he served as lieutenant governor.

Jane was born on March 27, 1724, five years after the Coldens settled at Coldingham and was probably taught botany by her father sometime in the late 1730s. Skilled in drawing, she made ink outlines washed in with neutral tints of 340 plants. Many of the drawings were accompanied by detailed descriptions and local folklore. For instance, she wrote that *"Asclepias tuberosa* [butterfly weed] is an excellent cure for the Colick. This was learn'd from a Canadian Indian and is called in New England Canada Root. The Excellency of this root for the Colick is confirmed by Dr. Pater of New England and Dr. Brooks of Maryland likewise confirmed this." Another plant, *Pedicularis canadensis* "is called by the country people Betony [now wood betony or lousewort]. They make Thee [tea] of the Leaves, and use it for Fever and Augue." Her interest in the uses of wild plants was understandable since one of women's housewifely duties was knowing what herbs to use as medicine.

Botanically, though, she made a few discoveries of her own. One — *Hypericum virginicum* (the marsh St. Johnswort) — she called Gardenia after Alexander Garden of South Carolina, a correspondent and friend of both Jane and her father. Garden had sent her a specimen he had collected while visiting them in New York, just after Jane had found her own specimen. So, "using the privilege of a first discoverer," she was "pleased to call this new plant Gardenia in compliment to Dr. Garden." However, the name was not adopted for that plant but for the showy, white, hedge plant of the South — *Gardenia jasminoides* — an honor bestowed on him by English botanist John Ellis who was a mutual friend of the Coldens.

Another of her plant descriptions was sent to Linnaeus via John Ellis in 1758. She had called it Fibraurea, a translation of its still-popular name, "goldthread;" Linnaeus called it Helleborus, which was later changed to *Coptis groenlandica.* Ellis suggested that Linnaeus name the plant for Jane, since she "merits your esteem and does honor to your system." But because her father already had a plant named for him — Coldenia — "I suppose you should call this Coldenella, or any other name that might distinguish her among your Genera."

Unfortunately Ellis's suggestion was ignored. So was the suggestion of Quaker Englishman Peter Collinson, another botanical friend of the Coldens, who asked Linnaeus to name a plant for "the first lady that has so perfectly studied your system." With all the new plants flowing in to Linnaeus from America to be named it is hard not to believe that he simply had no interest in naming a plant for Jane.

In fact, Jane did not mind pointing out Linnaeus's lapses. About *Clematis virginiana* (Virgin's bower) she wrote, "Neither [does] Linnaeus take notice that there are some plants of the Clematis that bear only Male flowers, but this I have observed with such care, that there can be no doubt of it."

Although her father's friends respected her botanical accomplishments, her collecting services were often taken advantage of, which may be why her benefactors tried to persuade Linnaeus to honor her. They knew how much she had done for them and for botany. Her father also tried to give her credit, sometimes even overstating her accomplishments. In a letter to the Dutch botanist John Fredric Gronovius, he claimed that she had learned a new method of using a rolling press with printer's ink to take an impression of leaves and that she had made three hundred plant impressions. Possibly they were all lost but one, because only one example of the technique has been found at the very end of her volume. In that same letter, Colden also enclosed samples of Jane's botanical writings; he believed some of the plants she described were new genera. "One is the Panax foliis ternis ternatis in the Flora Virg [*Flora Virginica*, published in 1739]. . . . Two more I have not found described anywhere, and in the others you'll find some things particular, which I think are not taken notice by any author I have seen. . . ."

Father and daughter obviously worked closely together in their botanical pursuits, Colden supplying his daughter with botanical books and colored plates and often even writing letters for and about her. Visitors to the household quickly learned of Jane's accomplishments, whether they were botanists — such as John Bartram of Philadelphia and Peter Kalm, an emissary of Linnaeus's from Sweden — or non-botanists — such as Walter Rutherford, a visitor from abroad obviously impressed with Jane. She was, he wrote, "a Florist and Botanist, she has discovered a great number of Plants never before described and has given their Properties and Virtues, many of which are found useful in Medicine, and she draws and colors them with great beauty." Still another visitor, convalescing fourteen-year-old Samuel Bard (later a well-known doctor and writer), came to spend the summer of 1756 with them and was immediately entranced by

Jane; she taught him how to botanize, which he continued as a hobby throughout his life.

She fell in love with a Scottish widower, Dr. William Farquhar, when she was thirty-five years old. They were married in 1759; one letter, to her sister, about how he hurt his back because he was holding her in his lap, glows with affection for the man she had chosen. There is no evidence that she continued botanizing after her marriage, which lasted a scant seven years. She died in childbirth on March 10, 1766, a couple of weeks before her forty-second birthday, and the child she bore died later that same year.

She did not live to see the Revolutionary War, but her father died just as it started, still loyal to the crown. Her volume of plant drawings and descriptions fell into the hands of a Hessian Captain — F. von Wangenheim — who wrote in 1782: "This work is a remarkable one because it is that of a lady who possessed such a love for botany that she learned Latin, and judging from its nature is so worthy and correct that it contains many even minute things."

Today the original volume is in the Department of Botany at the British Museum, but a facsimile was published by Chanticleer Press in New York in April, 1963, entitled *Jane Colden — Botanic Manuscript* — a fitting tribute to America's first woman botanist.

2

# *Maria Martin*

AUDUBON'S SWEETHEART

"I MUCH WISH that your Dear Sister our Sweetheart, would draw plants, and branches of Trees for Me to the Number of 15 or 20 Drawings for small plates — Anything not published in My Two first Volumes would prove a valuable acquisition, . . ." John James Audubon wrote to his "worthy friend," the Reverend John Bachman of Charleston, South Carolina, on June 12, 1836.

Their mutual "Sweetheart" was Maria Martin, youngest sister of Bachman's ailing wife Harriet and beloved aunt to his nine living children. Installed in his home along with her mother in 1816, when Bachman married Harriet, Maria had quickly become an indispensable part of the busy household, nursing sick and dying children, overseeing their education, and, in general, "being housekeeper and nurse," as Bachman commented in a letter to his daughter Jane. Seven of the nine children were daughters; she taught them the proper southern etiquette for young ladies, in addition to supervising their needlework and listening to their piano practice. She served as a mother substitute for her sister, who suffered from tic douloureux, a painful spasmodic neuralgia, during the last twenty years of her life.

In what spare time she had, Maria helped her brother-in-law by writing out the sermons he dictated to her. When John James Audubon entered their lives in 1831, she assisted in the artwork for volumes 2 and 4 of his *The Birds of America* and acted as Bachman's amanuensis during his collaboration with Audubon on *The Quadrupeds of North America*.

The Reverend John Bachman, a native of Rhinebeck, New York, had loved natural history from childhood. This love was further enforced during school days in Philadelphia when he accompanied or-

9

nithological artist Alexander Wilson, Audubon's predecessor, on field trips. Bachman's two specialties were mammals and birds, but during a trip he took north with Maria and his sister Eva in 1827, he also collected plants. That may have been when Maria first discovered that she preferred botany too, since she preserved the specimens he "pulled up." Bachman also instilled in Maria his own habit of referring to plants by their scientific names.

The trip, taken when Maria was thirty-one years old, covered parts of New York, New England, and Canada. It was a source of pleasure to her because she tried to observe things as she traveled, noting down what struck her as interesting and unusual. "Most Magnificent of all views" was Niagara Falls where they spent two days, she wrote to her sister Harriet, and she had been "highly gratified" by her visit there. In a letter to his wife, John also reported on Niagara Falls where he and Maria had taken a walk to see a "burning spring." For John, Maria was "an excellent travelling companion" who helped make the twelve-hundred-mile journey pleasant.

John was obviously the naturalist, Maria the student, and while she liked natural subjects, she was an artist rather than a field person. Most of her paintings were done from life in her garden or in those of her neighbors, but since in those days southern ladies did not go off by themselves, she may have been doing the only fieldwork acceptable — painting specimens near-at-hand.

Certainly her choice of subject matter did, in part, reflect the current rage for botany among educated women, but few, if any, women showed the interest she did in painting reptiles and insects, including butterflies and moths. Because of her obliging personality, it is difficult to know whether her choice of subject matter merely reflected the needs of Audubon and Bachman or stated her own preferences. Bachman did refer to her as "my artist" in a letter he wrote to Audubon's wife Lucy in 1833, mentioning that he had been studying insects and had had Maria "painting butterflies all summer, which I fear she does not relish particularly well." But once she learned how to paint insects by carefully copying from the illustrations in Thomas Say's three-volume *American Entomology*, completed in 1828, she continued to paint original watercolors of a wide variety of insects — caterpillars, beetles, flies, moths, and butterflies. Part of the butterfly study of *Oenomaus ortygnus*, which she painted in 1833, appears in plate 198, the Swainson's warbler. Audubon notes that both the bird and the butterflies were discovered by Bachman near Charleston and that the azalea and butterflies were drawn by "my friend's sister, Miss Martin." Another painting, of two white peacock butterflies, was later incorporated in plate 355, MacGillivray's seaside sparrow, and once again its discovery was credited to Bachman.

She did like painting birds after Audubon had taught her how, but her passion for them did not match her talent, since she had difficulty in setting the dead specimens up in realistic postures. Unlike Audubon, she had had no field experience in watching birds, although she was able to accurately copy them from Audubon's paintings.

Probably she did like botanical painting and, judging from the quality of her first efforts for Audubon, she had been painting for years. No doubt Audubon had merely seen her talent and utilized it. After all, as Audubon told Bachman in a letter from Edinburgh in 1834, "I know her [Maria] well — nay better than you do yourself and I am thereby assured that she will do all for my sake in her power." Earlier that year he had sent her a portfolio, some drawing paper, and a parcel of brushes, all of which he hoped she would soon wear out.

Her botanical painting for Audubon began after his second visit in 1832. Her first subject, the southern plant Franklinia, provided the background for Audubon's Bachman's warbler painting, plate 185 in volume 2 of *The Birds of America*. Bachman had first discovered a female bird, and then in 1833, a male. Audubon also named another bird for his friend Bachman — plate 165 was called "Bachman's finch," now Bachman's sparrow, and it illustrated "a male in full summer dress, which was presented to me, while yet quite fresh, by my friend Bachman. The beautiful plant on which it is placed, was drawn by my friend's sister, who has kindly rendered me similar services. . . ."

Scholars are still not certain how many botanical backgrounds Maria contributed to *The Birds of America*, but Audubon himself attributed eleven to her. She did a good deal of work on volume 4, sending over a dozen drawings of plants and tree branches directly to the engraver in London where Audubon's son Victor placed them on the appropriate bird portraits done by his father. In addition, Audubon arrived in Charleston in late 1836 with ninety-eight bird skins he had purchased from their collectors, Thomas Nuttall and John Kirk Townsend. He and his son John, working in the basement of Bachman's house, set them up in realistic poses. While Audubon painted the birds, Maria drew all the accompanying botanical and entomological specimens, according to Audubon's note on plate 373, the evening and black-headed grosbeak. And finally, in volume 5, Audubon gave Maria the most enduring of tributes. He named a bird — *Picus martinae*, now a race of the hairy woodpecker — for

11

1.   Black racer by Maria Martin. *Courtesy Charleston Museum, Charleston,* *South Carolina*

her, acknowledging "the aid she has on several occasions afforded me in embellishing my drawings of birds, by adding to them beautiful and correct representations of plants and flowers."

Sometime before 1836, when John Edwards Holbrook's *North American Herpetology* was published, Maria also found time to paint at least one reptile for Holbrook's book. Although Holbrook mentions in his preface Maria Martin's "accurate and very spirited drawings of Carolina reptiles," only one, the black racer, is definitely her work.

The Audubons continued to be a force in the Bachman household; Bachman's oldest daughter, Maria, married Audubon's youngest son, John Woodhouse, in June of 1837, and Audubon's eldest son, Victor, married Mary Eliza Bachman in December of 1839. Both marriages were tragically short, because the sisters died of tuberculosis within eight months of each other. In an attempt to save Eliza, Victor and Maria Martin took her to Cuba early in 1841, but she died soon after her return. Maria seemed to take some pleasure from the trip, describing in detail the structure of a coffee plant, but that trip and another she took in 1847 to Virginia Springs with a third Bachman daughter dying of tuberculosis, Julia, were sad excursions. On the latter trip, John and another daughter, Lynch, also went along, and while John served as a substitute pastor in the rural churches, Maria and Lynch nursed Julia, who died on the journey.

Maria was by then the only mother the Bachman children had since Harriet's death in 1846. Two years later Maria married John. "Maria," John wrote to his son-in-law Victor, "has been weak enough to take the old man with all his infirmities of mind and eyes for better and for worse and thus lawfully become his nurse and scribe." He had already been sick and had had to employ Maria as his amanuensis back in September when he and Victor had been working hard on *The Quadrupeds of North America*. John James had settled into senility, putting much of the work for that volume on John and Victor's shoulders, ably assisted by Maria.

The marriage seemed to be a love match as well, with John calling her a "first rate old girl" and Maria, as always, doing what was best for John. They did make at least one long trip together in 1851, taking the Erie railroad from Piermont, New Jersey, which followed along the upper Delaware River through scenery "romantic in the extreme, on one side of nature in all its rugged grandeur and on the other the sluggish Canal wending its long way like a silvery thread through wall and mountain," Maria wrote to Bachman's daughters.

Certainly marriage to the man who had been her intellectual companion for so many years must have pleased her, but never again were their lives as exciting and productive as during those years when they had worked so closely with Audubon.

Part II

# *The Naturalists*

Before there were botanists, entomologists, mammalogists, and ornithologists, there were naturalists — men
and women who delighted in all aspects of the natural
world and who moved from flowers to insects to mammals to birds with ease. Almost always those people
were self-taught, since scientific training could only be
had on a limited basis at a few colleges and universities
during the late eighteenth and early nineteenth centuries. But even today the naturalist tradition continues
among amateurs who may or may not have had scientific training in school.

Most of the prominent women naturalists entered
the field in the late nineteenth and early twentieth centuries at the same time that the men had already begun to specialize, hence the women naturalists in the
following chapters depended on the male specialists for
help. Naturalist Mary Treat corresponded with male
botanists as well as entomologists to learn about the
species she had discovered, Graceanna Lewis and Martha Maxwell were often assisted by male ornithologists,
Annie Montague Alexander relied on male ornithologists, botanists, paleontologists, and mammalogists to
classify her collections, and Ellen Quillin worked with
male botanists and herpetologists in both her botanical and museum work.

The personal lives of those same women naturalists were similar in that most were either unhappily

*married (Treat and Maxwell) or unmarried (Lewis and Alexander). Although Alexander was independently wealthy and Quillin supported by a husband, the other three did not have the luxury of doing just what they liked; therefore, much of their lives was spent trying to earn a living, usually by appealing to those who attended their lectures, read their books, and visited their museums.*

*The women naturalists unconsciously followed the two patterns set down by the preeminent male naturalists of the late nineteenth and early twentieth centuries — John Muir and John Burroughs. Maxwell and Alexander, like Muir, were explorer-naturalists who gloried in being alone in the untouched wilderness; Lewis, Treat, and Quillin, like Burroughs, preferred exploring nature near-at-hand. Only Treat, though, wrote books that reached the same kind of people attracted by Burroughs's and Muir's books and which, incidentally, made her a handsome living.*

*It remained for another woman naturalist, Mary Hunter Austin, to write a philosophical nature book with a broad appeal. A contemporary of Alexander, Austin extolled the Inyo County area of California in her classic THE LAND OF LITTLE RAIN before Alexander explored the area. Austin claimed she had written the book in a month, but she had spent twelve years there following coyotes and observing how they hunted for food, watching a spring, seeing bobcats bring down rabbits, badgers, and rats, and trailing elf owls from the spring where they hunted mice at night to their daytime burrows. To Austin the coyote was "my friend," "the little gray dog of the wilderness," and she once saw five coyotes kill an antelope and share the feast with an eagle, buzzards, and hawks. But Austin, also part of a failed marriage, did not sustain her early promise as a naturalist; instead, she became a popular novelist and lecturer, one of the best-known women writers of her day, whose friends included H. G. Wells, Jack London, Calvin Coolidge, and Lincoln Steffens.*

*Still another unhappily married woman, Emma Bell Miles, found her solace in nature and in a specific place, the Appalachian Mountains of Tennessee. Living in poverty with four children, she managed to convey her love of nature in her book, THE SPIRIT OF THE MOUNTAINS. Unfortunately the book was not a best-seller as was Austin's, but it was an accurate portrayal of the lives of the mountain people as well as a paean for the mountains themselves. To her, the mountains had "three special characteristics which . . . are perhaps not to be duplicated in all the world. They are silence, blue air, and an endless variety."*

*Women naturalists, like the men, have always been a special breed of people, willing to put up with discomfort, ill health, even poverty to pursue their passionate love for nature. And all of them could have been described in the same way Lily Solomon of New York City recently described another woman naturalist, Farida Wiley, who died in November of 1986 at the age of ninety-nine. "If there were no birds she knew the flowers, and if there were no flowers she knew the plants and the weeds and the trees and the grasses and the mushrooms."*

3

# Graceanna Lewis

## QUAKER NATURALIST

—⟡—

GRACEANNA LEWIS, a Quaker from Chester County, Pennsylvania, was, in many ways, typical of nineteenth-century American naturalists. Every aspect of the natural world fascinated her, and although she began with an interest in birds, throughout her long life she moved from one subject to another in an effort to understand the whole spectrum of nature.

Unlike many other naturalists, however, her underlying reason for studying nature was based on her Quaker beliefs. "I love nature," she once wrote, "because it teaches me better to comprehend its Author." It had been, after all, Graceanna's religion that had given her an opportunity to lead a more challenging intellectual life than most women of the restrictive Victorian era. The Society of Friends educated both men and women in schools that especially emphasized the study of natural history.

Graceanna Lewis was born on August 3, 1821, the second of four daughters, to Quakers John and Esther Fussell Lewis. Her father died when she was only three years old, and her mother was left to raise the children. Fortunately, Esther was both bright and resourceful. She also made certain her daughters were well educated. Having been a teacher herself, she taught the girls until they were old enough to attend the Kimberton Boarding School for Girls, which was run by Friends, Emmor and Susan Kimber.

The elder Kimbers believed in encouraging inquiring minds by teaching such challenging subjects as astronomy, botany, and chemistry, and their several daughters helped with instruction. One daughter, Abigail Kimber, was a practicing botanist and helped to identify and catalogue plants in the area. So strong was her influence that Graceanna became interested in botany and even found an unknown plant in her own garden.

Graceanna, in later writings, credited three people with influencing her to become a naturalist. First was her mother. Esther had enough interest in the natural world to keep a diary that recorded observations of solar and lunar eclipses, an eclipse of Mars by the moon, and the appearance of comets, meteors, and auroras. In addition, she kept weather and plant-blooming records. Her observant nature even led to a discovery that gave financial solvency to the fatherless family. While she was gardening, Esther noticed the reddish soil and decided her property contained iron ore. She was right, and eventually she had the land stripmined by a Phoenixville company that paid her $.50 a ton. For several years she received tidy sums ranging from $453.00 to $1700.00 per annum.

Esther, then, was the strongest influence in Graceanna's childhood. And the training she received both at home and at Kimberton enabled her to become a teacher of botany and astronomy at her Uncle Bartholomew Fussell's boarding school for girls in York, Pennsylvania. As part of the course, she took the girls on plant identification walks. On one of those walks, she wrote to her mother, she discovered two wildflowers she had never seen before. She also taught her students the stars and constellations and traced the paths of planets.

But, unfortunately, the school lasted only two years, and after a third year of teaching at a school in Phoenixville, Graceanna returned home in 1845. Graceanna never married nor ever seems to have been interested in anyone. Her biographer, Deborah Warner, suggests she did not envy women their unlimited capacity for childbearing and that among her immediate family members, she had observed the problems continual births caused women. Since the Society of Friends instilled in women a sense of their own worth aside from marriage and motherhood, many of them did not marry, including two of Graceanna's three sisters and many of her friends.

Friendship among educated Quaker women was a very important part of life, and Graceanna's closest friend and the second powerful influence on her life was Mary Townsend, sister of ornithologist John Kirk Townsend. Adept at careful observations, especially those of insects, Mary begged people to "treat [them] with kindness," an unusually enlightened idea for the time. She even published a book anonymously in 1844 entitled *Life in the Insect World; or, Conversations upon Insects between an Aunt and Her Nieces.*

Graceanna considered it a "privilege to be the chosen friend of the sister of a naturalist," and when Mary died in 1851, Graceanna mourned her deeply. "After a long period, I wished for a *study* kindred to hers. I occupied the leisure of a country home in observing the birds which visited us, and dreamed of preparing a little work as a companion to that of my friend," she later told author Phebe A. Hanaford.

Graceanna was also involved in social reform, and she devoted a good portion of her time to abolitionist causes before the Civil War. Later she worked on women's rights and temperance issues. Another part of her life was spent keeping her mother's farm going and doing the womanly chores, along with her sisters and mother, that went into a well-functioning household. Esther, concerned for her three unmarried daughters and the one, Rebecca, who was married to a good but impractical man, divided her farm. She gave land to Rebecca and Edwin where they could build their own home to house their seven children, and she erected a second home, named Sunnyside for Graceanna, and her other sisters, Mariann and Elizabeth. Shortly after that, in 1847, Esther died, leaving her daughters a farm flowing with the proverbial milk and honey — 180 apple trees of fifty-two varieties, as well as currants, grapes, strawberries, gooseberries, blackberries, raspberries, and pear, cherry, plum, and quince trees. The death of their grandmother Rebecca in 1850, left the sisters alone except for the nine-year-old daughter Ellen Bechtel, of destitute parents, whom the sisters decided to raise as their own. So although they did not have husbands, the three women still enjoyed the privileges of motherhood.

The next decade and a half was devoted to farming, raising Ellen, and finally, struggling through the Civil War. After it was all over, both her sisters were dead, Ellen was a married woman, and Graceanna, a vigorous forty-five years of age, had already begun a serious study of ornithology with the encouragement of two Quaker amateur naturalists, Ezra Michener and Vincent Bernard. Both men shared what they knew with Graceanna but, realizing their own limitations, widened her contacts by introducing her to more advanced Quaker naturalists in Philadelphia.

Graceanna had been observing birds for many years, ever since she had been inspired by her friend Mary Townsend. She began with "no plates and no specimens,— nothing but a book of verbal descriptions, with the technical terms of which I was unfamiliar. It took me three weeks to know the common song sparrow." She enjoyed sitting under a cherry tree when the fruit was ripe watching the variety of birds that fed on the cherries. And slowly she accumulated an ornithological library. Early in her study she was supplied with Alexander Wilson's pioneering work *American Ornithology.* She also studied naturalist Thomas Nuttall's *Manual of Ornithology of the United States and Canada* (1832–34).

Then she received a copy of *The Birds of North America* written by Spencer Fullerton Baird, John Cassin, and George N. Lawrence. Using it she could identify all the bird species around Sunnyside and observe their habits. "To wander at will, in field and wood, with the ear open to catch any note or song of bird, and the eye trained to notice the least flutter in the branches, cannot fail to result in an interesting knowledge of bird-life," she reported.

Around 1862 she had been introduced to the third great influence in her life—ornithologist John Cassin, one of the authors of her cherished *The Birds of North America*, who had been made Curator of Birds at the Academy of Natural Sciences in Philadelphia. A fellow Quaker, Cassin respected Graceanna's obvious intelligence and eagerness to learn. He was basically a "closet naturalist," interested in taxonomy rather than exploring, who described 194 new bird species that had been sent to the Academy, mostly from Africa. Graceanna found him to be a kind and caring friend, one to whom she could always go for advice and help—"He had knowledge, I had not; and he rejoiced in imparting it to me." Furthermore, "he never seemed to think it strange a woman should wish to study."

He opened the Academy to her, overflowing her table with books he recommended and referring her to the museum collections. When she decided to offer a series of four parlor classes in ornithology in 1865, John Cassin was the first of three men who lent his name and recommendation to the brochure she circulated describing her lectures. Quaker entomologist Joseph Trimble and amateur naturalist Vincent Bernard were her other supporters. She proposed to cover everything from the geographical distribution of birds to their usefulness as checks on the insect population. In addition, her lectures would be accompanied by "numerous elegant engravings and specimens, and also with charts prepared for the purpose."

It was probably also Cassin who encouraged Graceanna to write to fellow Pennsylvanian, Spencer Fullerton Baird. Baird was then assistant secretary of the Smithsonian and primarily interested in encouraging naturalists all over the country to collect specimens for the museum he had boosted with his own collections in Washington, D.C. Baird, an untiring letter writer, never turned down a request for help or advice from budding naturalists. If he did not know the answer to a question, he always found someone else who did. Graceanna's first request, for a copy of T. M. Brewer's *North American Oölogy*, was easy to fulfill. Later, he was able to help her find a good microscope, but when she began asking more sophisticated questions about crystals, he wrote to Professor Himes for an answer that Baird then sent on to Graceanna.

Needing a support system in her studies, she moved to Philadelphia where she could be near the Academy of Natural Sciences and her mentor and friend, John Cassin. With his encouragement and help, she was even able to identify a new bird species, *Agelaius cyanopus*, which Cassin proudly acknowledged in the *Proceedings of the Academy.* He referred to her as "one of several ladies who have most diligently studied in the Library and Museum of this Academy. . . ." To his friend, Baird, he called her "a good naturalist," and admitted that she was able to notice bird variations that he had overlooked.

One of the best years of Graceanna's life was 1868. Her dream to produce a book on nature had been partially fulfilled when Part I of her *Natural History of Birds* had appeared. She described it as a book for the "man of ordinary culture," but she became too involved with speculations concerning bird classification based on embryology, still an open question in scientific circles. This made the book difficult for non-scientists to understand, and yet she had not developed her ideas well enough to suit the scientists either. Nevertheless, reviews were cautiously favorable, and Graceanna began soliciting for six hundred subscribers willing to pay five dollars each to support the publication of the proposed nine further sections of her book. Cassin and Baird promptly subscribed.

F. W. Putnam, editor of *The American Naturalist* and a zoologist himself, financed three thousand copies of a prospectus on the rest of the book. The prospectus was accompanied by an impressive number of testimonials based on the reading of Part I of her *Natural History of Birds.* The names would all have been familiar to American naturalists of the time and included Baird as well as George Lawrence, the third author of the Baird, Cassin, Lawrence *Birds of North America*, Dr. T. M. Brewer, who had written the oology book she had requested from Baird, and Alexander Agassiz, son of Louis Agassiz, the most popular scientist in North America, and, in his own right, also an able scientist.

And then, the following year, Cassin unexpectedly died. With his death, she lost a teacher whom she could never replace, and without him to support her presence in what was primarily a male enclave, the Academy of Natural Sciences, she went back to teaching in 1870–71 at a Friends' school in Philadelphia. She also continued to pursue her own research, publishing articles such as "The Lyre Bird" for *The American Naturalist.* She even managed to win enough support from three men, anatomist Joseph Leidy, George Tryon, who had succeeded Cassin as curator of birds, and Edward J. Nolan, academy librarian, to win election to the academy on May 31, 1870. However, the last nine parts of her bird book were never written.

She collapsed with what she called "an affection of the brain" in a letter to Baird. For over a year she recovered in Rebecca's home, and by 1873 she was again supporting herself by lectures and by writing for periodicals such as *The New Century.* She also resumed her studies at the Academy. On December 30, 1882, she wrote to her sister's children, "I have been painting a group of wood ducks today. It is very nice work and I like to do it. The ducks are drawn on stone like Uncle Charlie does his work, and then printed. Afterwards they are painted. The wood ducks are the prettiest ducks we have. They build their nests up on a tree, not on the ground like other ducks. When the little ones are ready to come down and swim in the water, the mother picks them up one by one and carries them down. She is afraid she will hurt them, so she takes hold by the down and skin at the back of the neck and lifts them very carefully like a pussy cat carrying her kittens and drops them so softly that they are not hurt in the least." Such a description illustrates that Graceanna had read about this peculiar habit of the female wood duck, probably in Audubon's description of the mother's carrying her young in her bill if the nest tree is not above water.

As a lecturer in zoology, she was as accurate as she could be. Baird had already acknowledged in an 1870 letter that "you possess a more profound knowledge of the philosophy of many branches of Zoology and Natural History than a large percentage of the men of the best reputation of the day." Quaker Maria Mitchell, an astronomer at Vassar College who was undoubtedly the most famous woman scientist of her day, called Graceanna, "a hard student and a genuine lover of nature. Her lecture was grave and dignified, and thoroughly scientific." The "scientific" label was particularly significant in a discipline where charlatans and showmen abounded. No longer were her lectures restricted to birds — she offered twenty lectures on plants for two hundred dollars, twenty on animals, again at two hundred dollars, and a general course, still at twenty lessons for two hundred dollars.

Her national prominence seemed secure when she was asked to deliver a paper at the Third Congress of Women held in Syracuse, New York, on October 13, 14, and 15, 1875. Naturally enough she spoke on "Science for Women." Her own philosophy about her life's work came through when she talked about the "personal duty" of a person to do what he or she can "accomplish better than any other." "There is," she continued, "an appointment by nature for a special work, and there must be a loss in the sum total of human welfare if the work be either left undone or transferred to other hands." Certainly her Quaker beliefs were obvious in this and in her further assertion that women in science worked principally for intellectual reward.

She chose her Quaker friend and former roommate during her early days in Philadelphia, Mary Peart, as an example of a talented woman in science. Mary worked as a scientific illustrator for Bowen and Company, a lithographic establishment in Philadelphia that supplied the Smithsonian and other science-oriented organizations with illustrations for their publications. Mary Peart displayed "marvellous accuracy in microscopic drawing, as well as her womanly desire to render her art of service to a sister scientist." This latter quality was one which women at the Syracuse meeting hoped to encourage—women helping women in their long struggle for the right to pursue challenging careers.

Certainly Graceanna's friend, Maria Mitchell, tried to help her when a job teaching natural history at Vassar opened up in 1877. Baird obliged with a letter of recommendation in which he mentioned her "great originality in research" and "some scientific communications which have been highly esteemed." He also considered her "unquestionably better acquainted with zoology as a science than any other person of her sex in the country," but both her discipline— zoology—and her sex were against her. Vassar wanted a geologist and, in the opinion of Maria Mitchell, a man, and Graceanna was turned down.

Her letter to her sister Rebecca about the Vassar job castigated men of science in their relationships with women scientists. "I do not look for a testimonial from Dr. Leidy at all. I know he was spoken to twice—once by Professor [Rachel] Bodley and once by Dr. Ruschenberger. Both times he made a memorandum in his notebook, but I do not think it is his memory at fault." So Leidy, who had supported her membership in the academy (which was for amateur naturalists), would not help her get a professional job at Vassar. "I do not hope at all—not because I have not the very best of recommendations, but because of the preference for a masculine representative in that chair."

From that time on Graceanna seemed to accept the role she had been given by others—that as a popularizer of natural history. Her lectures and the charts she designed to illustrate them certainly appealed to non-scientists, particularly her efforts to tie in the development of the animal kingdom with God's foreordained design of the universe. While her belief that God's purpose in creating man was

"to multiply beings attuned to the Divine Nature, destined to an im-
mortal existence in the midst of his everlasting harmonies," appealed
to the common, religious, people of the day who were still struggling to fit Darwin's ideas into a religious context, scientists like Baird
and Leidy preferred to analyze and catalogue specimens and ignore
the religious questions.

However, Graceanna still needed to support herself. In 1883, she
accepted a teaching job, this time in Clifton, New York, at the Foster School. In her letters to her sister Rebecca, she described her
varying natural history pursuits. Her discovery of algae growing in
sulfur water led her to a study of paramecia under her microscope;
a friend showed her fossils in a nearby sand bank; in April 1884
she collected and analyzed fifty plants, including a hepatica with
sharp-pointed leaves [probably the sharp-lobed hepatica, *Hepatica
acutiloba*].

To her nephew, Robbie, she explained how she taught her students to soak and sprout seeds so they could understand the way
seeds grow. She described the natural life in the school aquarium
and her efforts to force twigs to blossom in vases. She had also watched
a luna moth, "the prettiest of all that we have," emerge from its co-
coon and added the information that Robbie search for luna moth
cocoons "near walnut and hickory trees, whose leaves the caterpillar
eats." Clearly Graceanna knew something about every aspect of natural history.

Not all her time was devoted to teaching, however. During the
Philadelphia Centennial back in 1876, she had made a big hit in the
Women's Pavillion with her chart of Natural History accompanied
by a wax model that illustrated relations in the animal kingdom.
For this display she had received an award from the Centennial Judges,
who decided she was "doing very interesting and important original
work in some departments of zoology hitherto but little explored."
Such recognition must have pleased her, because she continued for
many decades designing charts for a variety of expositions. Her discovery of what she thought was an unusual algae near Foster School
led her to do a drawing of the "water-veil growing here in the Sul-
phur Brook" for the 1885 New Orleans Exposition. She also did a
drawing "of the microscopic structure of a feather," and she planned
to send "a moderate-sized chart of the Vegetable Kingdom and one
of the Animal Kingdom."

In 1885, Graceanna was sixty-four years old. The Foster School,
which was not a Quaker school, depressed her. Its emphases on evan-
gelical protestantism and on producing ideal young ladies, rather
than women with minds of their own, ran counter to her strong

Quaker training. Its intellectual isolation also discouraged her, and she missed not only her contacts in Philadelphia at the Academy of Natural Sciences but also the strong coterie of Quaker women who involved themselves in social issues.

This time she was able to resign her job and return to Pennsylvania, in part because her adopted daughter, Ellen, who had been widowed shortly after the Civil War, had remarried in 1881. Ellen's second husband, M. Simpson McCullough, was a well-to-do lawyer, and Ellen shared her new found luxury with her stepmother. She settled on Graceanna a retirement stipend of twenty dollars a week and gave her generous presents on holidays. Best of all, Ellen and her husband owned a vacation house at Longport, New Jersey, on the Atlantic coast, and Graceanna visited her there every year. Both women collected algae, and Graceanna extended her natural history studies to seaweed and jellyfish. Back in Media, Pennsylvania, where she had settled in, she continued to read and write, developing still another interest—that of dendrology, the study of trees. In 1883, before taking the job at Foster's, she had attended free lectures at the Horticultural Hall in Philadelphia by Dr. Joseph Rothrock, who was later called the Father of Pennsylvania Forestry. Those particular lectures had dealt with mushrooms and toadstools, and she had found them "clear, practical and useful." No doubt she had met him at these lectures and continued her acquaintance, since he was a professor of botany at the University of Pennsylvania from 1877 until 1893.

In any event, Rothrock learned in 1892 that Graceanna had begun drawing the branchlets of shade and forest trees, including their summer and autumn foliage with their flowers and fruit, hoping to publish them as a book. Instead, Rothrock recommended to John Woodward, chairman of the Pennsylvania Forestry Commission, that he hire Graceanna to paint fifty watercolors of Pennsylvania tree leaves. She worked from dawn to dusk and finished the work in two and a half months, receiving $250.00 for her efforts. She entered them in the Chicago Columbian Exposition of 1893, where they won a bronze medal and a diploma. From those watercolors she once again expanded into charts, this time creating a series of eight, called Tree Leaf Charts, for school use at $0.50 each. She designed similar charts of choice wildflowers and handled the distribution and sales herself.

As decade succeeded decade, Graceanna's mind continued fertile and active. Her most entertaining and interesting writing was produced in the last decade of the nineteenth century and the first decade of the twentieth, when she wrote for both the *Friend's Intelli-*

2.   Brown thrasher by Graceanna Lewis. *Courtesy Friends Historical Library of Swarthmore College, Pennsylvania*

*gencer and Journal* and the *Delaware County Institute of Science, Proceedings.* In her piece for the *Friend's Intelligencer,* "Birds and Their Friends," published in 1896, she traced her own development as a naturalist and recounted a charming story about a wood thrush who had once picked up sticks and gone into her parlor through its open door. She and a friend were sitting in the parlor; they watched as the bird looked around, decided it was not a proper nesting place, and hopped out again. The wood thrush's song resembled "cathedral music and appeals to the religious element in our nature," she wrote, surely a sentiment that would have appealed to her Quaker readers.

She described Media, Pennsylvania, as "a meeting ground for both northern and southern species, and . . . a favorable point of observation for the young ornithologist." She also advised students to "make notes of the arrival and return of each specie, and keep a record of those seen during the year, with remarks on the habits to be observed for comparison in the future." All that was sound scientific advice, but in keeping with her beliefs, she explained bird migration, which was not understood at the time, in spiritual terms. Migration "attests a Power awakening reverence in the mind of the thoughtful student of nature." Furthermore, her microscopic study of feathers "awakened not only a higher appreciation of beauty but also feelings of adoration."

Her series for the *Friend's Intelligencer* on "Urbanista in Winter, Spring, Summer and Fall" in 1900 and 1901 also mixed her religious ideas with her scientific observations. Everything from spider webs to Carolina wrens intrigued her, and "the innocent pleasure to be found in the study of nature does not pall with age." She recommended studying nature as a way to stabilize "the character of men and women," and she inveighed against burning and raking leaves rather than letting them lie to enrich the forest soil. Poetically, she invoked the beauty of the first snowstorm of the season and talked about the joy of examining moss under a microscope.

Yet in her articles for the more scientific periodical, *Delaware County Institute of Science, Proceedings*, she did not stray from her scientific descriptions of what she had observed, and in her article, "At Longport, New Jersey, in September," published in 1909, she was painstakingly accurate in all her descriptions of jellyfish. She illustrated her wide reading on the subject, showing familiarity with Alexander Agassiz's seminal work on jellyfishes. All this at the age of eighty-eight!

But her age did not seem to stop her. While she tired easily, as she wrote to a friend in 1902, she still continued to paint pansies and roses. And she had not given up her scientific studies. In *The American Naturalist* she had read about a "Reclassification of Reptiles," which she was studying to see if she ought to adopt it, and she had already reworked her fish chart. Another new pursuit was extinct mammals. After all, she concluded, "I could not be satisfied that I was making a right use of the days that are left me without something of this kind."

So she continued, deeply interested in nature until the end of her life. That came on February 25, 1912 after a sudden stroke five days previously. But Graceanna Lewis had lived a vital, productive life according to her religious beliefs, and she remained convinced that "a reasonable acquaintance with the objects of nature may be a fitting preparation for our advancement in eternity."

# Martha Maxwell

### COLORADO NATURALIST

—————————————————————
～

NEWSPAPER AND MAGAZINE ARTICLES called her the Colorado Huntress, but Martha Maxwell, a diminutive housewife from Boulder, did not like the name. She preferred to be called the Colorado Naturalist.

Still, her hunting and taxidermy skills caused a stir in 1876, when her exhibit of stuffed wild animals, "Woman's Work," was one of the chief attractions at the Philadelphia Centennial. Representing the new state of Colorado, Martha spent her time answering questions about how she had killed and preserved her specimens. The realization that this genteel woman had gone off by herself on rugged camping trips into the wilderness to collect birds and animals made her a curiosity that people flocked to see. Furthermore, her unique skill in taxidermy and her idea of grouping her animals according to their habitat made her exhibit lifelike and fascinating to everyone.

Even the leading scientists of the day acknowledged the importance of her contribution. Ornithologists Robert Ridgway and Elliott Coues visited her collection at the centennial, and each man wrote a report about what he saw. Ridgway published a list of the 234 birds she had preserved; in his introduction to the list, he wrote that "it illustrates very fully the avian fauna of Colorado, while it bears testimony, not only to the great richness and variety which characterize the productions of the new state, but also to the success which has crowned the enthusiastic and intelligent efforts of a woman naturalist." Since Martha was proudest of her bird collection and thought of herself as a naturalist, such compliments from the foremost ornithologist of the day pleased her very much.

So did the praise of Elliott Coues, who made a mammal list of the forty-eight species in her collection. He emphasized her skill in mounting her specimens according to their habitat, claiming that the overall effect made natural history accessible to people from all walks of life. Certainly Martha's exhibit attracted a wide slice of humanity, and the *People's Journal* of New York declared that she "is doubtless the *living* heroine of this Centennial exhibition."

How had a quiet, unassuming woman become the star attraction at such a historic event? It had not been easy, but she had been blessed by a tradition of strong-minded women on her mother's side. For instance, her maternal grandparents were farmers in Connecticut, but when her grandmother Abigail decided to emigrate to northern Pennsylvania with some of her grown children, entreaties from her husband in Connecticut to return to him did not move her. She stayed and purchased a farm in the new community of Dartt's Settlement, Tioga County, Pennsylvania, and refused to return to her husband for several years. This was in the 1820s, when women were usually not so independent. In the meantime, her daughter Amy married Spencer Dartt, and Martha was born in 1831. Spencer died of scarlet fever shortly afterward, leaving a weakened and sorrowing wife, and grandmother Abigail took over the early raising of Martha.

This was crucial to the person Martha later became. Abigail loved nature and frequently took her small granddaughter into the woods to familiarize her with birds, squirrels, and wildlife in general. When Martha was nine years old, her mother married Josiah Dartt, a cousin of Martha's father, and Josiah became the father Martha had never had. He was a gentle, religious man who enjoyed reading and the study of nature.

In 1842 Amy, Josiah, and Martha set off for Oregon to convert the Indians to Christianity, accompanied by indefatigable grandmother Abigail and three of Amy's brothers. By the time they reached Byron, Illinois, malaria had killed many of the pioneers heading west, including Abigail. They buried her in Byron and then continued only as far as Baraboo, Wisconsin, where Amy's brother, Joseph Sanford, had already settled. There the Dartt family put down their roots.

Within a few years, Amy and Josiah had two daughters, Mary and Elizabeth. No sisters were ever loved as much as Martha loved them. Mary, especially, became her dear friend and confidante throughout her life.

They settled in a rough cabin on the edge of the wilderness, and because of Amy's frail health, Martha grew up quickly, pitching in with the hard work of farming and child care. Josiah was often away

3.   Martha Maxwell with her display at the Philadelphia Centennial. *Courtesy Colorado Historical Society, Denver, Colorado*

on various business ventures, so the women had to handle emergencies by themselves. One day, when Mary was a toddler and Martha was thirteen, Martha spotted a rattlesnake coiled next to Mary on the rough cabin floor. Grabbing her father's gun, Martha aimed and fired, killing the rattlesnake and leaving Mary unharmed. Martha had never handled a gun before; when Josiah returned and heard the story, he immediately taught Martha how to use it properly, and she became a dead shot.

As she matured, Martha made plans. She was determined to go to college and have a career. Her stepfather, with his love of book learning, agreed with her ambitions, although he was able to give her very little financial aid. He did manage to scrape together enough money to start her at Oberlin College in Ohio, and she continued to work her way through with some help from him. She led a precarious existence though, skimping on food, warm clothing, and heat, sustained by religion and a sense of her own worth. Eventually her monetary sources dried up completely, and she returned home to teach school for a winter.

That was when she met one of Baraboo's wealthiest citizens. James Alexander Maxwell owned a store, grist mill, and large home. He was also a widower with six children, two of whom were college age. Intrigued by the bright daughter of his friend Josiah, he made a proposal to her. If she would chaperone his son and daughter at Lawrence College, Wisconsin, he would pay her way there also. Naturally she accepted his offer with alacrity, hoping to complete her education.

She did not, however, wish to accept his marriage proposal. She parried for a time until he approached her family. Josiah urged her acceptance, so she married James despite the hostility of James' older children towards her. Although he was forty-two and she only twenty-two, he was properly devout, well-to-do, and lover-like in his letters to her.

For a few years, things went well with the couple, but then James was ruined by the panic of 1857. All that remained of his wealth was his house. In 1858 their daughter Mabel was born, but fortunately, his first family was raised. Then, in 1860, he and Martha set off for the gold fields of Colorado, leaving two-year-old Mabel with Amy and Josiah.

James and Martha followed the Omaha-Denver Trail with other gold seekers and settled in the rough mining town of Nevadaville. Like many others, they quickly discovered that finding gold was not easy. In fact, instead of finding money, they lost what little savings they had taken west with them. To make money, James began driving cattle from the east to their owners in Colorado, and Martha had a rough boardinghouse built. She took in between fifty and seventy-five men, and with the money she earned, she invested in land and a mining claim.

Her hours were long and hard, but she did find time to notice the majestic land she lived in. Her boarders often brought her bouquets of wildflowers from the nearby mountains, and she wrote home to her stepsister Mary that "you don't know how strange it seems to find such forms of beauty on these ruged [sic] and almost barren mountains where one might naturally look for sublimity but could hardly expect to find such delicate beauty."

The same year the boardinghouse was started, 1861, it burned down in a general conflagration that took most of the rest of the town as well. However, after a winter in a rented cabin, she and James moved to a cabin on the land she had bought with her boardinghouse savings. As soon as they left it for a few days, their claim was jumped by an itinerant German taxidermist. This was legal at the time, but she did pay him a visit and try to persuade him to move out. She also noticed his stuffed animals and, at that moment, a light went on in her head. She asked him to teach her how to preserve the animals, but he refused, fearful that she would become more adept than he and take away what little business he had.

Uppermost in her mind, though, was reclaiming her property. Accompanied by her husband, she hid near the cabin and waited for the German to leave. After a couple of weeks he did, and she and James moved back in. The cabin was filled with the taxidermist's work, and while they waited for his return, Martha carefully studied the specimens.

The next day the German appeared and was in a violent mood, but James held him off. Amid bitter recriminations, the German removed his possessions, and once again the Maxwells had a home. Almost immediately, on January 1, 1862, Martha wrote a letter to her family asking them to send a book of hers that was "an instruction in the fine arts. . . . I wish to learn how to preserve birds and other animal curiosities in this country." She had found the calling that would make her an independent, contributing member of society. No longer would she be lonely for the company of other women — she could spend her time studying and collecting the wild creatures of Colorado, and she would educate humanity by displaying them in all their diversity.

It took a long visit back to Wisconsin — 1864–68 — however, before she could really begin her career. She needed to learn more about taxidermy and natural history in general. When she arrived at her parents' home, she found her stepsisters attending school. She met and was inspired by their natural history teacher, Professor E. F. Hobart at the Baraboo Collegiate Institute. With his help, she located a local man, Mr. Ogden, who had had some experience in stuffing animals. Soon, with instruction from him, she began learning the art of taxidermy.

At first she did not like what she produced. The skins were always too large for their frames, so she invented a new approach — a combination of skin preparation and sculpture. She molded the frame of the animal in plaster and then covered it with the skin she had preserved. She also insisted on making authentic replicas of the backgrounds in which the animals were found.

The Dartt home rapidly filled with examples of her work. In the meantime, back in Colorado, James sold their claim and used the money to start a sawmill business in partnership with his son, James P. Maxwell. After a year or so in her parents' home, Martha moved into the old Maxwell home in Baraboo to help care for James' ailing father and her three unmarried stepdaughters. The strain was too much for her, and in the winter of 1866 she entered a newly opened sanitarium to recover from "a greatly run-down constitution and an exaggerated case of neuralgia." Apparently she recovered so quickly that she was helping out with the other patients after a few weeks of rest.

This was the only time during her arduous life that she actually sought help, and it seemed uncharacteristic of her. Perhaps she was really escaping from the Maxwell household or maybe she was beginning to realize that her marriage was not made in heaven. James, after all, did not sell out and come east as she had expected, and finally she took another unprecedented step away from the Maxwells. Hearing of a town colony being formed in Vineland, New Jersey, she took her daughter Mabel there, joined the colony, and purchased a three-acre tract. Mabel was put in school while Martha grew and sold vegetables to support herself and her daughter.

That action brought James to her side at last. Whether that was what she wanted or not, he did persuade her to rent (and later sell) the tract and return with him, first to Baraboo and then back to Colorado. Her stepsister Mary and their daughter Mabel accompanied them. From the moment Martha returned to Colorado her mind was set. Appalled by the reduction of the abundant wildlife she had remembered from four years before, she set out to study and preserve the animals of Colorado.

Sometimes she went camping alone. Other times she took Mabel along. Often she would go with James when he had lumbering business to attend to. A two-room stone house in Boulder was home to Martha, Mary, Mabel, and James. In addition, it was Martha's place of business, where she not only skinned and preserved specimens for herself but also for others. In this way she was able to earn a little money.

Years later her daughter Mabel, in her book *Thanks to Abigail*, described Martha's camping trips as very rough affairs. Their food consisted of beans and bacon supplemented by the fish Martha caught and the game she killed. They slept on the ground with no tents to protect them from the frost that sometimes covered them when they awoke in the morning. Mabel did not like camping and found it hard to sympathize with a mother she claimed "lacked any very strong maternal qualities. They may have been swallowed up in her artistic and scientific interests."

No doubt the daughter felt shunted aside by her ambitious mother, a woman who "had a deep love for all animal life, a passion for beauty, and an unsatisfied and unfocused need for self-expression in some form," as Mabel described her. Martha kept tamed wild animals in the house so she could study their habits. There was an antelope fawn named Dick who followed them around like a pet dog and a porcupine that climbed on to Martha's lap for affectionate pats. All this attention to the animals left very little for Mabel. Mabel said that as a child she had had to learn to make her own clothes while her mother was out collecting specimens. She also had to teach herself to clean and cook. It was Mabel who cared for James when he was at home, and she frankly admitted that her parents did not have a happy marriage.

Yet Martha continued to stick by James, even though, as she wrote to her sister Mary in 1870, "Here I have been from home nearly two weeks and have not heard a word from anyone except two dunning letters from Denver — I wrote James the very day I got here. As yet he does not deign a word of reply. Do you know what has become of him. Should you see him please give him my most sincere — *scolding.*" The letter was postmarked from Saint Louis, where she had gone to sell her entire collection to Shaw's Garden. James had been cheated out of his money by a Methodist minister, and she had decided to raise money to buy land at the mouth of Boulder Canyon. Whether he resented this or not, from then until the end of her life, Martha more or less supported herself.

Martha's letters to Mary, Mabel, and her parents survive, but no existing correspondence to or from James survives after the early years, so it is hard to piece together the dissolution of their marriage. In those days people did not bare their personal sorrows to the world. Just once did a letter portray a glimmer of their relationship, when she wrote to her daughter Mabel from the Centennial about college funds. "I know your father is getting old, but he is in good health and has never permitted himself to be injured by care or overwork — He has money . . . which he will not use for your schooling or for building a house. He has nobody but himself — and the church — to support and the farm which has had so much of my life and sweat worked into it, might to [sic] go a good ways toward that support. So that I do not feel that I am to be sensured [sic] on his account. . . ." James, at least in Martha's eyes, was weak and lazy, content to let his wife pursue her ambitions and support herself and their daughter with little help from him. On the other hand, James had expected a demure housewife and had instead gotten an independent, hard-driving, and creative career woman. At his age, it was probably too late to change his preconceived and society-approved notions of what a proper wife should be.

Seemingly undaunted by her personal problems, as soon as she sold her first collection, Martha began her second. She would arise

early in the morning so she could observe the habits of the creatures. Mabel described her as "moving quietly, she would crawl
through underbrush, over rocks, up mountains and down streams
until she had found her quarry. Then she would stand, infinitely
patient, silent as a tree, watching the birds and animals." She was
fearless in her pursuit of specimens, once getting trapped by a herd
of buffalo, but she managed to shoot the buffalo she wanted for her
collection.

She did not enjoy killing animals, and when she was home she
practiced strict vegetarianism. She was a naturalist, not a hunter and
trapper, she reminded her admirers. Those skills were merely a means
to the end she sought. "All must die sometime; I only shorten the
period of consciousness that I may give their forms perpetual memory," she wrote. According to one journalist, she set out on her expeditions "attired in a thick frock, falling a little below the knee,
a tight-fitting jacket with rolling collar, beneath which passed a handkerchief tied in sailor fashion; stout, laced shoes going well to the
knee, and any kind of head-gear that happened within reach; with
a large netted and fringed game-bag swung over the right shoulder,
a powder-flask, a double-barrel fowling-piece and a well-trained dog."
Once she climbed a high mountain in the midst of a thunderstorm
to capture a ptarmigan. Another time she was almost shot by a man
who thought she was an Indian. By 1873, she had built up another
impressive collection.

This time she decided to set up her own display. After a collecting
trip to California, she started her Rocky Mountain Museum on the
main street of Boulder. For twenty-five cents, museum patrons were
treated to the sight of several rooms filled with habitat groupings
of the wild creatures of Colorado. Word quickly spread of the amazing
little woman who had killed and preserved her own museum specimens, and she began receiving notice from the scientific community.

Spencer Fullerton Baird, assistant secretary of the Smithsonian,
specialized in wooing such people as Martha Maxwell. Martha sent
him two bird specimens in 1874, and when he answered, he asked
her to find out if they were the same species (they were). In addition,
he sent her catalogues of birds and mammals and offered to lend
her books on American natural history. At that time his colleague,
Robert Ridgway, began corresponding with her and paying her for
the specimens she procured for him. One specimen was a small owl
that Mabel had pointed out to her sitting on a tree in their yard.
Martha shot it and sent it to Ridgway, who declared a new subspecies of the common screech owl. He named it *Scops asio* var. *Max-
wellae* or Mrs. Maxwell's owl, the Rocky Mountain screech owl.

Martha's collection also positively ascertained the existence of a rare mammal, the black-footed ferret, that only Audubon had mentioned before. Most scientists had considered him in error until Martha produced three of them in her collection.

Though her work was stirring up interest, it was not making her any money. Her daughter, Mabel, had entered Oberlin College, and Martha needed to make money so "we may be able to give our daughter as good an education as she is capable of receiving, and my next ambition is to build up a temple of science that shall be a credit to *our sex* and an acquisition to the world," she explained. Finally, Martha was persuaded to move her home and museum to the larger town of Denver.

About that time, Colorado began making plans to participate in the 1876 Centennial. The legislature asked Martha if she would display her collection as part of the Colorado pavilion. They would not be able to pay her a salary, but they promised to repay her for her transportation costs. Martha agreed, hoping to sell mineral specimens and postcards of herself and her collection to earn college funds for Mabel and living expenses for herself.

She received far more fame than fortune for the whole Centennial venture, and often she had to put up with cruel jibes from women who thought she had brought shame on their sex by daring to exhibit her collection to the public. Nevertheless, when a reporter from the *Philadelphia Times* asked her what she would do if she inherited a large sum of money, she replied that she would "go back to the Rocky Mountains and pursue my studies — that vast field which is open to all who love nature."

But when the Centennial ended she did not even have the money to ship her collection home. The legislature refused to honor its promise to pay her transportation costs, and Mabel barely had enough funds to continue attending college. Desperate for money, Martha accepted the offer of a man to rent the collection and pay to move it to Washington, D.C., if she would accompany and display it. She did not like the offer or the man and stayed only a short time in his employ before moving the collection back up to Philadelphia where, she had been told, she and her collection could become part of a permanent exposition soon to be set up there. In the meantime, she moved up to Boston, Massachusetts, to live with her sister Mary's family and to assist Mary, who was an aspiring author, in writing a book about Martha's collection. Mary called it *On the Plains and among the Peaks; or, How Mrs. Maxwell Made Her Natural History Collection.*

While in Boston, Martha went back to school. She studied zool-

4. Martha Maxwell in her hunting outfit, 1876. *Courtesy Colorado Historical Society, Denver, Colorado*

ogy and chemistry at the Massachusetts Institute and was delighted when she learned to use a microscope. But all too soon she had to return to Philadelphia to display her specimens and to try to find a publisher for Mary's book. Eventually the Philadelphia firm of Claxton, Remsen, and Haffelfinger accepted the book, and it was published in 1879.

By then her dreams had fallen apart. She had hoped that Mabel would join her in her career when she graduated, but instead, her daughter wanted to teach, find a husband, and start a family. After that the heart seemed to go out of Martha, although she continued to work hard; she set up a lunch counter at the exposition to earn money. When the exposition ended she helped a lady dress hundreds of dolls for Christmas. "Glorious occupation! Intellectual! Scientific! I *hate it* — but must live I suppose and may be glad to do what is worse," she wrote to Mary.

Other schemes to make a living from her collection attracted her, and in 1880 she moved herself and her collection to the up-and-coming sea resort of Far Rockaway, Long Island. During the bitter winter of 1880–81, she skimped on food and heat. Unlike the time at Oberlin when she had done the same thing, however, she was no longer sustained by her hopes and dreams for the future. In her last letter to Mary, written on March 2, 1881, she said, "I have lost all energy and ambition — wonder what will become of me — perhaps a big wave will come and stir me up! . . ." The wave came on May 5, 1881, when she heard that her beloved stepfather was dead.

Her landlady noticed the change in her and wrote to Mabel who was happily engaged and teaching school in Wisconsin. Mabel arrived in Long Island just in time. Martha died in her arms on May 31, 1881, a victim of blood poisoning from an ovarian tumor, according to a local physician.

Her tragic story does not end there, however. Mabel buried her on Long Island, and then she and Mary entrusted the collection to J. P. Haskins of Saratoga Springs, New York, who was supposed to find a buyer for it. Instead, he exhibited it to make money for himself during the next twelve years, storing it carelessly in a barn when he didn't need it.

Martha's work had not been forgotten, and Mary was asked to show it at the Columbian Exposition in Chicago. She went to retrieve it from Haskins in 1893 and was shocked at its condition. Realizing that the cost of restoring it would be prohibitive, she wrote to a friend connected with the new Peabody Museum at Yale University about it. He expressed interest in obtaining the collection, but Haskins refused to give it up unless he was paid an exorbitant sum. Yale backed out, and the collection remained with Haskins until his death in 1916. Not much was left by then, and what was left was stored out in the snow on a vacant lot during 1917 and 1918. Mary, learning about this from an admirer of Martha's work, Henry W. Shoemaker, contacted the University of Colorado at Boulder. The university wanted the collection, but a New York taxidermist who was called in to evaluate what was left told them there were not enough surviving specimens to faithfully portray the habitat groupings Martha had set up.

Despite the devastation of her collection, Martha did leave an enduring legacy. Not only had she revolutionized the art of taxidermy, but she had pioneered the idea of habitat grouping in museum work. In addition, by persevering in her chosen field, she had proven that women could excel in something other than housework.

Today, in the Smithsonian's refurbished Arts and Industries Museum, a small remnant of Martha's work remains as part of a permanent representation of the original Centennial exhibition. It is still labeled "Woman's Work," just as it was in 1876 when she was the wonder of the Centennial.

# Mary Treat

## NATURALIST OF THE PINE BARRENS

To MARY TREAT, the Pine Barrens of New Jersey were filled with fascination. She called them "Nature's gardens, where she nourishes the sweet wildflowers in her own mysterious way," gardens filled with "flowers not to be met with in any other part of the world." Not only flowers but also birds and insects of the Pine Barrens lured her out from her home in Vineland, New Jersey, to study nature and to report her observations in popular magazine articles and books.

Despite her spirited defense of the beauties of southern New Jersey, she was not a native of the state. She had been born in Trumansville, New York, on September 7, 1830, the daughter of an itinerant Methodist minister and his wife. When she was nine, her family moved to Ohio, where she was able to obtain intermittent schooling, both in public school and at a girls' academy. Then she lived with a sister in New York before marrying an Ohio doctor, Joseph Burrel Treat, when she was thirty-three years old and he forty.

Treat was described as being interested in natural science, particularly astronomy and electricity. Only after her marriage did she begin her serious study of nature, although she later said that she had been interested in nature since childhood. The first several years of their marriage were spent in Iowa, and then they moved to May's Landing, New Jersey. It was easy to pursue their natural science interests there, but they felt intellectually isolated in the small town. They decided in 1868 to move to Vineland, New Jersey—the same mecca that had seduced Martha Maxwell shortly before. Unlike Martha, Mary planted roots there that lasted a lifetime.

At that time Vineland was a relatively new community. Land had been purchased for the town by Charles K. Landis in 1861. He wanted to build a harmonious community known for its industry, beauty, education, agriculture, and humanitarian principles. Fruit culture was particularly important to Landis, but he was discouraged by the prolific insect pests, so he offered rewards to growers who were able to produce "the best half-acre of fruit trees kept the cleanest from tree grubs, curculios and apple moths." Such problems encouraged the Treats to begin their studying and writing about insects.

The first evidence that Mary was interested in insects appeared in 1869, when she wrote to C. V. Riley, then the editor of *American Entomologist*, described a green beetle she had found, and asked him to identify it. During the following eleven years ten articles on insects by Mary appeared in the magazine on such diverse topics as the tomato worm, the pupa of the girdled sphinx moth, and the enemies of the oak. She had become not only an identifier but also an observer of insects, able to describe the life histories of polyphemus, raspberry, and verbena moths. Like all naturalists, though, she moved with ease from specialty to specialty, writing articles about birds at the same time she was studying insects and plants.

Her husband, meanwhile, after initial enthusiasm for Vineland, drifted away to New York City, helping to nominate suffragist Victoria Woodhull as the first female candidate for U.S. president in 1872. Apparently the Treats' marriage was already in trouble, probably because he was a womanizer, and until his penniless death in a New York hotel in 1878, they lived apart most of the time.

In true, decorous Victorian fashion, Mr. Treat was never mentioned, and Mrs. Treat had to make her own way in the world, with no material support from him. This she did by writing about the natural lives she was observing.

Having little in the way of books to guide her, she wrote to the men who knew the fields she was interested in—Asa Gray in botany, Auguste Forel, Samuel Scudder, Henry C. McCook, and Charles V. Riley in insects—and sent specimens and descriptions to them for verification. Gray was particularly helpful, suggesting likely places for her to collect, and in return was rewarded with the specimens she sent to him. It was through Gray that she also became a correspondent of Sir Joseph Hooker, director of Kew Gardens in London, and Charles Darwin.

She and Darwin shared a common interest—the specific mechanisms of carnivorous plants—and he quickly recognized her expertise in the subject, mentioning in his book *Insectivorous Plants* that "Mrs. Treat of New Jersy has been more successful than any other observer" in understanding how bladderworts (*Utricularia clandestina*) capture insects. At first she had thought, like Darwin, that in-

43

sects pushed their way in headfirst but later she changed her mind after long, careful hours of observation. "I soon became so deeply interested," she wrote in her book *Home Studies in Nature*, "that I scarcely took note of time, and the small hours of the morning frequently found me absorbed in the work." She put the minute bladders, or utricles, in water along with microscopic creatures, such as water bears. Watching through her microscope, she finally discovered "a depression at the entrance of the utricle, a pretty vestibule that seems to attract the little animals into the inviting retreat, where just beyond is a fatal trap or valve which if touched springs back and engulfs the unwary adventurers." When she sent her observations to Darwin, he capitulated at once, saying, "It is pretty clear I am quite wrong about the head acting like a wedge."

She did not stop with bladderworts; she studied other carnivorous plants as well — *Drosera* (sundews), *Dionaea* (Venus flytraps), *Pinguicula* (butterworts), and *Sarracenia* (pitcher plants). Sundews were common in the pine barrens of New Jersey, but she was able to study Venus flytraps, which are found only in a restricted area within fifty miles of Wilmington, North Carolina, through the generosity of Dr. Wood of Wilmington. He sent her thirty plants of *Dionoea muscipula* so that she could answer Darwin's query about whether one leaf could digest more than one fly. Some, she found, could digest up to three flies, while others could only manage one or even none. In the true spirit of scientific investigation, she experimented with her own finger, putting it into a leaf. In less than fifteen minutes she felt considerable pressure on her finger. After an hour, the pressure increased slightly and her arm began to hurt. Finally, totally unnerved, she removed her finger.

Pitcher plants were also plentiful in the barrens, but she again enlisted help from C. V. Riley, by then the well-known entomologist to the U.S. Department of Agriculture, in identifying the nests of insects built within fresh pitcher plant leaves before they started trapping insects. She believed that the sticky secretion inside the pitchers intoxicated the insects, but when she put her observations in writing, Gray immediately objected saying, "You know none of the botanists agree with you." "I cannot help it," she answered. "It must go in [to her article], for I have now *seen* it for myself, and I know *it is* so." Twenty years later botanists corroborated her observations.

In the summer of 1875 she received northern species of butterworts from Cornell and was so fascinated by their possibilities that she spent the first of several winters in Florida living in a cottage on the banks of the Saint Johns River near Jacksonville studying southern butterworts. Three species — *Pinguicula pumila, P. lutea* and *P. elatior* — kept her busy through the season. She decided first that they were annuals and second that they were carnivorous as well as herbivorous, consuming both pollen and the insects she put on their leaves.

She also continued her bladderwort studies in Florida, disagreeing with Dr. Chapman's *Flora of the Southern States*, which claimed there were nine species of bladderwort in the entire South. "I have found more than nine distinct species in Florida alone," she retorted.

She not only found bladderwort species in Florida but also rediscovered a water lily (*Nymphaea flava*) depicted by Audubon in his white American swan portrait. Botanists had previously dismissed the lily as a figment of Audubon's fertile imagination, but Mary discovered "acres and acres" of the beautiful plant, "a living testimony to Audubon's truth and skill."

Furthermore, as she botanized from her rowboat, exploring the shores and coves of the Saint Johns River, she made still another find — a new amaryllis lily. Sereno Watson of the Gray Herbarium at Harvard decided this was a new species and named it in honor of Mary — *Zephranthes treatae*, or the Zephyr-lily.

That was not the only thing named for Mary. Entomologists, too, honored her. Auguste Forel of Switzerland named an ant *Aphaenogaster treatae* for her, while Gustav Mayr of Vienna bestowed the name *Belonocnema treatae* on a cynipid oak fig root gall, which she found on a Virginia oak tree in Florida.

It is not clear where she discovered *Aphaenogaster treatae*, a widely distributed ant that lives from Ontario to Georgia and west to Nebraska and Texas, but there is no doubt that she studied and collected ants both in Florida and New Jersey, climaxing her work with ants in her book *Chapters on Ants*, published in 1877. Mary sent a letter in January of 1878 from Green Cove Spring, Florida, to Samuel Scudder of the Boston Society of Natural History. She wrote, "I have found a *harvesting* ant here, allied to the 'agricultural ant' of Texas. Dr. McCook (author of *The Natural History of the Agricultural Ant of Texas*) — says, it is a *big* discovery. Here ants do not hibernate, and I have been studying them for more than a month and find them wonderfully curious and interesting. I have also found a *new Camponotus* working in wood, but they are hibernating at present."

In a letter written a year earlier, she had enclosed seven vials of ants that she had hoped he could identify. She had been studying

5.   Drawing of Mary Treat in her Insect Garden from *Home Studies in Nature.*

them in New Jersey for an entire summer, because it was in New Jersey, and specifically in her backyard in Vineland, where she did much of her insect work.

She described the area as being less than an acre, one quarter of which was woodland. In the woods, she had discovered two new species of burrowing spiders — *Tarantula tigrina* and *Tarantula turricula* — and had twenty-eight nests under observation in one season. Since the former worked only at night, she watched their activities by lamplight. She also observed digger wasps, which killed and buried spiders as food for their larvae. By the end of the season only five of the burrowing spiders remained.

Most of the backyard was surrounded by an arbor vitae hedge 15 feet high and 150 feet in circumference. There she established what became known as her Insect Menagerie, but which she described as her Arachnidan menagerie, since so many of her observations were of spiders and their "relentless enemy," the digger wasps. Centered inside the hedge was a large, drooping, maple tree under which she observed the life history of harvester ants from early spring until late autumn. Ornamental plants and two bird baths, which were "large, shallow, earth-colored pans . . . set into the ground," completed the setting. In addition to the resident spiders and insects, she also received live "insect gifts" from people all over the country. Although she established them in as natural an environment as possible, she sometimes manipulated her study objects to observe them better and protect them from their natural enemies. For instance, she put some of the burrowing spiders in candy jars to watch them construct their burrows. Others she allowed to dig their burrows in the ground, but she covered them with "oval glasses with a small opening at the top, which I can close at pleasure. These I set over each burrow to keep my pets from the ravages of . . . the digger wasp. . . ." All of these close observations almost convinced her that "the more I limit myself to a small area, the more novelties and discoveries I make in natural history."

But in her best and most popular book, *Home Studies in Nature,* first published in 1880, she makes it clear that she did wander ten miles or more over the Pine Barrens in search of flowers and ferns. At one point, she found a rare local fern, *Schizaea pusilla,* which was later discovered by bryologist Elizabeth Gertrude Knight Britton in Nova Scotia. She also had to explore the barrens in every season to write her forty-one articles for *Garden and Forest* on the flora of the area.

Bird study was another of her interests. She fed birds in the winter and watched them build their nests and raise their young in the spring and summer. Since Elliott Coues's *Key to North American Birds* was available to her, she did not need to correspond with ornithologists. Beginning with "Notes on Birds" for *Hearth and Home* in 1870, she wrote thirteen articles about her bird observations from 1870 until 1896. The catbird was her favorite, although she was sympathetic to all species, even the raptors, which she watched take songbirds. She commented that they needed to eat too, which was definitely an enlightened attitude at a time when raptors were usually killed as "varmints."

Mary Treat was popular with all who knew her. Even Asa Gray, who was not known for his sense of humor, once said that "most of the letters I have to respond to are done from a sense of duty; but yours are a *treat.*" Certainly her letters convey the sense of a person eager to learn more about what she has been observing and then to share it with others. She even started a young ladies club in 1893, inviting them to meet with her every two weeks to discuss botanical, entomological, and ornithological topics. The women were impressed with her innate reserve, which wore off after five or ten minutes when she became more talkative and even humorous.

Those young ladies came to the new home Mary was able to buy for herself in 1888 — "a little home nest," as her friend Anne M. Lane called it, "surrounded by flowers and singing birds." In a little woods on the west side of her lawn she planted a wild garden of indigenous plants that she had gathered in the Pine Barrens. And there again, she replicated her old insect menagerie by planting a "circle of evergreens, in which was her study grounds, for her studies in entomology."

Despite her amateur status, her work was respected by her male contemporaries. Samuel Scudder, in fact, as one of the founders of the Cambridge Entomological Club, made certain she was elected a member. Otherwise, she was known as a popularizer of natural history. But unlike many people writing about nature at the time, both for children and adults, her work was as accurate as she could make it. She also proved that well-written, truthful nature writing could be lucrative.

Although her productive writing period lasted less than thirty years, she made enough money from book royalties to see her through a long, invalid old age. Never robust, the five-foot-tall, one-hundred-and-ten-pound woman, was crippled by a fall and was forced, in 1916, to leave her beloved Vineland and live with her sister in Akron, New York, where she died at the age of ninety-three in 1923.

They brought her back to Vineland, though, to join her husband in the Siloam Cemetery — the woman who believed that "Southern New Jersey has ever had an irresistible fascination to the botanist, unequalled by any other section of the Union."

# Annie Montague Alexander

## INTREPID EXPLORER

ANNIE MONTAGUE ALEXANDER was a quintessential naturalist. Deeply in love with the outdoors, she was particularly interested in botany, ornithology, mammalogy, and paleontology throughout her long, active life. In addition she had the skills and necessary grit to pursue those interests, because she was a tireless and daring explorer, a compulsive collector, and a crack shot.

Born in Honolulu, Hawaii, on December 29, 1867, she was, from the beginning, her father's daughter. Her father, Samuel Thomas Alexander, along with his best friend and later brother-in-law, Henry Baldwin, pioneered in raising sugar cane on the island of Maui. Samuel, with his boundless energy, innovative ideas, and gift for raising money, and Henry Baldwin, with his business sense and dogged determination, formed a corporation known as Alexander and Baldwin, Inc.

Annie was two years old when her father and her uncle purchased their first piece of land. Until she was fifteen she lived in the family home at Haiku on Maui while Alexander and Baldwin built up their original investment into a sound, profitable business.

Like her father, Annie was adventuresome and energetic and enjoyed the carefree life of a country-bred child in a land still largely unspoiled by exploitation. Her schooling began at home with a governess, but later she was sent to Honolulu with two of her siblings to attend a school for the children of missionaries.

In 1882, citing health reasons, her father moved the family to Oakland, California, where Annie attended public grammar and high schools. She was sent, in 1886, to La Salle Seminary for Girls in Auburndale, Massachusetts. Two years later Annie accompanied her family on the de rigueur tour of Europe, where she was left in Paris to study art. She apparently had considerable talent but unusually weak eyes that began to suffer from the close work required of an artist. Threatened with blindness, she was forced to give up her study and return home.

Her next attempt at a career—that of a nurse—was also foiled by her weak eyes, and so she settled into a life of travel and exploration as her father's chief companion. But travel was not enough for Annie. She needed something more to occupy her mind and energies.

When her close friend, Martha Beckwith, invited her on a trip into California's Sierra Nevada, she eagerly accepted, since she admired Martha, who became a teacher at Mount Holyoke College. Throughout their lifetimes, Annie's letters to Martha continued to reveal the private Annie behind her public stance. It was Martha, on the mountain trip, who collected flowers and studied birds and who taught Annie about them, and it was also Martha who introduced her to geology. "But what a fever the study of old Earth that you thought should be a part of my education has set up in me," she wrote to Martha in 1901. "I really am alarmed. If it were a general interest in geology there might be something quite wholesome in it but it seems to centralize on fossils, fossils! and I am beleagured."

Annie also started attending lectures at the University of California in Berkeley and was spellbound by Dr. John C. Merriam's lectures on paleontology. She quickly made the happy discovery that fieldwork did not hurt her eyes, and in 1901 she organized her first paleontological field trip to the Fossil Lake region of Oregon.

Her family, she wrote to Martha, "do not seem to quite approve my new ambition. I do not want to be selfish yet it seems to me we have the right to a considerable extent of disposing of our lives as we think fit." She must have had an independent income by then, which she could spend with no questions asked, because when she began financing expeditions under Merriam's tutelage, she told only Martha and another woman, Mary Wilson, who went along on the early field trips, about her financial backing.

In the summer of 1902 she explored Shasta County, California, on an expedition led by Vance C. Osmont, assistant professor of mineralogy at the University of California. They were joined by a Stanford professor, two other men who were expected to do the hard work of digging, Katherine Jones—undoubtedly as a companion for Annie—and, for part of the time, Annie's mentor, Dr. Merriam, who, she wrote to Martha "respects me thoroughly."

And well he might. Annie quickly gained a reputation for finding all the fossils. She seemed to have an uncanny talent for choosing the right place to dig, but perhaps that was because she would "push through thick brush to the most obscure places with the hope that for that reason they may not have been already visited." With such a method it is no wonder she made the "find of the trip"—three saurians—and that she liked paleontology "more and more." She called it "this study of our old, old world and the creatures to whom it belonged in the ages past. . . . Perhaps the study is all the more interesting because it is incomplete. There is so much yet to find out. . . ."

The following year she led and financed a party in the black limestone region of Shasta County. There she discovered her first creature new to the scientific world—a reptile from the upper Triassic age that was named *Thalattosaurus alexandrae* in her honor.

She also took up a new pursuit in 1903—collecting the skulls of wild animals. By the first of March she had already amassed forty different species of mostly carnivorous creatures. It was obvious that one paleontological trip a year was not enough to keep such an active person content. "Why not take risks now and then? It adds to the zest of life," she observed.

With that her adventuresome father no doubt agreed; on March 20, 1904, she and he went to London, where they outfitted themselves for a long-planned hunting safari to British East Africa. After many hundreds of miles on foot, during which both father and daughter hunted, explored, and collected skulls, they stopped at Victoria Falls on the Zambesi River. Carefully they worked their way down a trail to the river's edge so that Annie could take pictures, while high above them workmen were excavating a bridge foundation, tossing rocks and soil down over the edge. Although Annie and her father had moved off to what they had thought was a safe distance, a huge boulder struck Mr. Alexander on his left side and foot. He did not survive the night, dying with Annie by his side.

She buried her beloved father in a small cemetery in the town of Livingston. The shock of his death made her more desperate than ever to find meaning for her own life; the following summer she resumed her paleontological expeditions, this time to the Humboldt Range in Nevada. In the American Canyon, she, her friend Edna Wemple, and Eustace Furlong, spent two months investigating a single outcrop of limestone formed during the upper part of the Middle Triassic period. While the men dug, the women "sat in the dust and sun, marking and wrapping bones. . . ." Sometimes, though, the weather was not so benign, and for the first three weeks they shivered from the wind and occasional sleet storms. It seemed a small

6.   Annie Alexander in the desert. *Courtesy Alice Howard*

price to pay for the "great variety in light and shadow in the landscape about us. Sometimes half a dozen distinct thunder showers
would gather and sweep across the valley of the Buffalo Sink below
us. There was a perpetual scurry of clouds from the northwest. They
left their snow on the higher elevations that looked truly Alpine as
the sun touched them. . . . All this we witnessed while keeping an

eye open for bone, taking in large draughts of bracing air, our warm jersey[s] buttoned up to our necks."

As the weather moderated, Annie preferred to sleep outside, where "half the universe shone down upon us, not a tree to break the wonderful arch of the Milky Way reaching from horizon to horizon." After such an experience, returning home to live within four walls seemed to stifle her. Besides, the work had been useful. They had found twenty-five specimens along with valuable fragmentary material.

Then, late that fall, her life took a new turn. She met the charismatic C. Hart Merriam, a cousin of her mentor, John C. Merriam, brother of ornithologist Florence Merriam Bailey, and the chief of the United States Biological Survey, who was fascinated when he heard about Annie's collection of animal skulls. He was full of tales about Alaska, where he had gone to collect during the Harriman expedition, and Annie's interest was piqued.

In May of 1906 she set out for the Kenai Peninsula in search of Alaskan bears. Along with Edna Wemple and government collector Alvin Seale, they arrived at the head of Disenchantment Bay. From the Malaspina Glacier they followed the Kenai River to Skilak Lake and collected big game. But the find of that trip was purchased from a local trapper—a new subspecies of grizzly bear that Merriam later named *Ursus alexandrae.*

Enamored of Alaska and overwhelmed by its potential, Annie spent two more summers there, amassing "the largest and most important collection [of Alaska big bears] in existence after that of the United States Biological Survey," C. Hart Merriam claimed. She also became interested in birds and small mammals and wanted "to learn how to put up a good bird skin—one can master the mechanical part with a little practice, but the real art lies in the finishing touches, shaping the specimen and making the feathers lie right."

By the end of her second expedition to Alaska, her collections were immense. But she had already decided what her life's work was to be. Ever since her father's death she had been searching for "something to do to divert my mind and absorb my interest and the idea of making collections of West Coast fauna as a nucleus for study gradually took shape in my mind." She was helped along in her thinking by C. Hart Merriam who had told her how rapidly indigenous game birds and mammals were disappearing in the West.

At just that crucial point she met the man who would make it all possible. Joseph Grinnell was a young Pasadena naturalist working at the Throop Institute who had also done field work in Alaska. He showed her his research museum in the small, back parlor of his home, complete with his own neat and scholarly records. He talked of the need for the West Coast to have its own natural history museum with an emphasis on California fauna, and he wanted the museum to be at Stanford.

Annie insisted the museum be housed at the University of California, where she had first taken the paleontological courses that had so inspired her. She put up all the money for it and extracted a promise from the university's Board of Regents that she and Grinnell would have entire control of the museum and its employees. It was Grinnell who suggested the name Museum of Vertebrate Zoology and Grinnell who was her permanent choice as director.

With the museum established, she planned another expedition to Alaska. This time she was accompanied by a new female companion, "a dandy girl," she told Grinnell. Louise Kellogg was an Oakland, California, schoolteacher who enjoyed herself on the expedition every bit as much as Annie. Both Annie Alexander and Louise Kellogg began their separate, voluminous field notes on this trip. While Annie's notes were matter-of-fact and businesslike, Louise's were far more personal and showed an enthusiasm for all she observed. For instance, Louise "almost stepped on a porcupine busily eating around the base of a small spruce. I made a whistling sound and he promptly presented a bristling back in such a funny fashion that I stepped around to the other side and repeated the sound. Around he flounced again but all without cessation of his busy meal. Then I shouted at him and with that he decided I was a real enemy and scuttled off into the underbrush in his clumsy fashion." She also adopted two goslings, feeding them mosquitoes and cornmeal. They followed every one around the camp and "had a fine feast of cornmeal sitting on top of an owl Mr. Dixon was skinning."

With the arrival of Louise on the scene, the camp work was evenly divided. Louise did the cooking, while Annie tended to the dishes. She also saw to it that Annie did not overtax herself. "My friend Louise never failed me. She must needs go with me and see that I quit work when the long shadows began to creep down the hills," she told Martha.

Louise was thirteen years younger than Annie—twenty-eight to Annie's forty-one—and had a degree in classics from the University of California. She too was close to her father, whom she often accompanied on hunting expeditions into the California Suisun marshes after waterfowl. In addition to being a dead shot, she also enjoyed fishing, once using a fishing rod to "collect" a bat by hitting it over the head as it flew past her.

In January of 1909 the museum was ready for occupancy. Needing to fill the museum's yawning spaces, Annie and Louise organized their next big expedition, this time to the Quinn River crossing in Humboldt County, Nevada, to collect fossils. Along with Merriam, Furlong, and a man named Heindle, they dug for bones and found the remains of woolly rhinoceroses, camels, and mastodons, among other things. The "other things" seemed to be any creatures that would make good museum specimens — mammals, birds, lizards. That trip was their last paleontological expedition until 1922, although Annie had also helped found and fund the University of California's Department of Paleontology in 1908–1909.

Over the next thirteen years, they directed their energies into collecting small mammals and birds with a secondary emphasis on botanizing. Like naturalist-explorers of old, Alexander and Kellogg refused to specialize. Every natural object was grist for their mills, and before they were done, their collections boosted not only the Museum of Vertebrate Zoology but the Museum of Paleontology and the University Herbarium. In fact, over their lifetimes, they collected 6,744 mammals, birds, reptiles, and amphibians for the Museum of Vertebrate Zoology, 17,851 plant specimens for the University Herbarium, as well as thousands of fossil specimens for the Museum of Paleontology. Annie had founded the Museum of Paleontology in the 1920s and helped finance it in much the same way that she continued to finance the Museum of Vertebrate Zoology.

In the fall of 1911, Annie and Louise set up housekeeping together in the California Suisun marshes, purchasing a four-hundred-acre farm on Grizzly Island. There they discovered endemic races of the song sparrow, marsh wren, river otter, lowland mink, California meadow mouse, and Suisun shrew.

For several years, farming and raising prize-winning cattle absorbed much of their time. Eventually the confining nature of raising cattle, and a longing to once more resume their far-flung explorations, persuaded them to sell their herd and go into a less demanding, more seasonal type of farming raising asparagus. Since asparagus was a spring crop, they had their summers for field trips and their winters for visits to Hawaii or the desert.

Hawaii, in fact, continued to exert a strong hold over Annie, and she often spent several winter months there visiting friends and relatives. But despite her love for her native home, she felt that she could only have fit in on the islands if she had had a husband and children. Sometimes she went by herself; in 1910 she spent her time watching and collecting birds, and in 1919 she stayed alone for several days on three-acre Popoia Islet and trapped Hawaiian rats, dispassionately observing one as it walked past her feet and along her side over her skirt, a situation most women would not have sat still for! Other times Louise accompanied her; in 1920 they collected 150 species of shells for Dr. Clark of the Paleontology Department. Late in her life she wrote to Mrs. Grinnell about the beauties of the Hawaiian sea and sand and wondered why she did not retire there. But she answered her own question — "Perhaps I shall when I can't climb mountains anymore." She probably should have added "or explore deserts."

That time never came for her. Always there was the lure of mountains to climb and deserts to explore, "great, unreclaimable country . . . where there is nothing to tempt the enterprising spirit of man to conquer and subdue," "lonely places that make no demand upon my strength." In April of 1922 they ended their long hiatus at the farm as Annie and Louise resumed their full-time field trips to the wild, lonely places. At an age when most people begin to slow down — Annie was then fifty-five and Louise forty-three — they sped up, going into the Mojave Desert with chisels and jackknives to dig up camel remains, horse specimens, and a few deer jaws.

After that, they began to concentrate their efforts on small mammals — gophers, shrews, mice — which they trapped, often setting out and checking six dozen steel traps a day. In spare moments they also collected plants and observed birds. More and more the deserts attracted them, and in the next decade they thoroughly explored the arid regions of Nevada, Arizona, Idaho, New Mexico, Utah, Colorado, and California. Sometimes they ran into uncomfortable situations — heavy rains and unbearable mosquitoes near Provo, Utah; sultry heat that reached 136 degrees in the sun in Cassia County, Idaho; gnats and small flies in Mud Springs, Arizona; and tents that heated up to 110 degrees in southern Colorado.

Driving conditions were another problem. In Arizona at Tanner's Crossing they drove up a wash to look for gopher signs; instead, they broke through the crust into a mud hole that appeared to have no bottom. But the rewards of their travels were great. On one trip to Utah in the autumn of 1929 they collected 177 mammal specimens along with 4 birds and 1 amphibian. According to Grinnell's official report, three species were new to the museum's collections and two were probably new to science. They also found 8 specimens of the Colorado wood rat and 1 of the Arizona striped skunk, constituting the first records of these species for Utah.

During the summer of 1931 they discovered a new species of shrew in the Graham Mountains of Arizona. E. Raymond Hall, Grinnell's assistant, enthusiastically proposed calling it *Sorex alexanderi,* "in recognition of Miss Alexander's many contributions to our knowledge of mammals." Annie countered, "Shall we not call it *Sorex grahamensis* for you know my aversion to having things named after me." It was obviously neither the desire for immortality through nomenclature that motivated Annie nor a thirst for fame. To Annie and Louise the work was all that mattered.

They disappeared into the desert for long stretches of time and made their own entertainment on holidays. One Fourth of July in Nevada they ate kangaroo rat, which they decided was as good as chicken. Then, "Louise noosed two large gopher snakes with her fish line and two rattlesnakes which were too helpless even to buzz their rattles when they were dangling in the air. We made a Fourth of July picnic out of going to the spring, putting chains on at the mouth of the canyon, climbing a grade and crossing several gullies without much trouble in spite of the sand." Not everyone's idea of a glorious Fourth.

Christmas in Palm Springs was celebrated by spending the morning hiking six and a half miles to Palm Canyon, where they identified birds and set out their traps.

To them there was no place like the desert for collecting, and Annie was particularly interested in exploring Death Valley for gophers. In February of 1936 they found the desert cold and rainy, but they persevered, crawling under barbed wire fences, setting traps at night in the rain, and tramping over lava beds.

Near the end of 1936, they set out to explore the desert mountains of Inyo County in eastern California. They found the area dreadfully cold, especially since they were camping in tents, even though their camp stove was stuffed with wood that they took from deserted cabins. Even their specimens were frozen solid when they went to collect them. Worse yet, the traps froze to the ground and they had to be pried loose with a screwdriver. On December 8, 1936, at Deep Springs Lake the thermometer registered zero degrees although the weather was clear.

As usual Annie wrote a steady stream of letters back to Grinnell. Then, after a letter postmarked December 11, there was silence. On January 14, after consulting with Annie's old friend Edna Wemple (McDonald), he wrote a letter to Annie asking if she needed to be rescued. This he entrusted to two young men who worked at the museum, Ward Russell and Bill Richardson.

They knew the women had been heading for the Saline Valley, so they drove to nearby Big Pine and discovered that the roads were blocked with snow. Russell engaged Norman Clyde, a well-known winter explorer of the Sierra Nevada, to try to find them. It took him two days to reach their camp.

He was greeted by two cheerful but grateful ladies. Their supplies had been running low, and they had been busy chopping up dead pinon logs for fuel to cook their supply of pink beans and cornmeal and to melt the buckets of snow water they hauled a half mile to their camp. Keeping warm was also necessary, since the temperature ranged between ten and twenty degrees. An added aggravation was the lack of gophers. They had found only one in the whole area.

Since their enforced stay was contributing nothing to vertebrate zoology, they relieved Clyde of some of his provisions — eggs, bacon, butter, sugar, cookies — and sent him back to Russell and Richardson with a blank check. They were to hire a Caterpillar tractor and bulldozer to get them (and their car) out.

They had never been in any real danger. Miners, stranded by the weather at nearby Bunker Hill Mine, knew that Alexander and Kellogg were camped nearby. They shared their extra food with the women, but despite an airplane flying over with promises of eventual rescue for the miners, it took Annie's money and Russell and Richardson to effect a rescue for all of them. Annie's single entry in her field notes was typically terse. "Big Pines. January 26 Rescued!"

Such experiences seemed to spur the women on. For science, nothing was impossible. No matter that they were now two aging women. "I consider the sixties a very appropriate period in one's life to do field work — an out-of-doors quest that will always have, I believe, a certain charm and excitement about it," Annie informed Grinnell. One quest — for gophers in the Mojave Desert — proved a boon to science. Before Alexander and Kellogg explored the area, gophers were considered scarce there. But after collecting ninety-three specimens of gophers from twenty-three localities, they proved that gophers were widely, though sparsely, distributed over the Mojave Desert. For such findings, Annie and Louise would range over deserts, climb up and down canyons, and hike miles laden with steel traps or plant presses.

Then, in May of 1939, they received the stunning news that Joseph Grinnell had died. Annie was saddened to lose "so bright, so ardent a spirit" and went to the cemetery to pay her last respects "to the man who has had such an influence on my life." To his widow she wrote, "Throughout the years [he] never seemed to lose sight of the fact that I was his backer in this splendid and inspiring enterprise, was ever solicitous to keep me in touch with what was transpiring at the museum, to shield me from worry and that I should share in all the triumphs that came our way."

With Grinnell gone, she and Louise gave up most of the mammal work and put nearly all of their still considerable abilities into bo-

7.   Annie Alexander and Louise Kellogg camped in the desert. *Courtesy Alice Howard*

tanical collecting. "I like the mechanical work of drying specimens, the walks through the woods, the sunshine that strikes through the pines in the early mornings and I dread going back to the city," she wrote to Mrs. Grinnell in 1940. Together, she and Louise climbed 9,730-foot-high Hayford Peak, "a hard pull but it repaid us for we saw five mountain sheep near the summit." And in the Eureka Valley of Inyo County, California, in May of 1942, they discovered a new species of grass. It was named *Swallenia alexandrae*, a new genus as well as species that is still rare enough to be on the federal endangered species list.

    And so they continued year after year until November of 1947. For months they had been planning their first foray into Baja California. Annie bought a Dodge "Power Wagon" with four-wheel drive, eight speeds forward, and a sturdy winch on the front bumper. In addition, they had a cage with heavy wire sides constructed on the pickup body of the truck and a carrying rack made for the top to hold light equipment. They took a much younger woman botanist from the University Herbarium, Annetta Carter, with them.

It was a wonderful trip — thousands of miles by automobile interspersed with pack trips into the mountains. Often they camped by the roadside "where there weren't too many cacti or rocks and whenever darkness was about to overtake us." Annie found the country exciting and interesting, a place with weird vegetation and few, but kindly people.

On December 23 they packed their way into the Sierra de la Laguna. There, camped among the oaks and pines, they explored and collected until December 29 when Annie celebrated her eightieth birthday. It must have been the high point of her life to have reached such an age and still be able to live her life as she wished, "a part of nature, footloose in the mountains," and accompanied by friends who shared her ideals.

Finally, after nearly three months in the field they returned home with more than forty-six hundred botanical specimens, some of them new to science and others representing extensions of previously known ranges.

Annie had two more years of field trips before, in the fall of 1949, she had a stroke and remained in a coma until she died the following September. Her ashes were returned to Hawaii on the hillside overlooking her childhood home.

Louise never quite recovered from her loss, but she and Annetta Carter took several more botanical trips together to Baja. It was not the same, of course, and although Louise lived until 1967, her memories of her life with Annie remained more real to her than her seventeen years without her. After all, the team of Alexander and Kellogg had been unique — two women united in purpose, wandering over the deserts and mountains of the West in quest of specimens to enhance humanity's knowledge of the natural world.

# Ellen Quillin

## FLOWERLADY OF TEXAS

ELLEN QUILLIN, like many women naturalists, found her niche in museum work. Yet she began her scientific career as a field naturalist, and a field naturalist she remained throughout her professional life as the founder and first director of the Witte Memorial Museum in San Antonio.

She was born in Saginaw, Michigan, on June 16, 1892, the daughter of immigrant parents from Toronto, Canada. Her father was a farmer imbued with the importance of education, so much so that he donated land for the erection of a country schoolhouse. After all, he had six daughters to educate, and although he knew five languages from talking with immigrant neighbors, he had little formal education.

They lived frugally, growing all their own food in addition to raising crops for market. One of Ellen's chores was weeding the carrot patch. One day, as she worked in the sun, Sunday school acquaintances from town rode by in their carriage, and when she waved at them they turned away. Standing snubbed amid the weeds she made a vow that someday she would be an important person, a teacher, in fact, since teachers were highly respected in her town.

Ellen inherited her determined character and her reverence for nature from her father. He worked hard, clearing more land for farming, but he always stopped to move birds' nests into safer areas before cutting down trees. And despite hard times, he continued to add to his holdings every time he accumulated a little money.

Ellen loved to read and borrowed as many books as she could carry from the local library. At school she studied hard, and by the time she was ten years old, she was helping teach reading and arithmetic to students in the first through the fourth grade. When she was twelve she passed a test that qualified her to attend high school. Her proud father bought her a bicycle so that she could ride the four miles to and from school every day.

To her mortification the high school principal had only assigned her to two classes because of her tender age. After a week of crying herself to sleep every night, she was outside the principal's home one morning just as he was leaving for school. She begged him for more classes, and he grudgingly gave her another. The following week she was back again, and he added a fourth subject to her curriculum.

She sailed through high school, excelling in math and science, and was known as a "forward" student. Socially, though, because she was so young and poor, she had a harder time. That did not stop her from enrolling promptly at the University of Michigan in Ann Arbor, with her parents initially furnishing the money for her expenses. When they could no longer help, she took a door-to-door job selling cosmetics and was so successful that she quickly made six hundred dollars.

They called her Fair Ellen on campus because of her perfect complexion. Majoring in science, she was the only girl in her economic geology class of sixteen and her physics class of three hundred. When she enrolled in a mineralogy course, she was the first female to take the subject in five years. In 1913 she earned her A.B. degree. Then, with her parents' blessing, she fulfilled a childhood dream of moving to Texas.

Jobs for out-of-state women teachers were not plentiful, but again her persistence paid off. She talked herself into a teaching job in San Antonio, offering to take on an elementary class of Mexican boys with repeated failures. She learned Spanish so that she could read to them, and she made some progress. But to her surprise and with no explanation, she was suddenly transferred to the Main Avenue High School as a botany teacher, and her salary was doubled to ninety dollars a month.

That was when she began her first book—*500 Wild Flowers of San Antonio and Vicinity*—which grew "out of an effort to aid beginners at the high schools of San Antonio in identifying and learning the habits and economic value of the flowering plants of this vicinity." At first she took the streetcar as far as it would go and then walked miles in the country, collecting wildflowers and putting them into her verbasculum. It wasn't long, though, before she met another collector, oologist Roy Quillin, who owned a Ford roadster. Together they collected flowers, birds' eggs, butterflies, and lizards on weekends and during vacations, creating a mildly scandalous sensation, since they were not married. Oblivious to such talk, she dedicated the book in 1921 "to Mr. Roy Quillin, oologist, for his assistance in the field work and for widening the horizon of this work through his unusual powers of observation."

She had never been a fashion plate. In college she had made do with two middy blouses, two skirts, one sweater, one coat, and one pair of silk stockings. In the 1920s she locked away all her party clothes, declaring that social life interfered with scientific work. And in the field she always wore knee britches and boots, the latter essential in a state with a high density of poisonous snakes. Certainly her portrayal of Flowerlady in a children's book, *Texas Tales and Trails*, is a portrayal of herself — "the straight khaki-clad figure . . . [with] heavy 18 inch laced boots, the queer little close-fitting khaki hat that gave no shade, and the four foot persimmon stick she used to probe in the bushes. . . . Flowerlady was well known to the mothers of her neighborhood by the teen-aged boys that congregated wherever she stopped to pack flowers in her dull metal collecting case, 'hunt bugs,' or make notes in a mysterious little black-covered book." She further maintained, in a book proposal she circulated on nature-science, that her work was authentic because she did her own field work and consequently her stories were all part of her own experience.

Teaching had been her first goal, writing books based on her field work her second, but in 1922 Roy launched her into her life's work. He had heard about a wealthy old man's collection of Texas memorabilia that he housed in a barn. H. P. Attwater of Houston was partial to San Antonio and wanted to sell it to the city for five thousand dollars. Roy suggested that Ellen, en route north that summer to work on her master's degree at the University of Michigan, stop in and look at the collection.

Attwater, an Englishman who had come to Texas by way of Canada, had spent much of his spare time collecting what he called "Texas marvels," such as a ninety-foot-long grapevine as well as bird skins and native pecans, wool and silk. Ellen thought his collection was both valuable and beautiful, and she immediately had ideas about how to display it. She had been bitten by the museum bug.

Once she returned to Texas and to teaching school, she began organizing her high school students to earn money for the collection. It would be housed in the school, an invaluable teaching tool that would also be open to the public. She was, according to one former student, a very popular teacher, so the students worked hard for her. Ellen and her friend, vice principal Emma Gutzeit, organized a Tag Day on downtown San Antonio street corners. Female students, armed with cigar boxes and tags they had made, asked for donations from passersby. High school boys hovered protectively behind the girls while parents supervised the whole operation as chaperons. Two hundred cigar boxes were filled that day despite pouring rain, and a total of $826.36 had been collected, far short of the $5,000.00 they needed.

So Ellen stepped up her campaign and secured the loan of one oversized Texas jackrabbit, a small Texas cottontail rabbit, and a stuffed wingless bird from New Zealand, the apteryx, from Mr. Attwater's collection. With these props she made the rounds of clubs and PTAs and, overcoming her innate shyness, became a public speaker. Clubs donated money, the students held two more Tag Days, and the proceeds from an Elks concert and two high school plays were also added to the collection.

Probably the most creative idea was the suggestion of one of her students, Richard Eckhardt, whose family owned a five-hundred-acre field covered with a beautiful wildflower, the Texas bluebonnet. His parents were going to plow the field, but before they did, why not pick the flowers and sell them? So, one fair day in early spring, the field was filled with high school students, the girls in dresses, the boys in suits. Some students picked flowers, others carried water to the pickers, and others bundled the flowers into one-dollar bunches to be delivered immediately to buyers. The Bluebonnet Day Sale netted $1401.57. They earned enough money by early 1924 to buy the collection, and they had an excess of twelve hundred dollars to use for exhibit cases.

Actually Mr. Attwater was paid in installments, and the collection was installed in October of 1923, five months before the final payment was made. Ellen was promoted to director of nature study and science at the Main Avenue High School, and she was given rooms for the museum next door to her botany class.

Almost immediately the museum mushroomed. Vocational students built traveling exhibit cases for exhibits to be taken to other schools. People began donating things, particularly animal skins, which forced them to hire a taxidermist. More money donations came in, and a museum association was formed. The two school rooms quickly became too small for the ideas of many of San Antonio's citizens.

This time Ellen and Emma approached the mayor of the city, John Tobin, an old family friend of Emma's. After some cajoling, he promised them a site—San Pedro Park—and after still more fast talk he promised them seventy-five hundred dollars if they promised never to come back to his office. But Ellen did, in 1925, to get him to keep his promise for a building contract. She and Emma had obtained more funds from prominent citizens plus a donation of cobblestones to use as building material. Tobin, though, extracted another promise from Ellen before granting the building contract — that she not get married until the museum was a success. In the end, he also authorized seventy-five thousand dollars for the construction of the museum.

A windfall of sixty-five thousand dollars from Alfred Witte changed the location of the museum and gave it its name. It was to be named the Witte Memorial Museum in honor of the rich, unmarried man's parents, and it was to be built in Brackenridge Park rather than San Pedro Park. Of course, the Museum Association complied, and in January 1926 Ellen was elected first director of the museum with a salary of one dollar a year. The following October the museum building was finished and opened to the public with departments of art, history, geology, archaeology, natural history, and transportation. With Mayor Tobin's blessing she finally married Roy on July 29, 1927. The mayor needn't have worried that marriage would divert her from her career. As Mrs. Frank Drought later commented, Roy "never appeared on the scene. You would never have known she was married."

Yet all indications point to an amiable partnership with as much time as possible spent collecting and exploring the state. Both before and after her marriage Ellen took photographs wherever they went: sedges on Padre Island in 1924, sand dunes and sea oats on Point Isabel, Texas, in 1925, and round-ups at Waggoner Ranch near Vernon, Texas, in the 1930s. Native homes and bat roosts, the treeless plains of West Texas and Point Aransas — all were faithfully recorded. Perhaps their favorite place was the rugged, and at that time relatively unexplored, Big Bend area. On one of their first visits there they were accompanied by Dr. and Mrs. Albert H. Wright of Cornell University, and both couples were looking for natural history specimens. But Ellen also became intrigued by the remains of the Basketmaker civilization, which she wanted for the museum. She begged food and money from private donors for archeological digs, and in 1928 the Martin L. Cummins–Ellen Quillin exploration expedition was organized. Its purpose was to make contacts and go over the field to plan future museum archaeological digs. In fact, her friend Emma Gutzeit and Miss Virginia Carson led two expeditions in 1931 with the dictum to reproduce in color as many pictographs on the cave walls as possible. While Ellen stored sixteen Basketmaker skeletons under her guest room bed, Roy built sixteen wall display cases in his workshop for them.

Roy had a full-time job with Mobil, according to Charles J. Long, who accompanied them on some of their field trips for the museum. Long was impressed with their marriage built on mutual interests, like the chrysanthemums they raised. Both were fond of lizards and pheasants. They bought a home outside of San Antonio and explored the state in their Model T Ford. He called her Mother, even though they never had any children. Her constant concern with helping and educating youngsters — first through teaching, second through the museum, and then through a series of excellent children's books she wrote in the 1930s — certainly qualified her as a surrogate mother for many children.

Her writing career flourished, beginning with her self-published book on San Antonio wildflowers in 1922, illustrated with forty-one original photographs by Ellen. It was, according to an advertisement for the book, "an unusual botanical book in that the layman can use either the key or the descriptions in identifying the plants listed." It was the first work of its kind published on Texas plants, and it emphasized both the economical and ornamental value of the plants.

In the midst of starting the museum, she was also busy writing what was her most important book — *Texas Wild Flowers, A Popular Account of the Common Wild Flowers of Texas.* Despite "too little time and strength, too much hunting buzzard eggs, too much museum," the book appeared in 1928, "dedicated to the children and flower-loving public of Texas." The majority of photographic illustrations had been taken in the field by Ellen "under natural environmental conditions." Beautifully written and illustrated, the book was filled with folklore and history as well as common names, typical locations and plant uses.

In 1930 she followed that work with *Texas Cacti, A Popular and Scientific Account of the Cacti Native to Texas,* which appeared in the *Proceedings of the Texas Academy of Science.* The book was co-authored with Robert Runyon, who was listed as a photographer of wildlife and a member of the Texas Academy of Science. She, on the other hand, as first author, was a Fellow of the academy. From that work emerged several more popular books on cactus growing, a strong interest of Ellen's. She also branched off, in the 1930s, with her children's books, writing nine books for a nature-science series, published by the Turner Company of Dallas. Some of her intriguing titles included *Along the Creek, Little Creatures with Many Legs, Queer Animals, Feathered Flights, From Seed to Tree, Bits of Rock, Drop of Water,* and *Out in Star Land. Thin Wings,* written with Charles H. Gable, set out the purpose, not only of that book, but of the whole series: "to arouse an intelligent curiosity about this world

8.   Ellen Quillin with her botanical collecting case. *San Antonio Light* Collection. *Courtesy Institute of Texan Cultures, San Antonio, Texas*

of Nature." It was an attractive book about insects, with real-life illustrations, and was based on the resources of the Witte Memorial Museum and Brackenridge Park.

Such a literary output based on field observations would not have been so amazing if she had not, at the same time, had incredible difficulty in keeping the museum going. Her honeymoon with city officials lasted less than a year. When she refused to canvas votes for the party in power, they immediately cut off the six hundred dollars per month they had promised her to cover running costs of the museum. She reacted by moving the museum employees and their families into the museum and holding fund-raisers to purchase food and clothing for them. When proceeds from barbecues, dances, and lectures were not enough, after the depression set in, to support the three families, she accepted a plan by herpetologist W. C. (Bill) Bevan to build a Reptile Garden, the first of its kind in the country.

The idea of imprisoning snakes was repugnant to her, but she was desperate for funds, and, as it turned out, it did more good than harm. Not only were the museum employees supported but the many destitute people who collected snakes, alligators, and turtles for the garden were also helped. Earning fifteen cents a pound for live rattlesnakes, ten cents a pound for chicken snakes, and fifty cents apiece for young alligators, it seemed a small fortune for them. The Reptile Garden was built in the park to the left of the museum using donated labor and building materials of cheap, wide, knotty boards, barbed wire fencing, and discarded metal roofs. A wooden fence enclosed the snake pit, which had a viewing bridge for spectators and a pool for the alligators and turtles.

Eight hundred guests, paying ten cents each, attended the opening day of an enterprise some people condemned as too dangerous. They listened to speeches and watched as bags of nonpoisonous snakes and lizards were poured down the chute into the pit. Children who had been taught how to handle snakes were eager to show off their pets and to participate in the proceedings. Chicken snakes are strong climbers; when they were released and climbed up every tree in sight, a mild hysteria broke out. Ellen was standing next to the viewing bridge handrail when she realized her leg was encircled by a snake that had firmly attached her to a bridge post. She stood immobile until the excitement had died down and the chicken snakes had all been recaptured. When the zoo director, Fred Stark, came up to speak of her, she said, "Fred, please see what is just under my dress." Gingerly he lifted the hem of her dress and visibly relieved, exclaimed, "Oh, pshaw! It's only a chicken snake." He quietly and quickly picked it off, and no one even noticed.

The Reptile Garden was in operation ten years and became known as an important reptile research center, especially for its antivenin work. Various gimmicky entertainments, such as snake-handler shows, rattlesnake fries, and turtle races were held over the years, attracting 750,000 paid admissions. Without the Reptile Garden receipts, the museum would have collapsed, but naturalist "Ellen D.," as the museum employees called her, never liked the Reptile Garden. However, she tried to use it for educational purposes by handing out circulars of snake facts and promoting the benefits of snakes to both humanity and the environment. Nevertheless, she was relieved when they no longer needed the money from the Reptile Garden, and she immediately turned the snakes over to the Reptile House of the San Antonio Zoo.

By then the museum had become an integral part of the city with enough funding to pay employees' wages, including a salary to Ellen.

But she refused to take more than a token amount. Robert K. Winn, chairman of the Art Institute in San Antonio from 1953 until 1958, maintained that "she was getting, maybe, three fifty or four hundred dollars." Both he and the Frank Droughts gave vivid descriptions of Ellen in those years. The Droughts described her as energetic, delightful, and able to laugh at herself, a woman who kept a pet tarantula on her desk which she fed crickets she collected in the park at night. "She cared deeply about 'the museum,' and she remembered all of her students, and she had a real affection, and she'd never let the ties lapse," Mrs. Drought said. Mr. Drought was intrigued by her drive and ambition and was surprised that such a woman had married.

Mr. Winn focused more on her eccentricities, although he maintained that she was "very nice," albeit demanding. If he let her think she was the originator of an idea, she would go along with it. On the other hand, she wore "the same little georgette evening dress from the time I knew her until she retired from the Witte." Her refusal to attend most parties and luncheons, which she considered boring, was sometimes detrimental to public relations for the museum, he asserted.

Nevertheless, there was no doubt that the museum thrived under Ellen's direction. Inevitably, though, retirement came; in 1960 she stepped down. In honor of Ellen the city of San Antonio declared an "Ellen Quillin Day" to recognize "that the status and stature of the Witte Memorial Museum be recognized as primarily the result of the work and devotion of one person, Mrs. Ellen S. Quillin, its Director," the mayor's resolution read. She had definitely become a very important person just as she had vowed so many years ago in the carrot patch.

Part III

# *The Botanists*

―――――――――――――――――――――――――――
☙
―――――――――――――――――――――――――――

*Early in the nineteenth century botany became the acceptable science for women to study, so much so that Amos Eaton, a New York botanist and geologist, declared in 1822, "I believe more than half the botanists of New England and New York are ladies." By 1840 Increase Lapham claimed that a study of plants and shells "seems now to be almost indispensable to an* ACCOMPLISHED *lady."*

*A recent study of women botanists of the nineteenth century by Emanuel D. Rudolph uncovered 1,185 women with an active interest in botany. Since his work was based only on published sources, particularly the botanical journals and club membership lists, Rudolph believes he has probably missed a good many more. Nevertheless, his statistics are revealing. Most of the women botanists were active in the latter half of the nineteenth century, only 28 percent were married, 23 percent made plant collections, over half were teachers, a substantial number wrote books, and they were most interested in flowering plants with a lesser concern for ferns and then mosses. Women from New York, Massachusetts, Pennsylvania, and California made up 53 percent of women botanists, followed by women in the Midwest, with the South producing the lowest numbers.*

*Few women botanists became professionals, but at the nonprofessional level women performed research, collected plants, and helped in founding and running botanical organizations. In Rudolph's words, "at the non-professional levels of botany in the United States during the Nineteenth Century women were an important constituency for the developing science." Like the men, however, some women botanists did become professionals, writing for scientific journals and even attaining professional positions. Those women—E. G. Britton, Kate Brandegee, Alice Eastwood, Agnes Chase, and Mary Sophie Young—will be discussed in the following chapters. So will two of the most prodigious collectors, Ynes Mexia and Kate Furbish. There were other enthusiastic women collectors who also made worthwhile contributions. A few of the most noteworthy will be treated more briefly in the following paragraphs.*

*Rebecca Austin, the wife of a gold miner and the mother of three children, typified the botanical collector with no scientific background. Anxious to be accepted as a reliable investigator, Austin kept painstaking notes while she watched the California pitcher plant DARLINGTONIA in ten patches scattered over three small valleys in Plumas County, California. She shared her discoveries with William M. Canby of Wilmington, Delaware, J. D. Hooker and Charles Darwin of England, C. Keck of Austria, and Asa Gray at Harvard. In his book DARWINIANA, Gray acknowledged Austin's observations of DARLINGTONIA CALIFORNICA, calling her its principal observer. Her work was published by C. Keck in Austria and by Canby in the United States. Canby also supplied her with the pocket lens she so desperately needed as well as copies of botanical papers, lectures, and books, such as Darwin's INSECTIVOROUS PLANTS. According to her first letter to Canby in 1875, she had already been studying the plants for six years and had discovered that they "propagate themselves by sending out underground stems at right angles to the parent stem, and also by seed."*

*Canby, himself an expert on carnivorous plants, apparently respected her work and continued to pepper her with questions that she, in turn, eagerly answered. The root of DARLINGTONIA, she discovered, was perennial, the heart-shaped orifice repelled rain water, the hood was thinner than other parts of the tube, winged insects were caught in the plant, and most of the leaves twisted in the same direction. She enthusiastically agreed to collect the flora of Butterfly Valley for him, calling herself a "beginner in botany." With access only to Wood's* BOTANY *and no time to study it, she knew the names of only a few California plants, she explained.*

*During late April and most of May, 1875, Austin "spent hours among [the] flowers; when time could not be spared from home duty, I have taken my sewing, chose a favorable position and spent hours in this way, to see if any* FLYING *insects lit upon or entered the flower." Her aim was to discover the pollinating agent of* DARLINGTONIA. *In eight days she saw only one green fly and a smaller flying insect in one flower. Yet when she looked inside the flowers she found dozens of spiders and webs, leading her to conclude that spiders were the pollinators.*

*All that summer she continued her observations on various aspects of* DARLINGTONIA'S *life cycle. She was engaged in the work of "our beautiful science," as she called it, and found* DARLINGTONIA *"a mystery, full of life and death. We know nothing of its wonders yet."*

*Near the end of the year Austin felt confident enough to sign her letter to Canby "your friend in science" after apologizing in a previous letter for being "very tedious in my reports to you, but then, I had no confidence in myself." Even throughout the winter she visited her favorite patch once a week, but in April of 1876 she reported "business troubles," and in June her home was sold. Still, she continued her collecting and investigations of* DARLINGTONIA *until late August when, "alas, in one short week I must leave them. I have loved them. They have been to me a help in lifting the mind out of the depths of sorrow. . . . They have given me a keen desire to look in the hidden laws of nature, and note her secret work, which is the 'same yesterday, today, and forever' and full of beauty and truth, if we could only see understandingly."*

*She followed with a couple of letters from her new home in American Valley, where she continued her* DAR-LINGTONIA *notes from the previous summer, and there the correspondence ends. Austin's life as a botanical col-*

*lector did not end, however, and she, along with her
daughter, Mrs. C. C. Bruce, moved in 1881 to Modoc
County and continued collecting. Austin's friend, Mary
Pulsifer Ames, who had helped her with her DAR-
LINGTONIA studies, was also a prodigious collector. Together the three women are credited with giving "the
foundation to our knowledge of the vegetation of that
region" [northeastern California], according to botanical
historian Joseph Ewan. For their pains, each woman
had a plant named for her—SCUTELLARIA AUSTINAE, COL-
LINSIA BRUCAE, and ASTROGALUS PULSIFERAE.*

*Near the beginning of her botanical collecting ca-
reer, Austin had been visited by another itinerant collector, John Gill Lemmon, who recommended her to
Canby and who also made use of some of her DAR-
LINGTONIA studies. Collecting had caught his interest
when fifty of the plants he sent to Gray in 1866 proved
to be new to science. Usually nervous and fidgety, he
sometimes jumped to erroneous conclusions but he certainly had no prejudices against female botanists. He
marrried one!*

*Sara Allen Plummer Lemmon, described as "brilliant
and charming" with "firm and aggressive attitudes," is
suspected of being the more talented of the two. They
took several collecting trips together before their marriage in 1880, which they followed up with "A Botanical Wedding Trip" into the Santa Catalina Mountains,
lovingly described by Lemmon in a lively account in
THE CALIFORNIAN. Mrs. Lemmon went properly attired
in "a short suit of strong material, the best of firm calf-
skin shoes, nailed along the soles and heels with gimp-
tacks, and reinforced by substantial leather leggings.
. . . A broad-brimmed hat with a buckskin mask, and
heavy gloves, a botanical portfolio, and a long staff,
completed her outfit."*

*They lived in a cave infested with pack rats, slept
on a bed of dried and brittle grass, and kept a fire burning at the entrance to keep out animals. Struggling with
heat, thirst, and aggressive cacti, they made three attempts before finally scaling on horseback the north
side of a mountain later named for them. That was only
the beginning of their years of collecting in California,*

Nevada, and Arizona undeterred even by Apache massacres in their collecting area.

Sara, it turned out, was more than a collector. She could also deliver excellent speeches on botany and paint botanical specimens. Her husband did not mind bragging about her talents, telling his botanical friend Harry N. Patterson, "Mrs. Lemmon has developed into a good platform speaker as well as botanist and flower painter. She accompanies me into the region to be botanized and often takes the hardest trip with me, while at all times her assistance is most valuable in making good specimens." He also persuaded Asa Gray to name the genera PLUMMERA with one species in it for her in 1881. In addition, Gray honored her with two species STEVIA PLUMMERAE and IPOMAEA PLUMMERAE, and his successor Sereno Watson named two more after her, ALLIUM PLUMMERAE and EUPHORBIA PLUMMERAE. Altogether the Lemmons discovered 3 percent of the vascular plants of California, and one researcher, Frank Crosswhite, even said, "There is evidence that she may have been responsible for much of the work that made her husband famous. . . ."

One botanist-writer, Katharine Dooris Sharp, who specialized in the flora of Madison County, Ohio, extolled the botanically inclined wives of male botanists in her book SUMMER IN A BOG, declaring that "the fame of many a woman in the past has been merged in that of her husband or other male relative and history fails to give her any credit." Since Sharp was an Ohioan she went on to list both unmarried and married botanists, eleven altogether, including herself, who had contributed to the state flora collection. Miss Josephine Kleppart had helped her father, the state agriculturist, by painting shrubs and flowers; Mrs. Wormley had learned to engrave to help her husband; Mrs. Sarah S. James had assisted her husband, Professor Joseph James, in his botany work. Mrs. Kellerman, wife of state botanist, Dr. W. A. Kellerman, had helped him write his ELEMENTS OF BOTANY and had published her own articles; Mrs. Laura Morgan, married to noted fungus expert A. P. Morgan, was an expert in her own right, had painted fungi, and had a wild Ohio mushroom named for her—HYDROPHORUS LAURAE. *And Miss Hannah J. Biddlecome, an expert on the mosses and liverworts of Ohio, had discovered several new species, including* TRICHOCOLEA BIDDLECOMEI.

Coincidentally, one of the most lamented of botanical wives was also an Ohioan. Eliza Griscom Wheeler Sullivant was the second wife of William Starling Sullivant, the "father of American bryology." She assisted him from the time she married him, at the age of seventeen, until she died of cholera fourteen years later. She also had three children and cared for his child from his first marriage. The best sketches and drawings in his monumental two-volume MUSCI ALLEGHANYENSES are hers. In addition, she was "scientist, analyst, and microscopist" and accompanied him on botanical trips. Sullivant called her "my indispensable collaboratrix," and her death so devastated him that it took him a year to send the letter he had written about her to Asa Gray. He, like Lemmon, gave credit to his wife. "I can say with strictest truth that more than half of whatever I have done in these pursuits is due to her. . . . She had acquired of Latin and German and French sufficient to read botanical descriptions with ease. . . . In the most difficult and delicate dissections and Microscopical examinations she was astonishingly successful . . . her knowledge of Musci [mosses] and Hepaticae [lichens] was very extensive." Sullivant, it seems, was not averse to women in botany. His third wife, Caroline Eudora, one of Eliza's nieces, also helped him by copying Wilkes expedition material and serving as assistant muscologist, in addition to bearing six children of her own. Although Eliza had been cheated out of having a plant named for her (the two mosses chosen turned out to be the same species already named PLAGIOTHECIUM RO-SEANUM), Caroline was luckier with a Hawaiian moss, HYPNUM EUDORAE from the Wilkes expedition.

A veritable army of women engaged in the fascinating study of botany—not only single women but also those with husbands and children to care for. Some believed they had been born botanists, and despite, as Katharine Dooris Sharp put it, "a look askance and a cold reception . . . disappointments, discouragements, adversities, there is no ennui, no heavy time to kill,

*when all around us secrets of Nature invite to reveal-*
*ment." Katharine was probably speaking for all women*
*botanists when she wrote that "the social doings of her*
*own sex lose something of their attractiveness to the*
*woman who botanizes." No doubt most agreed with*
*her observation that their reward would be a "heaven-*
*imparted kinship with nature which is the open sesame*
*to that kingdom of delight."*

# Kate Furbish

## THE POSEY-WOMAN

THE FRENCH CANADIANS in the wilds of Maine called her the Posey-Woman, a far more complimentary name than the "Crazy" and "Fool" she sometimes earned from people who observed her "alone for the most part, on the highways and in the hedges, on foot, in Hayracks, on country mail-stages . . . on improvised rafts (equipped with hammer, saw, nails, knife, rubber-boots, vasculum etc.) in rowboats, on logs, crawling on hands and knees on the surface of bogs, and backing out, where I dare not walk—in order to procure a coveted treasure." That was the way she did her work, she explained to William DeWitt Hyde, president of Bowdoin College, after she had presented her "Illustrated Flora"—sixteen large folio volumes of watercolor drawings of the state's plants—to the college in 1908.

Her self-appointed life task was to collect, classify, and paint the flora of Maine. Despite bouts of ill health and other, more mundane claims on her time, she managed to paint 500 mushrooms as well as collect and press 4,000 sheets of dried plants and 182 sheets of ferns, in addition to completing her "Illustrated Flora." Prominent male botanists recognized her talents; in her honor, Sereno Watson at Harvard University named a wood betony she had discovered in northern Aroostook County beside the Saint John River the Furbish lousewort. "Were it not," she wrote to him, "that I can find no plant named for a female botanist in your manual," (Asa Gray's *Manual of Botany*, which Watson was revising) "I should object to *Pedicularis furbishiae* for it is too often conferred to be any particular honor, but as a new species is rarely found in New England and few plants are named for women, it pleases me."

Kate did not start her life's work in earnest until she was thirty-six, although her father Benjamin first taught her to identify the local plants when she was a child. Kate, born in 1834 in Exeter, New Hampshire, had been the oldest of six children and the only daughter. A year after her birth, her parents moved their family and business to Brunswick, Maine, which became their lifelong home.

Like many young ladies of her time, Kate interested herself in genteel pursuits — painting and the study of French literature — and even spent a year at her studies in Paris perfecting her painting. Then, in 1860, during a visit to Boston, she attended a series of botany lectures by a former Mainer from Saco, George L. Goodale, who inspired her interest in science. Unfortunately a long illness intervened, and it was not until 1870 that she was able to begin her most productive botanical years. Three years later her father died and left her the family home and enough money to be independent.

Independence, for Kate, meant the freedom to collect "the plants in God's flower-garden," as she called wildflowers in the little explored backwoods of Maine. Traveling unarmed, knowing no fear, she was "a little woman with bowed face using her keen eyes along a forest trail or up a mountain path. She had the sort of eyes that are made for seeing, and nothing escaped the swift circle of her glance," according to one contemporary. The conditions she encountered were often rough — dense woods swarming with black flies, steep, rocky mountainsides, and swamps filled with fallen trees blocking her way, but only once was she actually thwarted. At Cupsuptic Lake in Oxford County she was beset by "such swarms of vicious mosquitoes" that she put an insect net about her head and waited for her guide, who had gone off fishing, to return. In fact, she was "not only lost to all sense of comfort, but the fallen trees made such a network that I had lost my bearings also."

Despite such adversity she loved the wilderness, even the deepest woods where botanizing was not particularly productive, because of the peace she encountered there. Wildlife was almost tame — scarcely fluttering at her approach — "the squirrel sits and gazes at you, scolds perhaps, but does not scamper away, and the cedar partridge hardly notices your movements at all." To those who asked her why she worked so hard to get "weeds," she always had a ready answer in the words of Longfellow. "We feel the presence of God in Nature there, Nature grand and awful, and tread reverently where all is so hushed and oppressive in its silence." Kate, like the Quaker naturalist Graceanna Lewis, equated her belief in God with her love of nature, and she had serene faith in what she was doing.

Often her faith kept her going when common sense should have prevailed. One time she decided to climb Mount Day because she wanted to reach the pond at its top. The best way up seemed to be along a ravine that started out easily but suddenly became precipitous. She pushed on ahead, and immediately one of her legs sank into a rotten log. She put her collecting basket on a ledge above her as she struggled to extricate her leg, all the while painfully aware of the sharp rocks directly below her. Suddenly her basket tumbled off the ledge, hitting her face and shoulders, and falling down far below her. Nevertheless, she did manage to wrench her leg free, only to sink into mud up to her waist. Finally, she stopped, rested, climbed down after her basket, then continued more cautiously up the mountain. The whole adventure took her eleven hours, but she found ample rewards for her labor — the pond and a new sedge.

Nothing stopped her, not even her discovery one day of what seemed to be inaccessible water plants growing far out in a river. She merely took three hours to build herself a raft and went out after them, as she explained later to the worried people she had been boarding with. Another time, in pursuit of an unusual beech leaf and a variation of *Trillium erectum* (wake robin), she climbed two miles up Mount Blue near Strong, Maine, clambering over rocks and fallen trees through a fog of black flies.

Most of 1879, 1880, and 1881 were spent in the swamps of Aroostook County in northern Maine where she was particularly interested in collecting orchids. She admitted it was hard work "requiring many a tumble and scratch," but she was well-armed with waterproof boots. On one trip in June of 1881 she not only found the Furbish lousewort at Van Buren on the Saint John River growing three feet high on the bank of the river, but she also noted 208 other plants, 50 of which were new to her list of Maine plants. Other wilderness expeditions in the Rangeley Lakes area during 1889 and 1890 yielded 37 new plants to add to a previous list published by L. N. Johnson and E. L. Rand.

Once she returned from her wilderness wanderings, though, she settled down on the second floor of her home to paint her discoveries. She did not consider herself an artist but rather a scientist, faithfully reproducing the plants, "free from all decorative effects." Even today botanists find her work so accurate and detailed that they can use her paintings in place of some of the best wildflower identification books. She seemed to follow no set pattern, however, using both gray and blue paper to paint on. Often her paintings were works of art, such as those she painted of the marsh marigold and pitcher plant, while others were far less detailed. Several, in fact, were drawn only in pencil. Volume 12, devoted solely to tree blossoms, "is said to be the choicest," according to one local resident.

9.  Kate Furbish at her easel. *Courtesy Bowdoin College Library, Brunswick, Maine*

During the thirty-eight years, from 1870 until 1908, that she did the bulk of her collecting and painting, she also lived the life of a typical Victorian lady. "One of the finest ladies I ever met," one Brunswick resident recalled, Kate was a lady who read to the elderly, kept house, dressed in a proper fashion, and attended church regularly. But such a life did not always come easily to her. Sometimes she rebelled by fleeing to Wells, Maine, to visit her father's relatives. They took care of her, and she was not asked to do a square of crazy patchwork quilt as she was in Brunswick. The women of Brunswick assumed, of course, that she would do the same work as other women in the community, sending her a part of the material, which she returned to the sender with "quite a sharp note." She longed for botanical friends in Portland, Maine, where she helped found the Josselyn Botanical Society of Maine in 1894, and she wished she could live near them, "instead of here by myself where I do not get an encouraging word once a year," she wrote to her young friend, Merritt L. Fernald, at the Gray Herbarium.

Fernald was as close to a son as Kate ever got, and he seemed to return her affectionate regard. She had discovered him one day in 1880 during her botanical wanderings—a young boy born and raised in Orono, Maine, out collecting plants by himself—and it was to him that she confided her frustrations as well as her triumphs. Her frustrations were chiefly lack of time and lack of good health, the latter often plaguing her and slowing down her progress. Beginning in 1897, she complained frequently of losing time because of illness and lamented how fast her life was ebbing away. At that time she was sixty-three years old and still had many productive years ahead of her, although her long treks into the wilderness had ended by then. She began limiting herself chiefly to places nearer home or relatives, for instance, the area around Wells in 1899 and the town of West Baldwin in southern Cumberland County during the summer of 1900. At West Baldwin, where she was staying with a friend, she discovered the rare alpine species *Cardamine bellidifolia* "growing in crevices of granite rock by a stream in a deep gorge" at an altitude of five hundred feet. Previously, the plant had been found south of Labrador only in the northern Maine areas of Washington County and the alpine regions of Mount Katahdin, according to Kate's note in the botanical journal *Rhodora.*

The year 1901 found her exploring the seacoast near Brunswick, but the following summer she felt well enough to travel up the coast as far as Cutler and North Lubec, her first venture down east. She even managed to collect a *Linaria vulgaris* "on a high ledge on one of the high points running out into Quoddy Bay."

During the years 1897–1905 she also made her mushroom sketches and noted on one of them that "there is something very fascinating to me in the study of the Boleti." And her friend Fernald, who admired her immensely, named a variety of the heart-leaved aster, *Aster cordifolius var. furbishiae* after her in 1897. He wrote that "through her undaunted pluck and faithful brush" she had done "more than any other to make known the wonderful flora of the 'Garden of Maine.'"

By 1908 she felt her life work was about finished, and it was then that she distributed her paintings to Bowdoin College, her fern collection to the Portland (Maine) Society of Natural History and her four thousand sheets of dried plants to the New England Botanical Club (now housed at the Gray Herbarium). The latter was praised as a pioneer collection from places in Maine previously uncollected. It represented the floras of more than two hundred towns and villages.

Three years later she was elected president of the Josselyn Botanical Society of Maine, which was perhaps her best outlet for sharing her botanical interests. Amateurs and professionals alike attended the winter and summer meetings and sometimes she even met Fernald there. The summer meetings included extended field trips led by distinguished botanists, and Kate was always along from beginning to end, often extending her stay in the study area to collect still more plants.

She was never finished collecting, despite dismal notes to Fernald to the contrary. In 1912 she was certain her poor health would prevent her from ever going into the field again. The following year she closed her home for the winter and moved in with relatives at East Livermore, since caring for her home had been impossible for a long while. Yet in 1915 she spent two weeks at Casco, where she waded into a bog to collect an unusual white, closed gentian. The bog water reached the top of her rubber boots "with a great deal of suction," but she was still delighted both with her find and with the seacoast town of Casco.

The following year she reported to Fernald that despite having to use a cane to walk, she still continued collecting Brunswick plants with the help of school children and other interested persons who brought her plants to name. Later, with snow-white hair at the age of ninety, she worked over the farm where she was staying searching for specimens. Although her legs were giving out and she told Fernald she was "tottering" to her end as fast as her "great constitution" would permit, her last lament to him ten years before her death was "I love my work too well to leave it."

On December 6, 1931, at the age of ninety-seven she died of cardiac hypertrophy. She was buried in Pine Grove Cemetery at Brunswick, and most people promptly forgot both the lady and her extraordinary work. And then in 1976, Kate Furbish became famous. The flower Watson had named for her, the Furbish lousewort, temporarily stopped the building of the proposed Dickey-Lincoln dam on the wild Saint John River. Always a rare and localized plant, it had been one of fourteen plants named to the endangered species list after being previously listed by the Smithsonian Institution as "probably extinct." It was then rediscovered by botanist Charles D. Richards of the University of Maine on the south bank of the Saint John River. The dam would have flooded the only known habitat of the plant and so, for a time, it forestalled the dam builders and made headlines around the world.

After a summer of intensive searching, five other localities for the plant were discovered downstream of the proposed dam—in all 162 plants. However, Richards assured the New England Corps of Engineers that the lousewort would be easy to transplant because it is easily pollinated and produces seeds. Engineers and politicians breathed a sigh of relief—a weed would not stop progress. The Congress did, however, and the dam was finally shelved.

Kate's name and work had been revived. Bowdoin College proudly displayed her botanical drawings, and bibliographical sources added her name to the scant list of known women botanists in American natural history. The Posey-Woman had found satisfaction in looking for unusual flower forms and had taken a special interest in them. In the end, one of those rare forms brought her a posthumous fame she had never dreamed of.

# Kate Brandegee

## ACCIDENTAL BOTANIST

"WHAT DOES THE WORLD care for me?" Kate Brandegee retorted, when botanist Marcus E. Jones asked her to write an account of her life. Although she had worked hard in botany, a profession she had entered by accident, she "would have preferred the study of birds or more strongly still, the study of insects," she claimed. However, once she gave up her medical practice for botany, she never looked back, and spent the rest of her life collecting, classifying, writing about, and growing the plants of California. But her efforts were often overlooked, even camouflaged, because she was a woman. First, Edward L. Greene, defrocked Episcopal priest and first professor of botany at the University of California, and then her second husband, T. S. Brandegee, received some of the credit for her botanical work so that the male botanists in the East would not know how influential a western female was in a profession they claimed as their own. No wonder, then, that Kate had no desire to recount her accomplishments to what she considered an uncaring world.

Nevertheless, she left a brief "Reminiscences" that outlines a small portion of her life. To help her in her collecting, she had been issued a general railroad pass, she explained, so that she could ride anything from Pullman to engine. Also, she had confined her botanizing almost entirely to California and the adjacent areas of Nevada, although she dismissed her botanical trips as "too numerous to catalogue." So thoroughly did she know California that botanists hoped she would write a flora of the state. She never did. Instead, she kept most of her knowledge in her head. "Unfortunately, her worst sin was caution," Jones contended, "which led her to put off publication too long."

Kate had been born in western Tennessee on October 28, 1844, and was the oldest of Mary and Marshall Bolling Layne's five children. Her mother was an accomplished weaver, her father a restless, volatile, sometimes violent man with a wanderlust that took the growing family steadily westward — to Salt Lake City, Utah, Carson City, Nevada, and finally, when Kate was nine years old, to Eldorado County in the Sierra foothills of California. Kate claimed "biology in any of its branches . . . always attracted me greatly, even as a child," the sole evidence of her early interest in the natural world.

Otherwise, it is known that she met and married a hard-drinking, Irish constable in Folsom, California, in 1866 named Hugh Curran and that she taught school so she could pay his debts. When he died in 1874 she was thirty years old and able, at last, to live her own life.

She chose to go to San Francisco and enroll as a medical student in the University of California at nearby Berkeley. In three years she had her medical degree, license, and membership in the California State Medical Society. What she did not have was a large medical practice. As she later put it, "A young doctor is not usually overrun with patients," especially, she should have added, a *woman* doctor.

Following her graduation, she took up botanical studies under Dr. Hans Herman Behr, vice president of the California Academy of Sciences in San Francisco, who introduced her to other members of the academy, and in 1882 she began collecting plants. She also volunteered to help out in the academy's herbarium that she claimed was in a chaotic state. At the same time, Edward Lee Greene, an Episcopal priest who loved plants more than preaching, also spent most of his time at the herbarium.

When the curator of botany at the academy, Albert Kellogg, retired in 1883, Kate was offered his position. This was an unusual honor for a woman, since the academy was the center for botanical research in the West at the time. But then, the academy had never discriminated against women. In the year of its founding — 1853 — it had resolved "that we highly approve the aid of females in every department of natural history, and that we earnestly invite their cooperation," a policy that was scoffed at in the East. Kate accepted the position, and a year later Greene was drummed out of the ministry because of "social vice." Greene then declared to Gray that he was curator of botany at the academy and Kate was merely his assistant. But he was never put on the payroll, and in 1885 he accepted a position as a full-time instructor in botany at the University of California in Berkeley.

Although Greene had no doubt been somewhat of a mentor for

Kate, along with Kellogg and Behr, their botanical philosophies were diametrically opposed. Greene was a "splitter"—eager to declare every plant a new species—whereas Kate was a conservative "lumper"—painstakingly checking out each species she and others discovered to make certain it had not been previously described or was not merely a variety of a known species. In addition, like Gray, she believed in evolution, while both Greene and Kellogg did not.

Kellogg and Greene also disliked the eastern botanists' priority in the naming of all North American plants and wanted to free the Westerners from dependence on them. Kate, while impatient with many of the Easterners' classifications of western plants, was not interested in joining Kellogg and Greene's separatist movement. In fact, she maintained close contact with the Gray Herbarium at Harvard University; in 1891 she wrote that she could not decide whether Greene was a knave or a fool, but feared he was a fool.

In addition to organizing the herbarium's collection and taking her own collecting trips, Kate decided to resurrect the early publishing attempts of the academy. Formerly, seven volumes of the academy's *Proceedings*, which recorded the reading of botanical papers announcing new genera and species, had been issued from 1854 until 1876. Unfortunately, the *Proceedings* did not get published in the same year as the reported meetings (the gap was as long as four years afterwards, which played havoc with assigning priority to the discoverer). Kate wanted a publication that came out on time and that printed editor-checked botanical manuscripts acceptable to the eastern botanists. She called her publication *Bulletin of the California Academy of Sciences* when she started it in 1884.

According to Marcus Jones, she was a "model in thoroughness in her botanical work," putting "the herbarium on a sound basis both in the mounting and arrangement of specimens." But her painstaking efforts to determine the correct status of species previously described by others was not appreciated by the "splitters." Nevertheless, the *Bulletin* continued for three years until a more scholarly *Proceedings* replaced it in 1888.

By then Kate had fallen "insanely in love," she wrote to her sister, with one of the most renowned collectors of the West, Townshend Stith Brandegee. People tittered at large, robust, outspoken Kate's attraction for the small, quiet, intellectual Yale graduate who, as a civil engineer, had collected plants while making preliminary surveys for railroad lines. When the railroad work ended, eastern botanists employed him in a variety of botany-related jobs. One of those jobs, for Professor C. S. Sargent at the American Museum of Natural History in New York, brought him to California. He was to supervise the collecting of trunks from every major tree species in the West.

He joined the academy and there he met Kate, whom he called the "leading spirit in the affairs of that institution." And, according to Kate, she gave Brandegee the benefit of her familiarity with California's flora. To him she was "Kate," to her he was "Townie" or "Dearest" in the letters she later wrote to Brandegee. They were married in San Diego on May 29, 1889, their happiness assured, Kate maintained, because of their "mutual affection and congenial tastes." Those taste were immediately reflected in their honeymoon destination. They walked five hundred miles from San Diego to San Francisco, botanizing all the way.

Shortly before their marriage, Townie had inherited forty thousand dollars, a fortune that gave them financial independence for the rest of their lives. In 1890 "desiring some publication that would allow freer scope to discussion and criticism Zoe was begun for me by Mr. Brandegee and Dr. Harkness" (Harkness was then the President of the Academy), Kate wrote in her "Reminiscences" many years later. At the time, however, still concerned about eastern prejudices against women botanists in powerful positions, Kate's role in Zoe was adroitly camouflaged. Neither she nor Townie was mentioned in any editorial connection until the eighth number of volume one was published. Then T. S. Brandegee replaced Frank H. Vaslit as editor. In volume two, number one, Kate's name appeared on the roster of five associate editors. But the Easterners had already guessed that the initials K. B. were Kate's, and when she was less than complimentary about a book published by New York Botanical Garden botanist Nathaniel Lord Britton, who was leading the "splitter" contingent in the East, he launched a counterattack based on her sex. (One wonders what his own professional wife, Elizabeth Gertrude Knight Britton, thought of that.) Although his protests were vituperative and unnecessary, he had surmised correctly that it was Kate who was the guiding light behind Zoe.

By volume three, another woman's name, Alice Eastwood, appeared on the masthead as an associate editor. Alice was Kate's protégée, whom she lured to San Francisco in 1892 as joint curator of the herbarium, offering Alice her entire salary, since Townie's inheritance made it unnecessary for Kate. Once Alice arrived, she was listed as editor of Zoe and introduced to the California Botanical Club started by Kate in 1891, the first such club on the coast.

Meanwhile, Kate spent her time trying to sort out Greene's botanical work; this culminated in a forty-page article in volume four, entitled "The Botanical Writings of Edward Lee Greene." Her dispassionate style could not hide the fact that she questioned many of his proposed new species and genera. Greene never replied to her article, but Marcus Jones, at least, considered her handling of his work "masterful."

Volume four, number four, announced that all further communications to *Zoe* should be addressed to T. S. Brandegee in San Diego, California. Alice Eastwood had been eased into full curatorship as Kate had planned, freeing the Brandegees to retire in 1895. In San Diego they bought a house on a mesa overlooking the city and built their own brick herbarium and library. They also started a botanical garden. "It was a botanical paradise," William Albert Setchell of the University of California's Department of Botany later wrote, "rare flowers blooming on all sides, mockingbirds, quail calling, and other native songbirds making the air musical with song." Kate could at last watch birds as well as continue her botanical writing in *Zoe* without the harsh criticism of factions in the academy. And both she and Townie could do more of what they did best—collect. Previously Townie had begun collecting in Baja California, and Kate had accompanied him on a trip there in 1893 along with Gustav Eisen, the curator of Zoology at the Academy of Sciences. She had returned a month ahead of them by ship, laden with the plants they had collected, and had been shipwrecked but had saved the plants.

After that she never returned to Baja, probably because the intense heat and humidity bothered her. She went instead on her own collecting trips to the mountains of California, which, she told Townie, suited her health. Increasingly Kate's health did become a problem. She was a diabetic before insulin treatment existed and had to watch her diet carefully. She desperately wanted to spend time checking western specimens in eastern herbariums, but most of her attempts to travel east were abruptly aborted by diabetic attacks. Once, in 1917, she did make it to the Gray Herbarium, but after only one day in New York, she broke down completely and rushed home. Earlier, in 1908 and 1909, she relied on Alice Eastwood to check specimens both in the East and in England.

Still, she took collecting trips with and without Townie. Often, in fact, one stayed home and tended to the plants the other in the field sent ahead. The few letters that survive from Kate to Townie portray a woman eager to collect plants but lonely for the companionship of her husband. "Write to me often to this address until I give you some other—for I am comfortless and lonely. . . . I wish I were with you tonight—but I have put my hands to the plough and will not turn back," she wrote from Giant Forest. However, "there are lots of plants, and I am by way of settling many things. . . .

10. Kate Brandegee on a mule, ready to start for the mountains from San Jose del Cabo, California. *Courtesy University and Jepson Herbaria, University of California, Berkeley*

Monday I will get sent to Alta Meadows which is a great deal higher than this and may stay a week."

Another undated letter from Placerville informed Townie that "I leave here at 6:30 tomorrow morning on a twelve mile walk to Auburn. Only went about twenty miles up in the mountains, but far enough. . . . All this day I have worked alternately pressing and drying plants." On July 2, 1908, at the age of sixty-four, she reported, "I am going next Monday to Eldorado County to walk from Placerville to Truckee — may be gone two weeks. . . . I have had considerable hardships in botanizing and perhaps in consequence — I am unusually strong and well."

In 1906, just after the San Francisco earthquake had destroyed the academy's herbarium, the Brandegees donated their entire botanical collections and library to the University of California in Berkeley. This doubled the university's facilities for research work and gave them the most complete representation of Pacific coast flora in the West. The Brandegees' herbarium was rich in type specimens, most of which had been named and described by them and consisted of one hundred thousand plants gathered mostly in southern California, Arizona, and Mexico. Citing Kate's health, they moved to Berkeley, where Townie was made honorary curator of the University Herbarium and where both he and Kate worked until their deaths.

They continued to collect despite incipient old age, and on one trip into the Santa Lucia Mountains, Kate broke a leg and had to be carried for miles over rough trails to reach shelter and medical assistance. But the rewards, for both, were great. They were the first to describe and name forty-five new species of California plants, and many California plant species were named after either Townie or Kate. Greene unkindly used her maiden name in naming the *Astragulus layneae* (the Layne locoweed) for her, she preferred "Layne" to "Curran" before she married Townie. But when she named a plant during that period, "Curran" usually appeared after the scientific designation, as in *Chorizanthe insignis* Curran. After her marriage, "K. Brandegee" followed the plant's name. Kate and Townie were also honored for their work in Baja California, since close to 160 plant species from there were described by one or the other. Twenty additional plants were named *brandegeei* for Townie or *brandegeana* for Kate by other scientists.

The Brandegees definitely reinforced each other in their common interest, and although some people questioned Kate's housewifely abilities (she was a poor cook and a slovenly housekeeper), few questioned her devotion to Townie. When she died in 1920, Townie, by then deaf, blind in one eye, and partially paralyzed, withdrew from social intercourse but continued his botanical work until his own death five years later.

Although Kate's accomplishments were later eclipsed by her far more famous protégée Alice Eastwood, she had labored hard to make the work of western botanists acceptable by eastern standards. Because she was forthright in her judgments, though, she did make enemies. Disgruntled male botanists accused her of vindictiveness, and Greene openly referred to her as a she-devil. But those who had no quarrel with her praised her "simplicity and directness of character in faithful friendship."

Probably Kate's greatest sin was that she was a woman who refused to be put down because of her sex. However, as she admitted in her answer to Britton's anger over her review of his book, "she is a woman, but pledges in extenuation of the damning fact that she was in no way consulted about the matter." By fighting such battles, Kate cleared the way for other western women to work both as collectors and as paid professionals in the field of botany.

# *Alice Eastwood*

## GRAND OLD BOTANIST OF THE ACADEMY

OF ALL HER OUTSTANDING TRAITS, Alice Eastwood was best known for her hardiness. Why else would the Arnold Arboretum have asked her to go to the Yukon in 1914 when she was fifty-five years old to collect willow samples? Evidently they believed her when she wrote, "I don't mind anything when I want to get something."

"Anything" in the Yukon consisted of a rough cabin, a defective wood stove, insufficient food, and a floor coated with ice during the late winter (April) when she arrived. In the spring and summer it meant hordes of mosquitoes, which she ignored as she resolutely collected willows and other botanical specimens. However, "it is one of my air-castles realized," she wrote to Miss Day back at the Gray Herbarium in Cambridge, Massachusetts. "But the job is not easy. Willows are about as bothersome to collect as anything could well be." Nevertheless, working alone, she hiked miles into the back country collecting trees and shrubs in their flowering and fruiting stages, and she made many new friends.

None of this was unusual for her. At the age of six, she had been introduced to the world of plants by her Uncle William Eastwood. Thrilled with the interest of his orphaned niece, this doctor and ex-perimental horticulturist gave her books on plants and taught her Latin plant names.

She was a serious-minded, conscientious child who had been born in Toronto, Canada, on January 19, 1859, the eldest child of Colin and Eliza Jane Eastwood. Unfortunately, her mother died when Alice was six, but before she did, she summoned the little girl to her bed-side and made her promise to take care of her four-year-old sister and fourteen-month-old brother. Solemnly, Alice agreed.

Perhaps her mother realized that her husband would not be as reliable. Immediately after her death, he parceled his children out to relatives and left for parts unknown. He did maintain sporadic contact with them, and when Alice was eight she lived with him for a time. But when the grocery store he started failed, he once again divided up the children. This time her brother was left with relatives, while she and her sister were put in Oshawa Convent in Toronto. Uncle William kept a careful eye on them and continued to influence Alice's botanical leanings, but at the convent she found another mentor, an old French gardener-priest.

The convent was dank and cold. It provided very little intellectual stimulation, and the food that was served was often inadequate. Yet Alice, the eternal optimist, made a friend of one nun, studied diligently, and watched over her sister. Her happiest hours were spent in the garden with the priest.

Then, in 1873, when she was fourteen, her life changed radically. Her father had made a new life for himself as a storekeeper in Denver, Colorado, and he offered a home to the sisters. The move to Denver was both a joy and a disappointment—a joy because Alice could attend East Denver High School, and a disappointment because her father barely made enough money to keep the little family going. Alice's persistence in attending school baffled him. He needed her to work and bring in money. So work she did, while also graduating as valedictorian in 1879. She then began her career as a high school teacher.

From all accounts, she was an excellent teacher, but she lived for the summers, when she would scrape together a little money and spend the season in the High Rockies, learning to identify wildflowers and collecting specimens for her herbarium. In those frontier times of the 1880s, she went far beyond the stage stops, traveling alone by foot or on horseback. She often encountered rough miners, cowboys and ranchers, but she always maintained that "never in all my experiences have I had the slightest discourtesy and I have never had any fear. I believe that fear brings danger." Carrying a gun, in her opinion, was showing fear, so she never carried one.

"What grand times I had in the southwestern part of Colorado," she wrote much later, "wandering around alone over those beautiful mountains where the alpine regions far surpass in abundance, variety and beauty of the flowers anything I have seen in any other region." She quickly became an institution in Denver. So when the famous English naturalist, Alfred Russel Wallace, visited Denver and said he wanted to explore Gray's Peak, she was volunteered as the only person equipped to be his guide.

11.   Alice Eastwood collecting in the California foothills during the 1890s. *Courtesy Special Collections Department, California Academy of Sciences, San Francisco*

Off they went together, the famous man in his sixties, the unknown young woman in her twenties, on what she called "a glorious adventure" for three days. They easily climbed 1,170 feet in a day, stayed the nights in rough cabins with miners, and finally ascended Gray's Peak. Wallace mentioned in his autobiography, *My Life*, that he found many new alpine plants and altogether was well satisfied with the journey. Alice, in her own account, wrote enthusiastically about her encounter with the great man.

One of Alice's favorite companions was Al Wetherill. He and his brothers had just discovered Mesa Verde on their land, and Alice was privileged to explore the area with them. On one trip, Al lost his way; after lowering her and the baggage down the steep slopes of Montezuma Canyon by rope, he went off to find help. She spent the night alone on a shelf between the top of the canyon and the river, but she maintained that she "wasn't at all worried. I knew if I followed the creek up that I would reach Monticello eventually

95

and I am a good walker." Thanks to the matches she always carried, since "if one is lost the smoke of a fire will tell your location and if the need is warmth, that also is met," she remained relatively warm and dry until a very concerned Al returned the next day to guide her out.

All through her twenties she continued teaching, collecting, and exploring. Every penny she made was shared with her family or used to finance her botanical summers. Her father had remarried in 1880, his fortunes had improved, and he and Alice were able to make some astute real estate purchases in the fast-growing city of Denver. By the time she was thirty-one, those investments paid enough to give her a small but assured income. That was what she had been waiting for. She quit her teaching job and decided to spend the rest of her life studying botany.

By then her reputation had spread to San Francisco, which, with its California Academy of Sciences and its able botanists, T. S. and Kate Brandegee, was a center for western botanical research. With her spare cash, Alice took the train to San Francisco to visit the academy. There she met and impressed the Brandegees with her knowledge and enthusiasm. They encouraged her to write articles for their journal *Zoe*, and when she returned to Denver, they decided to woo her back to San Francisco.

At first they offered her fifty dollars a month to help organize the academy's herbarium, but in 1892 they upped the offer to seventy-five dollars and the position to joint curator of the herbarium. Still, leaving her beloved Denver was difficult. Her biographer, Carol Green Wilson, claimed that about that time she was planning to marry a tubercular Eastern journalist who had come to Denver to get well. However, he died, and almost immediately she accepted the Brandegee offer. Alice herself, in her own biographical notes, never mentioned the romance if indeed there had ever been one. But then, she was always reticent about her private life; what mattered most was her life as a botanist. To Carol Green Wilson she insisted that, "I never had time for A man, but I've *always* had men friends. I just couldn't let anyone of them interfere with my work."

This, it turns out, was not strictly true. Several years after she moved to California she had at least one other romance, well documented in both photographs and letters, with the geologist Grove Karl Gilbert, whom she met on a Sierra Club outing. Gilbert, sixteen years her senior, maintained in a letter to his son Arch that "Alice and I have been lovers for years but for a long time I would not propose marriage because it seemed like asking her to give up a life that satisfied her to become the nurse of my broken health." In 1918, though, his health had improved, and he and Alice (then fifty-nine) had agreed to marry and raise Arch's infant son, since his wife had died in childbirth. But once again Alice's intended groom died just before the wedding date. Alice, it seems, did have at least two men in her life for whom she was willing to give up her career.

She moved to San Francisco in 1892 and was immediately elected a member of the academy. For the next fourteen years she spent her time organizing the academy's botanical collections, buying other collections for them with her own money as well as adding to them through her own expeditions. At her expense, she botanized in the Sierra and Coast ranges by stage, horseback, and on foot. She usually rode at least forty miles a day and attended to her collections in the evening and early morning.

Despite her bold spirit, she was not a loner. As often as not, she explored with other intrepid hikers, although as she confessed, "I am not a true mountain climber as I go only for the flowers and views to be had from the lofty heights." But go she did, clad in buttoned, denim skirts she designed herself with heavy cotton nightgowns as bustles. She could walk four miles an hour and never seemed to tire.

"The Hill Tribe," a group of San Francisco residents who enjoyed roaming nearby Tamalpais Mountain on Sundays, welcomed her in their midst. One member remembered her as "a hatless, short-skirted, broad-shouldered woman of wonderful strength — she used to trudge easily twenty miles a day with the sun in her serene bronze face and the wind in her flying hair, carrying her heavy plant presses on her back." She also helped lead a hiking group called the Cross Country Club, which included naturalist Annie Alexander. They spent their weekends exploring the Sierra Nevada and from that group came the first Sierra Club bulletins, which were accounts of what the members saw and discovered on those outings.

If her friends were not available, she did not hesitate to tackle mountain climbing on her own. One day she set off to collect on Mount Shasta. As she started up the mountain, she encountered a party of six men intent on climbing to the top who persuaded her to accompany them. Years later she recalled the joy she experienced during the descent, when she donned a burlap sack, diaper-fashion, over her skirts and slid down the snow-covered slopes on it. "Our path was a beautiful rosy pink from the snow algae of which I had heard but now saw for the first time. It was a wonderful experience and I have always wished that I could do it again. However, at the lower levels the snow was soft and my skirt became very wet along the bottom and heavy and for the first and only time [I] wished that I could have been dressed like the men."

By 1906, Alice had the botanical collections in good shape, and she had wisely separated out the irreplaceable type specimens and put them together in one place where she could easily find them during an emergency. Her foresightedness was all that saved 1,211 botanical items when the San Francisco earthquake and fire hit the city on April 18, 1906. She awoke that fateful day and noticed the tremor, but it did not particularly worry her, since it was felt less in her part of the city. After breakfast she went down to the academy but could not get in. No one was there, doors were locked, and buildings all around her had been destroyed. The academy was partially ruined, but what really worried her was the nearby fire. What if the Academy burned down?

At last she located a male friend who managed to get her into the front hall where others were frantically rescuing library records. But the botanical collection was on the top floor and the marble staircase was in ruins. "We went up," she wrote in a letter to *Science,* "chiefly by holding on to the iron railing and putting our feet between the rungs. Porter helped me to tie up the plant types, and we lowered them to the floor of the museum by ropes and strings tied together. Not a book was I able to save, nor a single thing of my own, except my favorite lens, without which I should feel helpless."

By the time they got everything to the street, the fire had reached the building next door. The military was letting no one take possessions out of the area, but Alice pleaded for her specimens and eventually had them transported out of immediate danger by private conveyance. From there, with the help of friends, she took them to Russian Hill and when that seemed threatened moved them on to Fort Mason. With all her concern for the academy property, she neglected her own private quarters, and as a result "all my pictures and books are gone and many treasures that I prized highly; but I regret nothing for I am rich in friends and things seem of small account." About the academy she wrote, "I do not feel the loss to be mine, but it is a great loss to the scientific world and an irreparable loss to California. My own destroyed work I do not lament, but it was a joy to me while I did it, and I can still have the same joy in starting it again." Which is exactly what she did. Undaunted and then forty-seven years of age, she set out for the mountains to re-collect the many specimens that had been lost. There was no money for the project; she used her own small income. For the rest of her life, she always spent birthday and holiday gifts of money on books for the academy.

The University of California at Berkeley offered her research facilities in the botany department, but for nearly six years her position at the academy remained in limbo. In addition to re-collecting the plants, she had to verify the plant names from the original specimens. She visited the National Herbarium in Washington, D.C., the New York Botanical Garden, and finally the Gray Herbarium at Harvard.

As usual, Alice quickly gathered new friends around her and obtained a job as staff assistant at the herbarium. She worked beside Kate Furbish's friend, Merritt L. Fernald, who she considered the best systematic botanist in the country. Alice's stay at the Gray Herbarium was "one of the happiest experiences of my life," but after working there for two years she took her savings and went to Europe to check original plant specimens.

It was like a homecoming for her — meeting well-known scientists and studying the collections at the British Museum of Natural History, the Royal Botanic Gardens and Kew Gardens in England, and the Natural History Museum of Paris. But finally she returned to Cambridge and received the call she had been waiting for. The California Academy of Sciences wanted her to rebuild their herbarium. They had decided to reestablish themselves in Golden Gate Park, which from Alice's standpoint was an excellent plan. Not only did she have a herbarium to attend to but she also had unlimited land to turn into gardens.

She enlisted the help of the park superintendent, Scotsman John McClaren, and together they worked to educate people about both the foreign and domestic species of plants they grew in the gardens. Every week she decorated the entrance lobby of North American Hall, the new Academy headquarters, with an educational flower show. Each specimen was carefully labeled with its name and country of origin. The show became the longest continual floral exhibition in the world. In addition, she drew up a tree map of the park.

Every Thursday she held botanical classes for interested park gardeners. One of those gardeners, Tom Howell, later became her assistant, and when she grew older and it became necessary for the automobile to replace walking, he drove her to places where she could still collect. In 1936 she reported to friends at the Gray Herbarium that she and Howell had "made some great collections this year in San Luis Obispo and Mendocino counties. We have our own car and Mr. Howell does the collecting (most of it) and I do the cata-

loging and caring for the plants in press. It is a grand partnership."
In Alice's opinion, Howell was "the most able of all the young botanists in the west," as she confided in 1938 to her friend agrostologist
Agnes Chase at the Smithsonian. That same year, from October 5
until October 30, she and Howell traveled almost four thousand miles
and collected close to one thousand specimens, exploring the Grand
Canyon, Bryce Canyon (which she called the most beautiful canyon
in the world), Zion, the Petrified Forest, and the Painted Desert. She
never did like to drive, though, and always maintained that "there
is no way so good for a knowledge of the plants as walking through
a region."

It was Howell's remembrances of her that have painted the most
vivid portrait of Alice Eastwood as a person. "She took delight in
flouting trivial social conventions," he wrote. She liked simple food
and clothes, chamber music, poetry, and the works of English and
American nineteenth century novelists, particularly Henry James.
Her favorite magazine was *The Saturday Evening Post,* and she read
mystery novels for pleasure and relaxation. She loved to talk about
food and memorable meals and enjoyed making jellies, preserves,
and pickles for herself and her friends.

As a teacher, she was experimental, interesting, and adventurous, using anecdotes and appropriate allusions to literature and the
arts. "With Miss Eastwood," Howell wrote, "nothing of knowledge
or wisdom was reserved — her table was a veritable feast spread out
for anyone who wished to sample or to partake deeply . . . anyone
with a sincere love of flowers or beauty could have known Miss
Eastwood."

She maintained her love of humanity and her almost childlike
belief in goodness all her life. Through the 1920s, 1930s, and 1940s,
she became the grand old lady of the academy, and honors were
heaped upon her. A garden club she had helped dedicated a redwood grove to her, the arboretum she had dreamed of became a reality, the Shakespeare Garden she started contained a rose-granite bench
the Botany Club dedicated to her. Because she helped found the American Fuchsia Society, nurserymen named a fuchsia for her. There
was also an Alice Eastwood lilac and an Alice Eastwood orchid. Two
botanical genera honor her — *Eastwoodia* and *Aliciella.* "But," as she
told Agnes Chase, "the most proper [honor] is that officially the name
of the Herbarium is the Alice Eastwood Herbarium of the California Academy of Sciences. As I built it and the botanical library from
the types that I saved and two books with no help from 1912 when
I began to 1930 when I was allowed an assistant, it is practically

12.   Alice Eastwood collecting "her" grass, *Festuca eastwoodae. Courtesy Special Collection Department, California Academy of Sciences, San Francisco*

my herbarium." After all, from 1912 until 1949, she had added 340,000 specimens to the herbarium.

With the invaluable help of Tom Howell, Alice also started a quarterly in 1932 called *Leaflets of Western Botany*, because they could not get their articles into the University of California's Herbarium publication *Madroño*. In addition, Alice was instrumental in forming the California Horticultural Society. Always on the lookout for botanical specimens, she encouraged other, younger female botanical explorers, such as Louise A. Boyd, who went to the Arctic and Ynes Mexia, who penetrated remote areas of Mexico and South America.

But despite all the honors she received, there was one she would never accept. Because she had been self-taught and had never received a college degree, she refused any honorary degrees offered to her. In that refusal can be seen a little of the curmudgeonly personality that Howell briefly alluded to. "Her impatience could be as violent as her kindness and generosity were great, and the force and bite of that impatience were dreaded by all who ever encountered it."

A bit of a rebel was Alice, who claimed that she followed the command of Emerson to "scorn conventions and you always can." Even in religious matters she was unconventional, mentioning in her notes the "absurdity of dogmas in religion and philosophy and the insoluble mysteries of time, space, life and infinity. One can build up any kind of a system on a predicated hypothesis. To me the feeling that comes from the order and law of the universe is truly religious and I think that every scientific person must be religious without any belief in a dogma of any kind."

Her work was her life, and she continued until she was ninety, when she officially retired. She kept her desk and continued to work in her capacity as curator-emeritus, while Howell took her place as curator. Then, at the age of ninety-one, in 1950, she flew to the Eighth International Botanical Congress in Sweden, where she was made honorary president. Members of the IBC sat her in the chair of Linnaeus, that tiny, indomitable woman who had followed the teachings of Linnaeus throughout her long and fruitful lifetime.

Her great friend Dr. Gustav Eisen declared at the celebration the academy held for her during her fiftieth working year, "There has never been anyone like her on earth and there never will be, if I am permitted to prophesy."

# Ynes Mexia

## BOTANICAL ADVENTURER

SHE CALLED HERSELF a "nature lover and a bit of an adventuress" for whom "collecting was secondary, even though very real and very important. . . . With it I have a job, I produce something real and lasting, . . . and I also see and learn much that I would not just idling along," she wrote to her "Dear Mentor," Dr. Philip King Brown, the man who had helped her recover from a nervous breakdown and who continued to counsel her throughout her life.

Ynes had emotional problems that crippled her for many years, and it was only at the age of fifty-five, when she began her botanical collecting trips, that she found a purpose in life. However, it took very little to destroy her self-confidence. One condescending letter from one scientist about her work set her back for weeks, even though the collections she had brought out of Mexico had earned paeans from renowned botanists at both the Gray Herbarium at Harvard and the Field Museum in Chicago.

Few people liked Ynes once they knew her well. Annetta Carter, now botanist emeritus at the University Herbarium, recalled her as an "adult, exploitative, spoiled brat." Ynes's good friend N. Floy Bracelin, "Bracie," who equipped Ynes for her expeditions and carried on correspondence related to selling Ynes's specimens, admitted that she had "a difficult temperament" with flashes of violence, traits Bracie attributed to Ynes's Mexican blood. Like many impulsive people, though, Ynes was extremely generous. She gave thousands of dollars to Vernon and Florence Bailey to help Vernon produce the humane animal traps he had invented. She also left enough money to finance a job for Bracie at the California Academy of Sciences Herbarium so that she could work with her friends Alice Eastwood and John Thomas Howell. She had enough personal charm to get along well initially with the wide range of people she dealt with on her Latin American trips, and she had a "flair," according to agrostologist Agnes Chase "for making other people serve . . . and work for her." But Ynes herself recognized her failings and, as she told Dr. Brown, "I am trying to be good and to think of others and to get away from being self-centered, but do not know if I make much progress."

Ynes did not have a normal childhood. She was born on May 24, 1870, in Georgetown (in Washington, D.C.), to Enrique Antonio Mexia, an agent for the Mexican government, and Sarah R. Wilmer Mexia. Sarah had six children from a previous marriage to Albert Ramsey that had ended in divorce. Mexia subsequently adopted her youngest son and daughter. Mexia was not a faithful husband and kept at least one American-born mistress in Mexico City, by whom he had another daughter, Amada.

Sarah refused to live with him for most of Ynes's childhood. When Ynes was three, Sarah took Ynes and her other children to live in Limestone County, Texas, on land owned by the Mexia family. Ynes's education was spotty at best, since she moved often. Her home base continued to be Texas until she was fifteen, except for short periods in Philadelphia and Ontario. Then, in 1886 and 1887, she attended Saint Joseph's Academy in Emmitsburg, Maryland, her mother's home state. Following that, she went to Mexico City, where she lived most of the next ten years in her father's hacienda.

Family letters indicate that Ynes frequently visited a nearby convent and that she had considered becoming a nun. Her father's will left his home and money to Ynes and her legal stepsister (he had cut his stepson out of the will because of the son's mental instability), but the will indicated that if Ynes became a nun all of his worldly goods would go to her stepsister. In 1897, Ynes surprised everyone by marrying a young German-Spanish merchant in Mexico City, Herman Lane, who was five years her junior. As Amada put it, she thought Ynes had preferred "single blessedness."

A year later Mexia died and his will was challenged almost immediately by his mistress and stepson, who joined forces to oppose Ynes and her stepsister's inheritance, the mistress claiming she had had a proxy marriage prior to Sarah's marriage to Mexia. Sarah had died back in 1896, still vowing to her children that Mexia was her legal husband, but it is obvious from letters Ynes exchanged with Sarah's oldest daughter that neither woman fully understood how many of Sarah's younger children had actually been fathered by Mexia before Sarah's divorce from her first husband. It was, in other words, a mess, and Ynes spent most of her short married life with Lane defending her father's will in court against the passionate and seamy testimony of both her stepbrother and her father's mistress. When she finally won, she generously shared the money with Amada as well as with her legal stepsister.

In 1904 Lane died after a long illness. Either then or perhaps even earlier Ynes started a poultry and pet stock-raising business called Quinta at the Mexico City hacienda she had inherited from her father. Apparently the business thrived under her management. Four years later, at the age of thirty-eight, she married D. Agustin Reygados, a twenty-two-year-old young man who worked for her.

The marriage was a disaster from the beginning. By 1909 Ynes had suffered a total breakdown and, leaving the business in Reygados' hands, she went to San Francisco to seek medical help. That was when she found Dr. Brown. After many sessions with him, she regained her equilibrium; her first decision was to dissolve her marriage.

Getting rid of Reygados, who had almost bankrupted her business, was not easy. Both he and his family begged her not to, but it was evidently her money and not her person that they wished to retain. Nevertheless, encouraged by Dr. Brown, she stayed in San Francisco, sold her business in Mexico City, went through with her divorce, and settled into intermittent social work. Still, she had periods of instability when she would retreat from the world, read books, and overeat.

Then, in 1920, she began taking trips with the local Sierra Club, and the following year she signed up as a special student at the University of California in Berkeley interested in the natural sciences. But the science that attracted her most was botany, particularly after she took a course in flowering plants from Professor LeRoy Abrams at the Hopkins Marine Station in Pacific Grove in the summer of 1925. She followed that course with her first botanical collecting trip, accompanying botanist Roxanna Stinchfield Ferris of Stanford University to western Mexico from September 15 to November 19, 1925. Her trip was curtailed by a fall from a cliff, which left her with an injured hand and fractured ribs, but nevertheless she returned with five hundred species, several of which were new, including *Mimosa mexiae*, which was named for her by Joseph Nelson Rose. Ynes had found not only purpose in life but her preferred collecting ground — Mexico. With her ability to speak Spanish and her familiarity with the customs and people of the country, it seemed a natural choice.

She wrote to one Sierra Club friend, "As trousers for women are unknown in Mexico, I compromise on a short skirt which I wear with my high moccasin boots."

Before returning to Mexico, she enrolled in Dr. Harold Bryant's Six Trips Afield, a University of California extension course. There she met Bracie, who worked as an assistant at the university herbarium. Ynes planned to collect botanical sets for several institutions to help finance her collecting trips. Needing someone else to act as her curator and agent, while she concentrated on the actual collecting, Ynes persuaded Bracie to take on the job of caring for the material.

Armed with an impressive gold seal from the University of California and partly financed by Dr. William Setchell of the University of California's Department of Botany, Ynes returned for a seven-month trip to western Mexico in September of 1926. She hoped to penetrate remote areas where no collectors had been before and to discover new plant species in the subtropical region.

She embarked on a Pacific mail steamer to Mazatlán, in the state of Sinaloa along the coast, where she met her good friend J. Gonzales Ortega, a civil engineer and amateur botanist familiar with the western Mexican coast. From there she proceeded south to the state of Nayarit and settled into the old inland city of Tepic, set amidst a fertile valley. With a reliable local guide and a couple of horses, she set out every morning to explore and collect plants.

Unlike most women naturalists, Ynes liked to have plants named for her. It gave her the kind of immortality she relished. Ynes called her specimens "permanent exhibits under my name in the Herbaria of the world for all time to come." Her article for the botanical journal *Madroño*, entitled "Botanical Trails in Old Mexico: The Lure of the Unknown," is replete with the names of new plant species she discovered. Several, including *Piper Ynesae, Zexmenia mexiae, Eugenia mexiae, Psychotria mexiae, Euphorbia mexiae, Peperomia mexiae,* and *Begonia mexiae,* were named for her by prominent male botanists. She even discovered a new genus during her expedition, a composite growing in a sandy streambed near the ocean in the state of Jalisco, now called *Mexianthus mexicanus.*

From Tepic she headed southeast into the higher mountains of Ixtlán del Río where she discovered a new nightshade, *Solanum nayaritense.* Then she went back north, still in the state of Nayarit, to the city of Tuxpan on the Río San Pedro. In that area she collected by dugout canoe and was attacked by biting gnats. At one point she got out of the canoe to lighten the load. She pulled her boots off and waded in the warm, shallow water. Soft mud oozed up between her toes and she felt beautifully enclosed in a world of blue water lilies and vine-covered trees while all around her flashed the brightly colored tropical birds.

Buoyed by such a different world, she made a foray north, back to the state of Sinaloa to collect in the thorny coastal jungle near Los Labrados and then caught a steamer south to the coastal town of Puerto Vallarta in Jalisco state, where she spent a month collecting near the coast and in the foothills. Again she paid the price in insect attacks, writing to Dr. Brown that "the collecting was very good, but oh! the animated nature! I was introduced to . . . infant ticks, about the size of the dot of the letter i. They swarm on you by the thousand if you rub up against them and are everywhere. They are too little to pick off and they walk and tickle you and then they bite and stay there, and raise a worse lump than a mosquito. You cannot rub them off, but with a piece of soft wax can get them one by one. . . ." Nevertheless, she concluded, "There was all the collecting in the world and the streams and woods and hills were beautiful so I really enjoyed my stay in spite of the bugs."

She had come "to this place because it was the farthest away, most tucked in and hidden little spot I could learn about," she informed Mrs. Brown. She put up her cot in a banana grove owned by a wood-cutter with nine children. A panther had killed two of his dogs the previous week, and she wondered how much protection her mosquito net and flashlight would provide if the panther returned.

It was from the woodcutter's hut that she proceeded by packtrain on a three-day journey to the crest of the Sierra Madre. There she stayed with a poor woman named Guadalupe and her three children. With the help of a local guide named José she explored the mountains, finding new plants every day. On one trip, she and José missed an obscure turn and went miles out of their way; they returned to Guadalupe's long after dark, having stumbled along a steep, rocky trail over the heavily wooded mountains for hours.

The following day they made an even worse trip. Searching for the source of the stream they had reached the day before, they were stopped by a precipitous cliff. With nowhere to go but up, she clung to the rock and shale with her hands, knees, and toes as she wormed her way up the cliff. "After a year or two of climbing I reached the first tree, and . . . I hugged its good, firm, solid trunk."

The mountains of Jalisco held her captive for the rest of her trip, but when it was over she had collected thirty-three thousand specimens, including fifty new species and one genera. No wonder Professor Benjamin Robinson of the Gray Herbarium praised her "noteworthy service in exploration." Ynes was also pleased that not one of her plants had been spoiled by the tropical heat. This is little wonder, though, since she had been trained in the art of collecting by none other than her friend and mentor Alice Eastwood. In addition to collecting the plants, she had also photographed many of them to show their size and growth habit as well as their habitat. Unfortunately, political unrest in Mexico kept her from returning again as she had planned.

She wrote to Dr. J. M. Greenman, curator of the herbarium at the Missouri Botanical Garden in March, 1928, that Professor Setchell was anxious for her to go to South America to collect but that she was not ready to start on such a long trip. In the meantime, she proposed a short summer collecting trip around the slopes of Mount McKinley, another area that botanists had not explored. In a subsequent letter to Greenman, she told him she had collected in different altitudes at widely separated localities. She did her collecting first at the upper edge of the timberline, near Savage River. From there she went by packtrain to Copper Mountain above timberline. Then she backpacked with dogs twenty-two miles farther and set up her principal station at Wonder Lake. Altogether, she collected sixty-one hundred plants.

Fourteen months after her return to California she headed south again, this time to Brazil. She settled in with Dr. P. H. Rolfs and his daughter at Viçosa in the state of Minas Gerais, where Rolfs headed the State College of Agriculture. In return for free room and board and college facilities for her work, Ynes agreed to collect specimens for their proposed herbarium.

Previously, Ynes had collected grasses on her Mexican trip and had sent them to A. S. Hitchcock, agrostologist Agnes Chase's mentor at the United States Department of Agriculture. Once Ynes was installed at Viçosa, Agnes, already collecting around Rio de Janeiro, decided to join Ynes. They did take one perilous trip together but it was obvious that the two strong women did not get along. Ynes postulated to Dr. Brown that Agnes did not like her because "I trod on the toes of her pet theories, prohibition and women's rights and her constant criticism of her own country's shortcomings. She is proud of having been in jail as a suffragette! It seems to me quite unnecessary in our country. . . ." As a recently naturalized citizen (1924), Ynes was probably fiercely patriotic, and Agnes's strong social consciousness had obviously offended her.

The women also did not have the same method of collecting. Ynes enjoyed roughing it by riding horseback and camping out, while Agnes preferred the train and what Ynes called "unspeakable little 'hotels' with bugs and dirt and infection." Chase, on the other hand, found Ynes to be a carping complainer. Then, too, Ynes did not consider herself to be a scientist but a collector for the adventure of it. Agnes, she found, was "almost a human grass . . . who lives, sleeps, dreams nothing but grasses and writing a book on them." And so the self-taught botanist and the self-taught collector parted ways. Ynes persisted in Viçosa with occasional collecting trips to other Brazilian regions for nearly two years before embarking on the greatest adventure of her life, "Three Thousand Miles up the Amazon," as she called her subsequent account in the *Sierra Club Bulletin.*

The first twenty-five hundred miles on the steamer *Victoria* through Brazil to Iquitos, Peru, were traveled in comparative luxury, and the few stops they made were never long enough for Ynes to collect. But when she reached Iquitos, she hired three male servants — José, Neptali, and Valentíno — and was taken several hundred miles upriver to the town of Barranca on the Rio Marañón, a tributary of the Amazon. At Barranca they set off in a dugout canoe, headed for the Pongo de Manseriche, the so-called Iron Gateway of the Amazon. She said, "I sat amidships under a little palm-leaf shelter, forgetting my rather hard 'box-seat' in watching the river and its life as it unfolded before me." She camped on sandy beaches each night, sleeping on her cot swathed in mosquito netting and bathing in a bucket of water "while the hypodermic needles of the mosquitoes unduly hastened the process."

After ten days they reached the Pongo, a seven-mile-long gorge known for its whirlpools and rushing water. At that time, mid-October, the water was low, making the passage difficult but not impossible. They were met at the other side by nomadic Aguaruna Indians, a branch of the Jivaro headhunters, who were friendly once they learned Ynes and her guides were Christians and not their Indian enemies.

And then the rains came, effectively marooning Ynes a few miles above the Pongo for three months. She quickly set up a camp routine. Neptali paddled her around in a small canoe so that she could collect plants as well as insects and birds. She taught José to dry and press her plants, and Valentíno cooked and helped with the plants. They bartered with the Indians for extra food and enjoyed eating monkey stew, parrots, and toucans. On Christmas of 1931 she set up a palm tree under her thatched shelter and trimmed it with wild red peppers and poinsettias.

Finally she persuaded the Indians to build a balsa raft for her to float back to Iquitos. Although Ynes found rafting "a delightful way to travel," it was not without its dangers, especially in the high waters of the Pongo. "If we were not scraping past the jagged teeth of a stranded tree by inches, we were watching the daily storms traveling

13.    Ynez Mexia's thatched hut in Amazonia, Peru, where she lived for three months. *Courtesy University and Jepson Herbaria, University of California, Berkeley*

toward our tiny ark, the strong wind catching our thatch like a sail and forcing us towards the inundated shore in imminent danger of smashing into the trees in the deluge of rain, lightning and thunder."

After two weeks they reached Iquitos. The rest of her trip was anticlimactic. Unable to ascend the eastern slope of the Andes on horseback because of the rain, she took a six-passenger hydroplane to San Ramón, Peru, where she transferred to a two-passenger open airplane to fly to La Oroya, the sixteen-thousand-foot terminus of the railroad from Lima. That train trip, from La Oroya to Lima, is still considered one of the great railroad adventures of the world, but to Ynes, who had rafted down the Río Marañón, it must have seemed tame.

All in all, she concluded, "In the two and a half years that I was in South America, I never was sick for ten minutes" (a slight exaggeration — she had suffered from amoebic dysentery for over half a year in Brazil). "I had no accidents and not a disagreeable incident, and that is a pretty good record for Latin-American countries where it is *said* a woman cannot travel alone!" Furthermore, she had collected sixty-five thousand plant specimens in Brazil and Peru. Of those, a little over one-tenth were ferns and allied genera, judged by fern specialist Edwin B. Copeland to be such "as we rarely see from the tropics, including in every specimen a practically complete representation of the features of the plant."

She returned to California in April of 1932. From then until she left for a second trip to South America in September of 1934, she contented herself with Sierra Club outings and at least one collecting trip to Nevada, Utah, and Arizona with Alice Eastwood and John Thomas Howell in 1933. She and Alice paid all the expenses, and Howell drove the car jointly owned by him and Alice. Howell and Ynes did the collecting, while seventy-five-year-old Alice pressed and catalogued the plants. Ynes memorialized the trip with her camera and apparently got on well with them, since Howell later remembered her as "a dear, good friend" who accompanied him down into the Grand Canyon, she on horseback, he on foot, collecting over a hundred kinds of plants, one of which, *Carex curatorium*, was new to science.

All the while, though, she had been negotiating with the U.S. Department of Agriculture's Bureau of Plant Industry and Exploration about making a trip to Ecuador for them. She wanted to search for the rare wax palm, *Cinchona*, which was supposed to grow at a greater altitude and lower temperature than any other palm, on the Volcán de Chiles, a peak on the border of Ecuador and Colombia. She was also looking for the Indians' plant sources for the fish poisons they used.

After arriving by steamer at Guayaquil, she took the train northeast to Quito and then due north to Tulcán, a border town in northern Ecuador. From there she continued on horseback, accompanied by an Ecuadorian guide and two pack horses. "That trail!" she later wrote. "It went up the side of a mountain so steep that in places I had to be hauled up, and then through choked forest and along precipitous slopes, apparently endless, where the sun shone tirelessly. . . ." At last she reached Volcán de Chiles, where she found two ivory nut palms and one species of quinine bark tree.

On that journey she had subsisted almost entirely on barley meal, beans, lentils, yucca, and green bananas. This may be why she snatched a handful of what looked to her like blueberries and was immediately attacked by pain so severe that she almost fell off her horse. First she was given molasses-water by the local people. When that did not help, they stuck an unwashed chicken feather down her throat to induce vomiting, and the emergency passed.

From northern Ecuador she proceeded to El Oriente, or the Eastern Region, the part of Ecuador east of the Andes. She found the going so difficult that she used oxen for both packing and riding. "It was loads of fun," she reported to Dr. Brown. "The pace was about two miles per hour, minus, . . . and I had plenty of time to watch the flora and admire the scenery!" She described the trail as "pure mulch and silt and every few yards dipping to a boggy trickle." But her ox "just ploughed serenely through the mud and water up to his knees, up to his belly, up to his breast and sometimes he laid his chin on the surface. But his legs kept moving like pistons, and he thought nothing of climbing a perpendicular bank twelve or fifteen feet high while I held on for dear life." Not only was her search for fish poison plants successful, but in a full year in Ecuador (September, 1934–September, 1935) she collected five thousand plant specimens of all kinds.

From Ecuador she went directly to Peru to join T. Harper Goodspeed's University of California Botanical Expedition to the Andes in search of garden plants and wild tobacco. Later he praised Ynes in his classic *Plant Hunters in the Andes*, calling her "a remarkable woman, . . . the true explorer type and happiest when independent and far from civilization. She always made light of the privations and dangers." He also gave her credit for showing his expedition how to cope with and adjust to Andean life. Despite being part of the expedition for over a year, from October 1935 until January of 1937, she mostly went her own way on funds provided by Goodspeed. She collected intensively in Peru and the foothills of the Argentinian, Chilean, and Bolivian Andes, and then worked through other areas in Ecuador, Peru, Chile, and Argentina. She reached the Straits of Magellan and collected, in all, nearly fifteen thousand plant specimens. Ynes had certainly covered a good portion of South America in her travels, but she died before she could write any articles similar to those on her Mexican and Amazonian trips.

Most of 1937 she spent back in the United States. In July she attended strenuous outdoor classes at the University of Michigan's Biological Station in Cheboygen, Michigan, learning a whole new flora and attempting to keep up with a class of much younger people. In addition to her age (she was then sixty-seven), she also complained of pain under her right ribs and in her chest to Dr. Brown.

Pain, however, did not stop Ynes from planning another collecting trip, this time to southwestern Mexico. She left on October 31, 1937, for the states of Guerrero and Oaxaca. Once again she endured rugged conditions, traveling by horseback six thousand feet up into the mountains, where she stayed with the natives and lived on a diet of beans and tortillas sometimes supplemented by a little milk or an egg. During one trip into the southeastern corner of Oaxaca

14.   Ynez Mexia on a horse in Patagonia, Argentina, June, 1936. *Courtesy University and Jepson Herbaria, University of California, Berkeley*

she was stabled with the horses and chickens. Bedeviled by mosquitoes, ticks, and sand flies, she dried her plants and enjoyed her adventure in the country she called "magnificent."

But severe stomach pains sent her back to California prematurely in late May of 1938, laden with thirteen thousand plant specimens. She was immediately hospitalized and died of lung cancer on July 12, 1938.

Ynes had persevered through adversity, and in only ten years she had ranged more widely and collected a greater number of plants than any other woman collector. She had, indeed, "found a task where I could be useful and really produce something of lasting worth, while living out among the flowers."

# Mary Sophie Young

## TRANS-PECOS BOTANIST

MARY SOPHIE YOUNG was probably the only woman botanist to use
a pair of burros and a roofless buggy on her collecting trips. Because of limited funds, she needed a cheap way to carry her camping gear and plant presses into the rugged Trans-Pecos area of West
Texas back in 1914, so she bought Nebuchadnezzar and Balaam
from a Mexican boy for eight dollars and paid a further nine dollars
for the buggy.

Although she had been told they were old, experienced burros,
they were young and intractable. So intractable, in fact, that the
normally soft-spoken and cheerful botanist once lost her temper with
them. After walking two miles just to find the burros, she spent even
more time and energy trying to catch them. Then, when she was
at last able to bridle Nebuchadnezzar, he refused to move. "Burros,"
she observed in her journal, "are a sore temptation to wrath. . . .
No amount of kicking or whacking would move him. . . . Nothing
but the choking process, hold his nostrils, so he could not breathe,
had the slightest effect. . . . Before I got through with him, he nearly
wore me out. I choked him six or seven times and he dragged me
all over the place during the process. If I had not been so furious,
I should have given up from sheer exhaustion." Finally he started
trotting, and Mary was off to collect plants in a nearby canyon.

Usually she made her daily jaunts from her campsite on foot. A
gaunt, determined woman of forty-two, she wore high leather boots,
an ankle-length skirt, a long-sleeved blouse, and a wide-brimmed
hat as she traipsed over the rocky, steep countryside. Sometimes she
and her young companion, Carey Tharp, were mistaken for tramps.
She and Carey were relegated to a rancher's barn one night, because

the rancher thought she was a quack "Yarb" or herb doctor—a person who gathered herbs and sold them as curatives from door to door.

Few people guessed that M. S. Young, as she signed her business letters, was Dr. Mary Sophie Young, instructor in botany at the University of Texas and an expert both on the plants around Austin and those of the Trans-Pecos. Those who did know her profession made fun of her rig and her life-style. "Is that the way educated people live? . . . What do you get out of it?" one man asked. Even Mary herself sometimes admitted that she tired of the dirt, the labor, and the often skimpy food rations. And although she looked forward to visiting the small towns along the way, she had "too much sinful pride to enjoy walking around any kind of a town in such clothes. They were my worst clothes at their worst. When we go back [to the town of Valentine], I am going to dress up as swell as I possibly can and walk all over that town."

She had been raised, after all, by genteel people. The youngest child of an Episcopal priest and his wife, Mary had been born in Glendale, Ohio, in 1872. Not much is known of her childhood, but at least some of her siblings were boys. Those brothers, she later remembered, had been reluctant to take their little sister on their tramps in the country. So she had promised never to complain and learned to persevere despite exhaustion. This early training certainly helped her in her later botanical forays.

She came from an educated family and entered kindergarten when she was four years old. This was followed by several years in Ohio public schools and at the Harcourt Place Seminary before she enrolled at Wellesley College in Massachusetts. Because she was shy and hard-working, most people overlooked her, but she had a strong academic record, graduating with a bachelor of arts degree in 1895.

Like many educated women of her day, she became a schoolteacher, first at Louis Academy at Sullivan, Missouri; then at Dundee (Illinois) High School; then in Kansas City, Kansas; and finally at Grafton Hill, Fond-du-Lac, Wisconsin. All the while, though, she was taking correspondence courses and summer sessions at the University of Chicago, and after three long sessions — 1906–1907, 1908–1909, and 1909–1910 — she finally received her Doctor of Philosophy degree in 1910 when she was thirty-eight years old. She had been an excellent student, according to the man she had studied under, Professor Charles J. Chamberlain, and her research specialty had been the morphology of the *Podocarpinae* (a family of coniferous trees and shrubs).

That same fall she was hired as a tutor in botany at the University of Texas and was promoted to instructor the following year.

Her principal duty was to teach the freshman botany laboratory and, probably due to her fifteen years experience as a high school teacher, she knew just how to handle the students. However, she believed in the Socratic method, always answering a question with her own questions in order for students to think puzzles through for themselves.

Students working only for grades did not appreciate her tactics, but those studying botany out of interest thought she was an excellent teacher. Those students were also invited to accompany Mary on her botanical tramps around the Austin vicinity. Armed with collecting can, lunch, and water, she walked miles over rugged territory in search of every kind of plant the area produced.

In 1912 she was given a course in taxonomy to teach as well as the full care of the university herbarium. Although she did not have much training in taxonomy, she instantly took to the work, especially since it required more field trips. When she was not teaching, she was out collecting specimens for the herbarium. Since Austin represents the meeting place of eastern and western species, it was a rich collecting area for Mary, and she was able to fill in many botanical gaps, enriching both the university herbarium and other botanists and herbaria with which she exchanged duplicate specimens. In exchange she received thousands of botanical specimens for the university herbarium.

Her intensive Austin collecting enabled her to write *A Key to the Families and Genera of Flowering Plants and Ferns in the Vicinity of Austin, Texas,* published by the University of Texas in 1917, and "The Seed Plants, Ferns, and Fern Allies of the Austin Region," which appeared as *University of Texas Bulletin no. 2065* on November 20, 1920.

In the summer months she went farther afield, accompanied by a young man who received a free trip in return for his help. This solved her problem of being a woman alone in a wild country, although she also went armed. A .25-caliber Colt automatic rested in the pocket of her skirt even when she was in Austin, since she often walked home late at night after working in the laboratory. In addition, she owned a .22-caliber six-shot revolver and could shoot both guns quite accurately, frequently supplementing their camp larder with rabbits. Carey Tharp, her seventeen-year-old assistant during her first trip into the Trans-Pecos in 1914, also used one of the guns to bring in game since Mary's funds were always meager.

To finance her trips she worked out a creative solution with the university. In return for her time, herbarium specimens, and copious botanical notes, the university would pay part of her expenses and she would pay the rest. This meant considerable scrimping on her part and meals that were not only monotonous (beans, bacon, rice, hardtack, biscuits, coffee) but often nutritionally poor.

Unlike most women in the field, Mary kept a complete journal during the 1914 trip — from August 2, when they left Austin, until September 15. The journal is an excellent account of the kinds of hardships and delights all field persons experience. It is full of laments about low food supplies, although Carey claimed that they always had plenty — rabbits for the shooting, green apples and peaches from nearby orchards, and the opportunity to buy food from nearby ranches. In fact, her biggest expense was train tickets from Austin to Marfa (forty-five dollars), followed by the burro rig, food, and replacement of worn-out clothes, particularly shoes.

The trip took her northwest into the Davis Mountains in Jeff Davis County, west to Valentine, south through Presidio County to Candelaria on the Rio Grande, and finally south of Candelaria to Hot Spring Canyon above Ruidosa, Texas. After camping in the canyon several days, they returned to Candelaria, where they sold the burros and went by stagecoach back to Valentine to catch the Southern Pacific home. In less than six weeks, they had covered several hundred miles of rugged terrain by burro and foot.

Interspersed with her journal are lists of the 403 plants she collected, detailed descriptions of their localities, sketches of canyons and mountains, and meticulous geological notes, since geology was another interest of hers. From August 5 to September 17, 1915, she collected 541 plants in the Chisos Mountains in Brewster County near present-day Big Bend National Park, from July 31 to September 15, 1916, she explored the Guadalupe Mountains area on the border of New Mexico and Texas, collecting 403 plants, and from September 4 to 19, 1918, she returned to the Davis Mountain area and collected 386 plants. In these later years, she kept only her botanical and geological notes, except for a beginning fragment of the Chisos trip. According to B. C. Tharp, Carey's brother and a professor at the University of Texas, she spent 1917 up in the Panhandle near Canyon. However, there are no notes at all of that trip in the Eugene C. Barker Texas History Center at the University of Texas, which houses her journals and notes.

One can only regret that she did not continue her journals. The 1914 account is filled with details, anecdotes, and touches of humor that give the reader a good idea of the mechanics of the trip as well as the personality of Mary Sophie Young. Using burros with their buggy, they set out for the Davis Mountains, with Carey in the driver's seat. They prodded the burros every step of the way, and that night, caught by darkness, they spread their blankets on the ground

15.   Mary Sophie Young and Nebuchadnezzar in volume 65 of the *Southwest-ern Historical Quarterly. Courtesy Texas State Historical Association, Austin, Texas*

beside the road after eating a supper of canned beans and sausage.

After two more days on the road, they reached the Kelly Ranch at the base of Merrill Canyon in the Davis Mountains, where they hoped to camp for several weeks. Caretakers for the ranch gave them permission to go into the posted canyon area; Mary called this the most beautiful place she had ever stayed, with the exception of the Alps and Glacier National Park.

They took over a dirty but deserted adobe house that sat on a hillside covered with blooming *Aloysia ligustrina,* an aromatic shrub of the verbena family. Mary cleaned its two rooms — the one serving as a sleeping and living room, the other for dressing and scrubbing. Meals were cooked and eaten outside. For the first time she washed their camp dishes, having used newspapers on the road, where, she explained, "no amount of dirt could phase us. We washed our faces on the average of once in two days."

They settled there for three weeks; while Carey often stayed home to study math, Mary was out collecting most days. She started with the dooryard — the talus from a gully — the same day she did her cleaning, but soon she was exploring by herself deep in the canyons, taking along a cake of chocolate and a teacake in lieu of lunch. Climbing one ridge to get her bearings for longer trips, she found "a glorious pile of mountains up there" and a view that was worth the climb to her.

The following day she and Carey headed toward Mount Livermore, at 8,382 feet the second highest peak in Texas, carrying canteens, knapsacks, two guns, Mary's botany can, and a lunch of baked beans, four teacakes, and two cakes of chocolate. After a time they lost the trail and could not even distinguish Mount Livermore from the other peaks, so they "aimed for the most attractive looking mountain. . . . We went up a very steep long slope, then around the top of that small mountain, only to find ourselves cut off from the next mountain . . . by deep ravines. We made our way partly around the canyons then crossed them where they were not so very deep. . . . Of course, there are no trails in these mountains, but what makes them so hard to climb is the fact that long grass and shrubby plants cover the rocks and loose stones in many places so that one is very much impeded and besides cannot tell where he is going to put his foot." Finally they were stopped on a bluff by a perpendicular cliff; there they had their lunch, and Carey did math problems while Mary collected in the area, which she called "botanically . . . quite different from anything else I have seen. It was beautifully painted with orange, yellow, and gray lichens, and decorated in every crevice with very many plants, ferns, selaginellas, liverworts. . . ."

On their way back, they followed a different canyon, in which they found one waterfall after another. At last they reached an almost impenetrable thicket, where Mary discovered a single, leafless, red-purple orchid. They walked in the stream bed and pushed their way through the thickets for hours, trying to find their way out of the seemingly endless canyon. Lost but determined, they pressed on and at last blundered back into familiar territory. It had been a long, strenuous hike, and Mary needed the next day to take care of her specimens, write up her notes, and bathe in the creek.

Three days later they packed up the burros and headed into the mountains again, still intent on reaching Mount Livermore. This time they got close to the top but were driven back by black clouds and thunder on the rock pinnacle. They spent the night camped along the trail below the ridge, dining on a young jack rabbit that Carey had shot, but they found that "one piece two inches in diameter and half an inch thick will last an average man all day if he chews constantly and his jaws stand the strain. Jack rabbit meat would make good sole leather. We are going to put a new heel on Carey's shoes from some of our jack rabbit that is left," Mary joked.

In fact, her sense of humor never deserted her as she learned "the characteristics of burros, how to treat (burro) wounds when they have worms in them, that hogs always have liver worms, how to cook frijoles, what jack rabbit tastes like, how not to cook cornmeal — a few things like that." Cornmeal was difficult to keep edible, and she spent most of one day picking weevils, worms, and webs out of their supply.

She made her third and last foray to Livermore alone, taking along one huge cold pancake and bacon—"not an attractive lunch. . . . O, for one grocery store!" As she climbed up the rocks she met her first and only rattlesnake, napping in a crack between two rocks. She bombarded it with rocks and succeeded in cutting off its rattles for Carey. Seeing a rattlesnake unnerved her, but she went on anyway, reasoning "that the chances of rattlesnakes on the way back would be just as great as those ahead. . . ." Having forgotten to fill her canteen, she chewed on pink oxalis, which she claimed quenched her thirst as well as water. That day she collected forty-five plants while climbing a small peak and beating her way back down another canyon choked with oak thickets.

Much of her time was spent doing chores—mending Carey's clothes, cooking, and helping Carey with his math problems. And as the days passed, they ate more and more beans and biscuits. Coffee grounds were reused several times and sometimes supplemented with Postum. Mary experimented with sugarless applesauce, made from green apples, as a substitute for vinegar in their beans; the result was dubious at best. Whenever they ran out of baking powder, they ate hardtack instead of biscuits; once, when she forgot to cover it, the kangaroo rats that lived in the house carried it off. This left them with only beans, cornmeal, bacon, and flour—a diet that she said made them drowsy and lazy.

Still she continued collecting, identifying, and preparing specimens, despite frequent heavy rainstorms. On the last day of August, after baking a supply of biscuits and teacakes with bacon grease, sugar, flour, and a fresh supply of baking powder purchased from a nearby ranch, they headed for the Mexican border. Rain forced them to camp under the buggy, which they draped with tent cloths, but the rain beat in. They awoke to find their blankets soaked and the road almost impassable with mud. Slogging along on foot most of the way, they arrived in Valentine "too dirty to go to a restaurant." Carey replaced his shoes, leggings, shirt, and socks while Mary purchased a large, stale loaf of bread. Another day of rain en route to Candelaria depressed the burros as well as the humans, but on they pressed over a road that had become a canal due to the heavy rains. At last they reached a ranch and stayed the night in the warm, dry barn, sleeping comfortably on bales of hay.

The following day the weather cooperated and so did the burros, even when they began the long descent down to the Rio Grande. The land had definitely changed—hills with level tops, no timber, a country of chiefly candlewood and creosote with some cacti, yucca, sotol, and mesquite. The heat was enervating, and when they finally stopped to camp they discovered that the "mosquitoes were very large and very hungry."

At Candelaria the next day they were treated to dinner by the only Anglo couple in town—the storekeeper and his wife—and after eating until they were ashamed, they bought their supplies, rented a tent, and left all of Mary's botanical specimens with the couple. They traveled the road from Candelaria to Hot Springs Canyon—a hard twelve miles over and up and down a thoroughly muddy road, but they were determined to reach their permanent campsite. It took them until midnight, pushing and pulling both buggy and burros up what seemed an endless canyon, and dropping on their blankets in the tent when they finally arrived.

They shared the campground with other groups, and food was easier to obtain, but Mary did not like the area as much as she had the Davis Mountains. The vegetation was limited, and she felt so lazy that she only wanted to eat and sleep. When she did go collecting, she found little to collect. To add to her discomfort, a plague of caterpillars rained down one night, and after that she spent much of her time killing them.

Nevertheless, on September 11 she finally went off by herself to collect in the nearby Chinati Mountains. It was hot, the hills were covered with loose stones, and "the vegetation — every bush — reaches out its claws and catches your clothes if it does not tear your skin." She was able to bring back thirty-three plants, despite sore feet from the loose stones that wore out her shoes. She mended them by removing the nails and putting in botanical dryer insoles — they had done their last mountain climbing.

Just before they broke camp to head back home, a man from El Paso who wanted to buy their burros and buggy took their pictures. He offered them as many photographs as they wanted plus a gun cartridge belt, and they accepted. Their grand adventure was over.

No doubt Mary's other trips were just as exciting. She continued to purchase burros and to take along willing male students. But time ran out prematurely for Mary. In February of 1919 she went to the hospital for what she thought was a minor operation. The doctor found her filled with cancer and sewed her back up.

Even though she was not told her condition was fatal, she probably knew, suffering pain in silence and always talking about what she would do after she was better. She died on March 5, 1919, at the age of forty-seven, leaving behind one bereft dog, many loyal friends, and at least eight students whom she had helped to support. Mary, unfortunately, was the exception to the rule that field botanists live longer than most other people. But during the nine short years she had botanized, she had made lasting contributions to the study of Texas flora.

# Elizabeth Gertrude Knight Britton

## MOTHER OF AMERICAN BRYOLOGY

ELIZABETH GERTRUDE KNIGHT BRITTON was a perfectionist. But then, to be the outstanding bryologist she was, perfectionism was not a bad quality to possess. Bryology, the study of mosses and liverworts, was considered one of the most difficult botanical specialties. In fact, before Elizabeth took up the study in the early 1880s, only William Starling Sullivant — who Asa Gray called the Father of American Bryology — had made an intensive study of North American mosses.

Gray had hoped other American botanists would specialize in bryology after Sullivant's death in 1873, but it was not until Elizabeth published what would be the first of 170 papers on bryology in 1883 that he realized Sullivant's mantle would rest on female shoulders.

Gray already knew Elizabeth as the discoverer of the rare fern *Schizaea pusilla* in Nova Scotia, the same fern collected by Mary Treat in the pine barrens of New Jersey. According to the account Elizabeth later wrote in *The Linnaean Fern Bulletin*, "We were paddling around the shores of Grand Lake, Nova Scotia, in a birch-bark canoe, searching for a nice beach, intending to take a bath. It was the middle of July, 1879, and we had gone all around the island where the loons nested . . . but nowhere had we found a smooth stretch of beach. Finally we crossed over to the shore where the bits of bark from the tannery had floated down in the stream and formed a delta on the shore where it emptied into the lake." There she encountered several interesing plants but was especially attracted to the orchid *Pogonia ohioglossoides* which grew on a bank a foot above the beach. "I knelt down to dig up a good plant of the orchid . . . and there, growing under the edge of the miniature bank, I found Schizaea pu-

silla." She had recognized the fern, because she had previously collected it in the New Jersey pine barrens. She sent off the Nova Scotia
specimens to several eminent botanists, including Gray. He was
pleased by her discovery, because he had once seen specimens of
the fern collected from Newfoundland but had thought them incor-
rectly labeled until Elizabeth's find in Nova Scotia. Gray promptly
wrote a notice of her rediscovery for *The Botanical Gazette.*

At that time she was twenty-one years old and had been a teacher
at her alma mater, Normal (later Hunter) College in New York City,
for four years. A native of New York City, she had been born on
January 9, 1858, one of five daughters, to James and Sophie Anne
Knight. Her family operated a furniture factory and a sugar plantation near Matanzas, Cuba, and a large portion of their childhood
was spent on the island plantation. One sister, Mrs. David Oak, who
later wrote a family history, described it as filled with "flowers, lots
of birds, white and green peacocks shrieking, the cackle of guinea
hens, a big fountain where we watched the tiny birds bath [*sic*]. . . .
We children had wonderful walks with Father," who knew all about
the wild creatures and told his children about them. Her sister also
claimed that Elizabeth's interest in bryology was awakened by visits
with their father to an old well near Matanzas. The well's masonry
both inside and out was covered with ferns and moss.

Elizabeth attended private elementary schools in Cuba until she
was eleven years old. Then she spent most of her time with her maternal grandmother in New York City while she finished up her education at Dr. Benedict's private school and then at Normal College.
She specialized in botany both in and out of the classroom; she joined
the Torrey Botanical Club in 1879 and wrote her first professional
paper on albinism in plants three years later, six months before
her paper on the discovery of the fruit of the moss *Eustichium
norvegicum.*

That same year—1883—she was made an assistant in natural science, thanks in part to glowing recommendations from numerous
influential people, including Asa Gray. Professor Newberry, who
taught geology and botany at Columbia College, called her "the best
botanist in the city. Botany is her forte, and in this her attainments
are very unusual" because of her ability to identify "the difficult families of the grasses, ferns and mosses. She is an enthusiastic and indefatigable worker and her methods are scientific and logical beyond those of any other woman I know."

A former student, Mary A. C. Livermore, testified to her ability
as a teacher, emphasizing her "clear and precise way of presenting
a subject . . . her faithful, patient, thorough manner, leaving no mi-

nutest detail unexamined." Addison Brown, a wealthy amateur botanist, praised her "keen observation," "enthusiasm," and "readiness to impart information" and mentioned "that she is ardently in love with the subject."

Certainly all those qualities remained with Elizabeth throughout her life, so much so that she had little patience with people who were less meticulous and less in love with the subject. To Elizabeth botany was a calling; it was also a discipline that could be taught to the masses, which is one reason why she devoted so much of her time to helping amateurs. Everyone was potential grist for the botanical mill, and she especially believed that bryology was a field women could excel in.

William Wood of the Normal College considered Elizabeth the second best botanist in the United States. He called her marriage in 1885 to Nathaniel Lord Britton, an assistant in geology at Columbia College, "the greatest check to the career of prosperous young women."

But she had made the perfect choice. "Nat," as she called him, looked so frail that many people doubted he would live very long. Looks, in his case, were deceiving. Even more of a workaholic than Elizabeth, with a greater interest in botany than geology, he became instructor in botany at Columbia two years after their marriage. No doubt they had met at the Torrey Botanical Club, where he had been elected a member in 1877 and had been serving as librarian since 1882.

After her marriage, Elizabeth immediately resigned her position at Normal College. But since Nat was interested only in flowers, he left the study of mosses, ferns, and liverworts to Elizabeth. And while they sometimes went on botanical collecting trips together in the eastern United States, Elizabeth often went with female friends, leaving Nat to his work at Columbia.

He had taken over the botanical collections at the college as soon as he became instructor of botany. One of his first duties was to classify the tropical botanical collections from Bolivia that Henry Hurd Rusby had given to Columbia. To classify the collections, Nat had to go to Kew Gardens in London, and Elizabeth went along.

They spent half of July 1888 and all of August and September in England. While Nat did his research, Elizabeth worked on mosses at the Linnaean Society in London. However, she was only allowed to work upstairs, since no ladies were admitted to the main floor. Their favorite place, though, was the Royal Gardens at Kew, with its outstanding herbarium, its botanical library, and its attempt to grow as many horticultural specimens as possible from all over the world. "Why couldn't we have something like this in New York?" she asked. That was all the suggestion either of them needed. Back they went to New York, and to the Torrey Botanical Club, bursting with missionary zeal.

On October 24, 1888, at a Torrey Botanical Club meeting, Elizabeth gave a talk on Kew, describing in great detail all its wonders. At the next meeting a committee, which included Nat but not Elizabeth, was formed to consider the idea of a botanical garden in New York. By January of 1889, an appeal for the garden had been issued from the club, and a list of forty-eight incorporators had been drawn up. Nearly every prominent (and rich) citizen of New York was represented.

They decided, after some dickering, to locate the garden in Bronx Park. Nat's initial proposal was modest; he was willing to make do with as little as twenty-five acres for a "public botanic garden in New York City," although he would have liked seventy-five acres. They received much more than they had bargained for. The city informed the incorporators that they had to come up with $250,000 in subscriptions within seven years. Judge Addison Brown immediately pledged $25,000. Another $25,000 came from Columbia College, which planned to turn over its herbarium, supervised then by both Nat and Elizabeth, to the garden once it was established.

By June 18, 1895, the $250,000 had been raised, and the commissioners of public parks set aside 250 acres of Bronx Park for the garden. New York's Board of Estimate pledged a further $500,000 for buildings, and a board of managers was elected. It sounded, except for Britton, like a Who's Who of American moguls. Cornelius Vanderbilt was the president, Andrew Carnegie was vice president, J. Pierpont Morgan was treasurer, and Nathaniel Lord Britton was secretary. Seth Low, president of Columbia College, was made chairman of scientific directors.

In 1896, Nat was appointed director of the New York Botanical Garden, and, at the age of thirty-seven, he resigned his relatively recent promotion as professor of botany at Columbia College. Using temporary quarters until the museum building was completed in 1901, he began to organize both an herbarium and a library.

Elizabeth was, as always, his helpmate, and they labored from early in the morning until late at night in botanical work as well as garden organization. Because of his earlier training as an engineer at the School of Mines, Nat was able to visualize and lay out excellent grounds for the garden. He was also a superb administrator. But their first love remained things botanical. With his good friend, Judge Addison Brown, Nat wrote an *Illustrated Flora of the*

*Northern United States, Canada, and the British Possessions.* Known today as *Britton and Brown* in botanical circles, it made plant identification possible not only for professionals but also for amateurs. This monumental three-volume work took eight years to write, from 1890 to 1898, and was written during the time he was getting the garden established.

Elizabeth also continued her botanical work. An article appeared in the *New York Times,* September 5, 1895, on the occasion of the forty-fourth annual meeting of the American Association for the Advancement of Science. In it, she was described as a "very charming and very clever New York woman, a fellow of the Association," who "has assisted Professor Britton in his work in the herbarium of the college, taking entire charge of the collection of mosses and ferns, and working often from nine in the morning until nine and ten at night. All this was done unofficially and without remuneration." Nevertheless, Nat did look after her interests; four years later she was writing contentedly to William Farlow, "I am again in a position where I can do my work with ease and pleasure in sight of our new botanical museum where the Columbia books and specimens are deposited, and with an experienced Western collector [R. S. Williams] to help me."

In addition, she was going on botanical collecting trips to the Dismal Swamp of Virginia, the Adirondacks, and the mountains of North Carolina, giving all the specimens she collected to the garden's herbarium. She was also writing articles for both popular magazines and scientific journals, as well as working on her own book about mosses. That book was never finished, probably because a bryology student she had helped, Abel Joel Grout, scooped her with his own book *Mosses with a Hand-Lens and Microscope* in 1903. In fact, she made it clear, in two letters to Farlow five years before the book was written, that Grout was not her favorite young botanist. "Dr. Grout," she wrote, "is an applicant for a high school position in Brooklyn to teach botany at $1500 a year and is likely to get it soon. But in my opinion Collins [W. F.] is a better man. He works more for the *love* of it and less for the *glory* and *money* that is in it! — and he is *neater* and more *painstaking* and *methodical.*" Later, she compared Grout to M. A. Howe — "Personally, I do not like him as well as I do Mr. Howe, but he is a 'slave' and knows how to 'grind.'" But Grout was a pragmatist, not a perfectionist. Instead of checking and rechecking his work, he published hastily. Elizabeth, on the other hand, was a stickler for perfection. Then, too, Grout was a doer and Elizabeth an idea person. She mentioned writing a popular book on mosses; he quickly did it. She suggested establishing a moss society and journal, and he immediately formed the Sullivant Moss Society and its journal *The Bryologist* in 1898. It was then that her letters to and about Grout became vitriolic— to her he remained the blundering, not-quite-bright student, even though she joined the society and contributed articles to *The Bryologist*.

But shortly before the publication of Grout's book, Elizabeth embraced a new cause, one that took precious time from her work as a bryologist. Whether she did it because she felt outflanked by Grout will never be known. But, to the sorrow of professional bryologists, just after the garden officially opened in 1902, Elizabeth helped organize a new society, the Wild Flower Preservation Society of America, a society she probably believed would hold no interest for ambitious young men. From then until the end of her life, much of her energies were devoted to the cause of saving America's wild-flowers and American holly from extinction.

Previously, Olivia and Caroline Phelps Stokes of New York had given the New York Botanical Garden a fund of three thousand dollars, specifying that the interest had to be used "for the investigation and preservation of native plants or for bringing the need of such preservation before the public." Using that interest as seed money, she launched her campaign with articles and lectures, reaching out to the common people to save the wildflowers. She spoke at garden clubs and schools, public meetings and women's organizations; she had placards erected in railroad stations and post offices; she supervised the making of colored slides and postcards of wildflowers, holly and other Christmas greens; and she wrote a long series of articles for the *Journal of the New York Botanical Garden*, which Nat had started, on "Wild Plants Needing Protection." After many years of effort, her work finally resulted in the passing of legislation that protected native plants. While chairman of the Conservation Committee of the Federated Garden Clubs of New York State in 1925, she engineered a national boycott against the use of American holly as Christmas greens. She encouraged, instead, cultivating holly from seed to sell for commercial uses.

However, she did not totally desert bryology. In 1905, she attended the Botanical Congress of Vienna and was one of three prominent worldwide bryologists appointed to a commission to decide on the nomenclature of mosses in time for the next Botanical Congress at Brussels in 1910. In 1912, when the New York Botanical Garden had been increased to four hundred acres, she was officially made honorary curator of mosses; this was merely a formality, since she had been caring for them all the time. She also continued her support of the Sullivant Moss Society, becoming president in 1916.

Her happiest hours were spent accompanying Nat on twenty-three of the twenty-five botanical collecting trips he made to the West Indies on behalf of the garden. Their favorite collecting grounds were Bermuda, the Bahamas, Puerto Rico, Saint Thomas, Cuba, Jamaica, and Trinidad. The expeditions were often arduous and uncomfortable, but there were rewards. "We are back from our trip to Jamaica," she wrote to J. F. Collins in 1906, "where we made a great haul of mosses, hepatica [liverworts], lichens and ferns . . . we had a good time and found lots of treasures."

During one trip to Puerto Rico, Nat spotted an interesting slender palm on top of a rough limestone hill several miles north of the road. As he wrote later in his report to the garden officials, "Mrs. Britton subsequently climbed up to it and obtained its ripe fruit." She was, at the time, fifty-six years old and still extremely agile. The palm was a species new to botanical science.

Elizabeth wrote several journal articles, conveying her sense of adventure and love of the land, about her experiences in the tropics. One of her most vivid accounts, "Fern Collecting in Cuba," which she wrote for the *American Fern Journal* in 1910, told of how they turned their backs on hotels and camped for two weeks in the Trinidad Mountains. "The slopes of the Trinidad Mountains," she wrote, "are full of deep valleys . . . with streams flowing down them into the larger rivers. To get into these and spend a day hunting for ferns and mosses is a joy and delight. Usually it necessitates a long horseback ride and some wading and scrambling after dismounting, with the occasional recompense of a bath in some cool, fascinating pool."

By the time she and Nat retired from the field, he had had five genera of plants and one of animals named in his honor; she, one genera of moss, *Bryobrittonia*. In addition, sixty-nine species and varieties of plants, living and fossil, and three varieties of animals honored him, while Elizabeth had fifteen species of plants and one of animals named for her. Significantly though, two species of plants, a palm and a beard-tongue, were named for both of them. And when they died, in 1934, within four months of each other, a double peak in Luquillo National Park, Puerto Rico, where they had collected together, was named Mount Britton in their honor.

Marriage had not been a mistake for Elizabeth. With Nat's help and support, she had been able to accomplish, as a woman, much more than many less fortunately placed women of her day. He financed all her botanical pursuits, both professional and popular, since she never received a salary in any of her positions after her marriage. When he published his *Flora of Bermuda* and *The Flora of Bahamas,* he gave her full credit for writing the moss sections.

They had had no children — whether by choice or accident is not known — but as Marshall A. Howe wrote in Nat's obituary for the *Journal of the New York Botanical Garden,* "In a way that was very real to them, the New York Botanical Garden was their child." Together they had made it one of the best botanical and horticultural gardens in the world.

# 14

## Agnes Chase

### DEAN OF AMERICAN AGROSTOLOGISTS

"I CAN'T TALK WITH YOU. There's not much time left," were Agnes Chase's opening and usually closing lines to any journalist who approached her about a story. She was in her eighties then, hurrying to finish her life's work—the study of grasses. A diminutive, "spry old lady" with the energy of a twenty-year-old, she was already a legendary figure in botany. One reporter called her "Uncle Sam's chief woman explorer;" others considered her the "dean of American agrostologists," because she knew more about grasses than anyone else in the world.

It had not been easy for Agnes. Her father was an Irish railroad blacksmith, who had died when Agnes was two years old, which left her hardworking mother, Mary Cassidy of Louisville, Kentucky, to raise five young children alone. Agnes was born Mary Agnes Meara in Iroquois County, Illinois, on April 20, 1869, but her mother changed the family name to Merrill after moving the fatherless family to Chicago.

Her maternal grandmother lived with them, and the two women worked to support the children. Mary Agnes, as she was then called, was allowed the luxury of grammar school; after that, she was expected to work to help with the expenses. The only story Agnes ever told of her childhood was an explanation for her love of grasses. She had once brought a bouquet of grasses she had picked, probably from a vacant city lot, to her grandmother and had tried to point out the minuscule blossoms on them. Her grandmother had insisted that grass had no flowers," but Agnes later declared, "I was right and she was wrong." Whether or not the story was apocryphal, it is the only evidence that she might have had early botanical leanings.

One of her first adult jobs was reading the proof and setting the type for an idealistic periodical called the *School Herald*, written by its editor William Ingraham Chase. He was a good man with vision who wanted to do something to enrich the lives of rural schoolteachers, but he had no head for business. His kindness must have appealed to a girl whose knowledge of men was probably limited, having been raised by women. Certainly he was a worthy substitute for the father she had never had.

She married the thirty-four-year-old Chase when she was nineteen. He was already mortally ill with tuberculosis; in the scant year of their marriage before he died, she was more nursemaid than wife. Nevertheless, she took his name with pride and ever after called herself Mrs. Agnes Chase. When she died seventy-four years later, her ashes were interred in his grave as she had wished.

Both were honorable, idealistic people who had undoubtedly loved each other, and William had made a wise choice when he married Agnes. How wise only became clear after his death. He had left her a legacy of unpaid debts, and instead of telling even his brother about her financial straits, Agnes quickly took another job reading proof for the *Inter Ocean* newspaper. Living on a diet of oatmeal and beans, she put most of her salary into paying off her husband's debts. Only after she had paid off the debts did his family learn of her sacrifices.

She had a close relationship with her brother-in-law and his wife and children, particularly their son Virginius. When she moved in with them for a short time to help keep house and mind the children and store that they owned, thirteen-year-old Virginius persuaded her to take him botanizing. Three years later both aunt and nephew were inspired by the plant-collecting exhibit at the 1893 Columbian Exposition. She began a special study of the flora of northern Illinois and Indiana in her spare time, while she continued working for the *Inter Ocean*.

Agnes had remarkable luck in her dealings with men—a kind husband, a nephew who spurred on her botanical interests, and then a chance encounter in the field with the bryologist Rev. Ellsworth Jerome Hill. He was retired from the ministry and did not have the money to pay an illustrator to draw the new species he was discovering. Agnes, it turned out, had great skill as an illustrator, and while he taught her all he knew of botany and also how to use a compound microscope, she illustrated his botanical papers. He also introduced her to Charles Frederick Millspaugh, the curator of botany at the Field Museum of Natural History in Chicago, who put her to work illustrating two museum publications, *Plantae Utowanae* and *Plantae Yucatanae.*

Such work was done gratis, but Hill seemed concerned that Agnes better herself. He urged her, in 1901, to apply for a job as a meat inspector for the United States Department of Agriculture in the Chicago stockyards. There, she could use her newly learned skill with the microscope to examine pork for trichina.

Hill was determined to spur Agnes on. In 1903, when he learned of an opening for a botanical illustrator at the USDA Bureau of Plant Industry in Washington, D.C., he persuaded her to apply for it. Although she was reluctant, to please her friend she took the test and passed at the top of the list. Hill's kindness had cost him a botanical sidekick but had started Agnes on her life's work.

For two years she illustrated publications by the Division of Forage Plants, but after office hours she worked in the grass herbarium of the USDA, studying the genera of the *Paniceae* and publishing her first scientific paper on it in 1906. By then she had been collaborating for a year with Albert Spear Hitchcock, the principal scientist in charge of systematic agrostology, again as an illustrator. But in 1907 she was appointed as his scientific assistant in systematic agrostology.

Again she had made a lucky connection with a powerful male, one that initiated a firm friendship lasting until his death. Whenever she went on field trips her letters to Hitchcock were frequent, long, and outspoken, covering a wide range of personal observations and convictions often unrelated to botany, because Agnes was not just a botanist but a militant suffragist, a pacificist with socialist sympathies, and a confirmed prohibitionist.

Whether or not Hitchcock approved of her extracurricular activities, he certainly did support her agrostological work. Like him she was a collector as well as a laboratory botanist, spending her spare time from 1905 to 1912 in the field. In 1906, for instance, she explored North Carolina from June 1 until 9; the Chesapeake Beach in Maryland June 24–27; New Jersey and Delaware during the last week in July; and Florida, Mississippi, Louisiana, Alabama, Georgia, and the Carolinas in September and October. She made several trips to the West, spending the summer of 1908 collecting in Wyoming, Idaho, Oregon, Washington, Montana, and Colorado. In 1910 she visited northern Mexico, California, and Arizona, and in 1912 she made a trip to Texas. In addition to obtaining specimens, she was also gaining a thorough knowledge of what grasses grew where in the United States, accumulating information she and Hitchcock would use in preparing his monumental *Manual of Grasses of the United States.*

Usually she financed her own trips, donating all she collected to the herbarium, just as Hitchcock did. In later years, both Hitchcock and Agnes donated their own agrostological libraries to the Smithsonian's herbarium, which greatly enhanced its value as a research center. To Hitchcock and Chase, then, learning all they could about grasses and teaching others what they knew was of primary concern.

Agnes was usually the only woman present at scientific gatherings, and she seemed pleased with her status as an equal among the male botanists and scientists. Agnes did not have time for small talk, a quality that probably forced the men to respect her. And certainly Hitchcock had good reason to champion her; without "Mrs. Chase's constant interest and assistance, it is doubtful if Hitchcock could have accomplished as much as he did," her close associate, Dr. Jason R. Swallen, wrote many years later.

During the fall of 1913 she made her first foreign expedition, spending two months studying and collecting the grasses of Puerto Rico. She went on horseback up mountains and across rivers; in addition to grasses, she added ferns and climbing bamboos to her plant presses. One fern (*Botrychium jenmani*) was new to island collectors.

Her articles in the *American Fern Journal* and the *Botanical Journal* about her trip were read by botanists, and over the years she continued to write numerous professional articles, but she was also dedicated to teaching the nonprofessional how to identify grasses. For those people she wrote her *First Book of Grasses,* "a primer . . . to give those with little or no knowledge of botany such an understanding of the structure of grasses as will enable them to use manuals of botany and other technical works." She hoped that such a book would make "our native grasses . . . better known and their worth and beauty . . . more fully appreciated."

Before her book was published, though, she fought another battle to educate people. In this she was joined by many other American women who wanted the vote as much as Agnes did. Twice she was jailed and force-fed after she had demonstrated in front of the White House.

All her social and political opinions, including her contempt for most politicians and her pacifism, were aired in the journal and letters she wrote as part of her first trip to Europe in 1922. She went primarily to visit the Hackel Herbarium in the Natural History Museum of Vienna and to find types of American species of *Paspalum* and *Axonopus* grasses, but her observations of people illustrated her keen interest in social as well as botanical problems.

She crossed the ocean on the ship "America" and made friends with one of her cabin mates who was a costume designer from Vienna. She, like Agnes, had made her own way in the world "struggling against prejudice and discrimination" from American men. "It is a great strain on one's self-confidence to be always on the unpopular side, as seems to be my fate, to be called a 'Calamity Jane' because I cannot but see below the surface, always being advised tactfully and untactfully to be 'like other people.'"

She took the Orient Express through Normandy and across Germany to Vienna. Her welcome at the Natural History Museum was warm and supportive, and she had the time of her life. Luckily she had learned German at a Berlitz school (her solution to picking up any language she needed), because no one there understood much English. She worked from 8:30 A.M. until 5:45 P.M. with no lunch break to make some kind of order out of the Hackel collection. When she finished she made a pilgrimage to Attersee to visit the seventy-two-year-old Edward Hackel. Together they went out to collect Alpine grasses, but only the *Sesleria cerulea* was in bloom, she reported.

"It grows in springy places on the steep mountainside in disintegrating rock. We scrambled around and got ourselves all muddy getting it." They also collected wildflowers near Attersee. The Hackels, she observed, were devoted to each other. Still, she was distressed by their poverty, they, like most other Austrians after the war, could not afford fuel to keep their home warm through the cold winter and spring. As hardy as Agnes was, the unremitting chill of both public and private places gave her pleurisy.

But at least the people were kind. The arrogant treatment she received at the herbarium in Florence, Italy, did not impress her, but she liked the herbarium and its people in Pisa. Her greatest praise, though, was reserved for Geneva — "Altogether the Swiss seem to me the finest thing in humanity I ever saw." It was there that she *"heard the nightingale!* . . . This place is simply heavenly. I had the whole day on the lake Sunday. . . . It was a wonderful day, and is going to be one of the 'glorious days' I treasure over and over again — like some days in Yellowstone Park, on the LoLo Trail, in Yosemite, several in Porto Rico, Florida, North Carolina and elsewhere."

She finished off her trip by visiting the herbariums in Leiden, Brussels, and finally Paris. Her first trip to Europe had definitely been a success. However, "botanizing in herbaria does not afford the same pleasure as does botanizing in the field, but it is not without its thrills of discovery. Current concepts of several species were found to be erroneous; that is, our ideas were those of later authors instead of those of the original ones."

She returned home to find her *First Book of Grasses* on the market, and the following year she was promoted to assistant botanist in systematic agrostology.

In 1924, she had another opportunity to botanize in the field. With the help of grants from the USDA, the New York Botanical Garden, the Gray Herbarium, the Missouri Botanical Garden, and the Field Museum, she sailed for Rio de Janeiro. Her plan was to collect grasses in eastern Brazil, an area that had been largely ignored by American botanists. The National Herbarium needed to increase its botanical specimens from that region, because, until Agnes's trip, they had been relying on specimens preserved in herbaria at Brussels, Munich, and Vienna.

She arrived in Rio de Janeiro on November 1, 1924, and the following day she began collecting in the vicinity of Rio that she claimed had not been spoiled at all for the botanist. The steep jungly slopes of the nearby mountains still contained the same grasses collected by Raddi of Tuscany over a hundred years before. She climbed narrow trails up precipitous slopes, certain that she was following in Raddi's footsteps.

Four days later she sailed north to Recife — a coastal city on flat ground built up by coral reefs and mangroves. She admired the beautiful city full of trees, flowering shrubs, and royal palms but was surprised at how densely populated its outlying districts were. The weather was very hot, and often she sought refuge under the caju or cashew trees — "wide-spreading trees bearing multitudes of fragrant small maroon flowers, buzzing with bees, and fruit in all stages of development . . . a blessing to a blistering botanist."

She found that "the wet meadows and stream borders offered the best botanizing," although with the grasses higher than her head and tangled up with aroids, ferns, and brush, it was not an easy area to penetrate. In addition, she discovered a half-mile-long bog that quaked and "billowed under my feet in a way that made me gasp."

From the local missionaries, her best and most accurate sources of information, she found out where to go inland to get an impression of the arid regions. To her dismay, large areas had been overgrazed by domestic animals, but at the end of the railroad line — at Garanhuns, 271 kilometers southwest of Recife, the land was in better shape.

With two women missionaries, she drove two hundred kilometers farther into the interior by car. They followed a newly-cut road to the Paulo Afonso Falls in the Rio São Francisco — an area that had never been visited by botanists. The last few miles were made by moonlight in a hand-pushed trolley car, and they hung their hammocks in an empty house where they camped overnight. To Agnes's great disappointment, the falls — a stupendous cascade almost twice as high as Niagara Falls — ran through "the most lifeless desert I have ever seen."

Her next destination was São Salvador, south of Recife on the inside of a small peninsula between the bay and the ocean. Since the peninsula was a succession of hills and hollows, her field book filled up rapidly. She stayed with American missionaries and covered their veranda and lawn with her plant dryers.

Sometimes by foot, occasionally by dugout canoe, she explored marshes and sandy savannas for specimens. On January 6, 1925, she returned to Rio de Janeiro. This time she was accompanied on her botanical wanderings by Maria Bandeiro, who was studying mosses at the Jardim Botanico in Rio. With Maria she made a trip to Itatiaia, the mountain that marks the confluence of the states of Rio de Janeiro, São Paulo, and Minas Gerais. At nearby Campo Bello, they hired horses and set out for Florestal — a combination forest and experiment station under the jurisdiction of the Jardim Botanico. They stayed there overnight, and then, with two pack horses carrying camping and collecting equipment, they set out along a difficult trail, "up over stones and through deep mud or across streams."

Once they were above timberline, they left the horses, intent on climbing a peak called Agulhas Negras, "the black needles," which lived up to its name. It rose abruptly and was composed of "steep, bare granite cliffs deeply furrowed vertically. We climbed up the furrows on all fours and crossed from one series to another over steep slopes covered with low bamboo most convenient to cling to. At the top of these furrowed cliffs is a great overhanging rock that seemed to stop all progress, but the way led through a crevice to one side and over and between boulders wedged in the crevice. The worst place was like a chimney flue, which we ascended with the help of a rope." Not a bad feat for a woman of fifty-six.

Her rewards were a magnificent view, one grass specimen, and several other plants. She made the two-day descent down to Florestal by foot "collecting as rapidly as possible" and arrived "with bulging portfolio, a big handkerchief tied around a bundle, and an armful besides."

Her last destination was Viçosa. This time she was the guest of Dr. P. H. Rolfs, who was building up a school of agriculture for the state of Minas Gerais. With Rolfs and his daughter, she made a horseback trip into the virgin forest of the Serra Sebastião. At the base of Serra da Gramma, they proceeded on foot with a man to cut the trail, a guide, and three more men from Viçosa. "This was the real tropical jungle of the school geographies, dense and dark, with palms, tree ferns, vines and bamboos all tangled together, with brilliant bromeliads up the trees, and multitudes of ferns." They made their way up the steep trail tripping and stumbling or sinking "into soft humus, up and up, then slipping and sliding down into a deep ravine, then climbing up again." They camped on open ground at the summit of the lowest of three peaks, and the next morning Agnes was out before the dew was dry collecting. On the way down she collected all the way, the party stopping whenever she requested.

Despite the hard conditions, Agnes seemed to enjoy exploring the mountains. Within a few days she, a boy from the Rolfs's farm school, and Miss Rolfs set off for Pico da Bandeira, taking the train to the village of Caparao. After hiring three riding mules, a pack mule, and a guide, they set off. Unfortunately, the guide did not know the way even to the purported resthouse halfway up the mountain, so they spent the first night camped on the shoulder of the mountain. They burned downed timber to keep warm — "a great comfort," Agnes reported, "as it rained till midnight and then cleared and turned very cold."

The next day they found the resthouse, which was only a low hut made of upright sticks, "partly chinked with mud, the roof a combination of wooden shingles and sheets of zinc." It had to be cleaned of horse manure and floored with loose shingles before it was habitable. Although there was a stone-and-clay mound in lieu of a real stove to cook on, Agnes practically burned the place down when she tried to use it, so they did without a fire for warmth during the night.

They left the guide behind the following day, since he could not even tell them which of the mountaintops they could see from the guesthouse was Pico da Bandeira. Choosing what looked like the highest peak, they made a hard climb to the top. Only then did the clouds lift and reveal a still higher peak. Later they learned they had ascended Pontão Crystal, 2,798 meters high, rather than Pico da Bandeira, which was 2,884 meters high. Nevertheless, the botanizing was good on Pontão Crystal, "so I probably did not lose much, still it was disappointing."

That was her last grand adventure in Brazil, and on May 31, 1925, "rejoicing in what I had found and regretting what I had not, . . . I sailed for home." She had collected twenty thousand plant specimens, five hundred of which were grasses. And once again, when she reached Washington, she was promoted, this time to associate botanist.

Four years later, at the age of sixty, she again sailed for Brazil.

16.   Agnes Chase at rest house below Pico da Bandeira, Brazil, from *Smithsonian Annual Reports. Courtesy Smithsonian Institution*

This time she was determined to climb the eastern side of the Pontão Crystal peak, which, she had understood, was virgin rainforest. She was accompanied by Ynes Mexia.

They took along four native men and their mules, but neither men nor mules did much to help the women as they struggled up the steep path in a heavy rain besieged by all manner of biting insects. When the men led them to a cave filled with fleas, the women rebelled, and after digging a trench, the men erected Ynes's tiny tent by tying it to a boulder at one end and a gnarled tree at the other.

Despite the weather and the insects, though, the women had collected all the way, Agnes claiming later that her knees were wobbly but the "grasses all about rejoiced my heart." The next morning, when the men came and tried to persuade them to come into the shelter, they refused because they had not yet gotten their plants in the press. All day it rained, and getting a fire started was impossible, but they labored through that day, "half-frozen, drenched, muddy and dirty." The night was even worse, because the trench overflowed with water and the wind whipped the tent moorings loose.

Finally they had their plants ready and began an arduous descent. This concluded what Agnes called the "hardest physical feat of my life," which left her with swollen feet, an infected toe, a severe cold, and laryngitis.

It took her several days to recover from the ordeal, which was justifiable in her eyes, because no botanists had ever been there before. "I feel my grasses are worth the climb, though I have only one new species, a beautiful *Ichnanthus*."

Such an experience might have deterred most people, but she continued to climb peaks and explore swamps for several more weeks in the area. She described her solo ascent of the Serra Curo Porto as "glorious, fatiguing, joyous, harrowing," and no wonder, since it meant climbing up jagged rocks while "millions of tiny gnats filled the air, got between my spectacles and eyes, around my ears and neck, stinging like red hot needles." She waded barefoot through icy streams and was lost at least once, but she always kept going, filling her press with enormous grasses. Then, in February of 1930, she went on to the southwestern Brazilian state of Matto Grosso where she encountered "rain and mud and terrible roads and more terrible places to stop at night, swarms of midges and little black and white flies that nearly drive one crazy, and chiggers that raise blisters. . . ." She took to singing hymns to keep up her nerve as she waded through swamp water, sometimes as deep as three feet and filled with biting insects. "The strife is o'er, the battle won," was an understandable favorite.

A driver took her in a car over the bad roads and she usually spent her nights sleeping in the car doubled up, after bathing in nearby streams by moonlight. Except for insect bites, she thrived on such a life, but she did find herself discouraged by the humanity she encountered. The people were slow and dirty with no understanding at all of basic sanitation and frightened of the wildlife. To her the only real dangers were the insects and the filth, and when she encountered army ants for a second time, she was relieved to see them in time to avoid more than a few dozen.

Her conclusions about the trip were both humorous ("If a woman wants to 'reduce' she can do so by botanizing in the far sertão of Brasil") and serious ("I shall have made, in these two trips, by far the largest collection of grasses ever brought out of Brasil"). In fact, she had collected over 4,500 grasses alone.

Those two Brazilian trips earned her the sobriquet "Uncle Sam's chief woman explorer of the USDA." She had added at least 10 percent to the world's knowledge of Brazilian grasses. Her 1929–30 expedition alone yielded between twenty-five and thirty-five grass varieties never before known to be in Brazil and at least ten varieties entirely new to science.

She was to make only two more trips abroad. The first, in 1935, was to France, where she worked at herbariums in Montpellier, Caen, and Paris. When she was not climbing mountains and swatting insects, she was working seven days a week on leave without pay and eating her usual meager vegetarian fare.

Her last trip, to Venezuela, was in 1940, a year after she had officially retired. This merely meant that she no longer received a salary for the same work she continued to do for twenty-four more years. She had been invited to visit the country by the Venezuelan Ministry of Agriculture, who wanted her to study their grasses and then help to develop a range management program based on native grasses. Officially she was the guest of Dr. Henri Pittier, director of the Servicio Botánico of the Ministry of Agriculture, who had been Venezuela's outstanding botanist for twenty-three years, and he supplied a car and chauffeur during most of her time in the field. But she did not always stay in or even near the car, walking six kilometers one day in the Andes near Mérida, crawling through fences or over stone walls so she could report firsthand on what the cattle were eating.

She visited several ecological zones in Venezuela — the Andes, the cloud forest, and the flat, windswept savanna of eastern Venezuela called llanos, which is alternately flooded with rain and parched with drought every year. Agnes arrived during an extreme drought, but despite the dried-up condition of most of the grasses, she managed to collect 419 grasses, 11 species new to Venezuela and 1 undescribed.

Perhaps her greatest contribution was to suggest that Venezuela needed a specialist in grasses. Miss Zoraida Luces, who had begun studying grasses on her own and had accompanied Agnes on most of her botanizing expeditions in Venezuela, was her choice for the position. Agnes further proposed that Miss Luces be sent to study grasses in the Grass Division of the United States National Herbarium. There she fell under Agnes's expert tutelage and lived in Agnes's home.

Agnes was known to encourage Latin American students in botany to study at the National Herbarium and often had them for meals or, in some cases, had them as boarders in her home. Even today elderly botanists, such as Dr. Ramón Feyrera of Lima, Peru, remember Miss Chase and her dinners with great affection. By then, she had become the grand old lady of agrostology who never missed a day of work despite, as the years passed, a tendency to be forgetful and do the same work twice, and being, as she called it, a *"little deaf."*

But she had so much she still wanted to accomplish. Hitchcock's *Manual of Grasses of the United States* had been first published in 1935, shortly before his death, accompanied by Agnes Chase's original drawings. It badly needed revision, however, which she did during her "retirement" years, along with a revision of *The First Book of Grasses.* She also wrote the preface for and did consulting work on the *1948 Department of Agriculture Year Book* called *Grass,* catalogued and filled insect-proof steel cases with the 10,031 grass-type specimens that she had been the first to describe, and completed and revised a card index on grasses. No doubt she agreed with her botanist-friend Alice Eastwood on the West Coast who wrote, "I have very little sympathy with this retiring people when there is no physical or mental deficiency. . . . You and I are the same so-called foolish enthusiasts who are glad to work for nothing."

And like Alice, Agnes had had no academic training and was proud of her self-education. She also had honors heaped on her as she lived on, receiving an honorary Doctor of Science degree from the University of Illinois at the age of eighty-nine and a Certificate of Merit at the Fiftieth Anniversary of the founding of the Botanical Society of America in 1956. In addition she was made the eighth Honorary Fellow of the Smithsonian Institution on October 1, 1958, clearly appreciated by Director Leonard Carmichael, who later wrote in his introduction to Agnes's revised *First Book of Grasses* that "the Smithsonian Institution is proud of its long and happy association with this truly distinguished scientist."

Inevitably old age defeated Agnes, but not until 1963 when she was ninety-five years old. Five months before her death, she quit working, and on her first day in a nursing home she died.

But what a triumph her life had been. The unknown, uneducated daughter of a poor widow had become the greatest living agrostologist of her time, and her death was mourned by scientists throughout the world.

# Part IV

# *The Entomologists*

~

Not long ago a minor furor developed when *Audu-bon magazine published a spoof entitled "Of Bugs and Women" by Paul Quinnett. Quinnett had noticed that his wife, the daughter of an eminent entomologist, disliked and killed any insect she saw. When he questioned her she maintained that every woman she knew disliked insects. A survey of his female coworkers in the office revealed that not one woman "thought any insect was interesting, cute, intelligent, worthy of study or emulation. . . . Thinking back," he continued, "I realize that I have never met a female entomologist, although surely there must be one. But in case there isn't, my theory [that all women have an inbred dislike of insects] is strengthened by that singular fact alone."*

*Quinnett's sweeping statement infuriated many women readers, especially those who were entomologists. Had Quinnett conducted even a modicum of research on the subject, he would have discovered that there have been women entomologists in America at least as far back as the 1830s, when Charlotte De Bernier Taylor, of Savannah, Georgia, and Margaretta Hare Morris, of Germantown, Pennsylvania, began to study entomology.*

*In fact, throughout the second half of the nineteenth century and well into the twentieth, women entomologists were active in field work, laboratory studies, teaching, and writing. Some women specialized in field*

*work, others became involved in studying insects be-
cause their husbands were entomologists, and still others
were active researchers with professional positions.
While the following chapters examine in detail the lives
and accomplishments of the most important women
entomologists—Annie Trumbull Slosson, Edith Patch,
and Anna Comstock—several other women need to be
discussed at least briefly.*

*Margaretta Morris and Charlotte Taylor were the
earliest known American women field entomologists.
Charlotte was the wife of a well-to-do merchant and
mother of two daughters and a son, but she still found
time to spend over fifteen years observing and drawing the parasites of the cotton plant. Not until 1859 and
1860 did she feel confident enough to publish her findings in an article for HARPER'S NEW MONTHLY MAGA-
ZINE called "Insects Belonging to the Cotton Plant." She
followed that with articles on both the natural history
of silkworms and of spiders, but at the onset of the
Civil War she left the South for the Isle of Man in the
Irish Sea, where she died of tuberculosis in 1861.*

*Margaretta's first paper, "On the Cecidomyia de-
structor, or Hessian fly" was published in the PROCEED-
INGS OF THE AMERICAN PHILOSOPHICAL SOCIETY in December of 1840. She followed this on August 6, 1841,
with a letter entitled "Observations on the Development
of the Hessian Fly," which appeared in the PROCEED-
INGS OF THE ACADEMY OF NATURAL SCIENCES. In it she
described using a magnifying glass to detect the fly larvae feeding on wheat straw, and had even allowed female flies to lay eggs on her finger. She declared that
the female lacked the hairy fringe on her wings that
the male possessed and was a different color from the
male fly described by Thomas Say in his classic AMERI-
CAN ENTOMOLOGY. In addition Margaretta described
the main predator on Hessian flies, which she called
the "ceraphon destructor."*

*Her next communication, in 1846, "On the Discov-
ery of the larvae of the Cicada septemdecim" concerned
the seventeen-year locust. In her paper she accused its
larvae of damaging the roots of fruit trees. She followed
up her information a year later by sending a box con-*

taining locust larvae to the academy and accompanying it with a letter claiming that those trees with mole tracks around them were not harmed by the locust larvae.

In 1849 she returned to the Hessian fly, with her paper "On Cecidomyia culmicoli" reporting that the insect was probably carried from country to country as eggs on straw. Her last report to the academy, in 1859, about finding a two-inch luminous larva in the woods near the Delaware Water Gap, coincided with her election to membership in the academy, the second woman (Lucy Say was the first) to be so honored and the first practicing woman naturalist. She had been proposed for membership by Graceanna Lewis's mentor, John Cassin, as well as by W. A. Hammond, James C. Fisher, and Joseph Leidy, other members of the academy.

Margaretta also sent papers to other scientific societies — one to the American Association for the Advancement of Science in 1850 entitled "Remarks on the Seventeen Year Locust," and a second the following year to the Boston Society of Natural History on the same subject. In addition, the New York State Agricultural Society published her "Tenth Family: Cetonidae" in 1850, and the AMERICAN QUARTERLY JOURNAL OF AGRICULTURE AND SCIENCE, another New York-based journal, presented her "Controversy respecting the Hessian Fly" in 1847. Margaretta signed her papers "Miss M. H. Morris," and they were always read by male members of the various societies she sent them to, since no self-respecting female would have considered reading a paper before an all-male audience. Apparently Margaretta's work was respected enough that she had no trouble finding men willing to present her papers.

Eight years after her election to the academy, Margaretta died at the age of seventy. She never married and had spent her life studying not only entomology but also botany, an interest she shared with her sister and companion, Elizabeth C. Morris.

Field work continued to fascinate women, even those who spent only a small portion of their lives on entomology. Probably one of the greatest female humanitarians of her time, Adele Marion Fielde worked in en-

*tomology only from 1894 until 1905; she specialized
in ants and wrote eighteen papers on ant behavior between 1901 and 1907.*

*Born in East Rodman, New York, in 1839, she led
at least three lives, starting out as a schoolteacher, then
spending five years as a Baptist missionary in Siam
(Thailand), and then fifteen years in Swatow, China,
becoming an expert on the Chinese language and writing
a dictionary of the Swatow dialect with English equiva-
lents. She also worked to improve the health of Chinese women, and during a leave of absence from the
mission field in 1883, she went to the Woman's Medical College of Philadelphia to take an obstetrics course.*

*A woman of restless intellectual curiosity, Adele had
another goal during her leave. She wanted to learn
about evolution, "God's method of creation." She found
her way to the Academy of Natural Sciences, and although it was not a teaching institution, Adele made
such an overpowering impression that the scientists
there took her on as their only student. There she
worked for two winters, studying and dissecting twenty-
six classes of creatures from amoebas to mammals and
doing original research on the regeneration of nerve
tissue. Her special mentor was Edward J. Nolan, the
talented librarian of the academy, but she also acknowledged help from Professor Heilprin and Dr. Benjamin
Sharp. Later she recalled the years 1883 to 1885 as the
most delightful period of her life, spending her first summer at Annisquam Biological Laboratory and the second at Nantucket with the Sharps, culminating her scientific studies as a delegate to the World Congress of
Scientists in New York, where she delivered a talk on
the Chinese conception of science.*

*Refusing the presidency of Vassar College, she re-
turned to China to teach the Chinese women obstetrics.
This innovation set the stage for the whole new field
of women medical missionaries. But she did not neglect her new interest in science, corresponding steadily with Nolan. She sent specimens of conifers to him,
a new species of insect to entomologist Samuel Scudder, and a box of SUCCINEA shells to conchologist George
Washington Tryon, Jr. And when retirement and a pension from the church was imminent, she resigned as*

*a missionary teacher; since becoming a scientist, she no longer subscribed to every tenet of faith and creed.*

*After traveling for three years in Asia and Europe, she returned to the United States and began a new career as public lecturer, science teacher, and publicist. She spent her summers from 1900 to 1909 at the Woods Hole Marine Biological Laboratory studying and lecturing, concentrating on the senses, activities, and behavior of ants. She designed the original glass house for observing ants; through a long succession of experiments, she discovered that ants remembered an odor for at least three years. She thought they "smelled" through the ends of their antennae. She also found that ants were blind except for seeing ultraviolet light, and together with Professor George H. Parker of Harvard, she tried to find out if ants could hear.*

*With all her scientific work though, she made other, more personal observations — "Individual ants have different temperaments. . . . Ants of some species are as varied in character as human beings. Some are irascible, others docile; some have strong maternal instincts, while others dislike the care of the young; some like quiet home life, while others like to go afield and roam about; some learn more quickly than others the things which I want them to do. Ants keep themselves and their young scrupulously clean."*

*And then, at the age of seventy, she made another life change. Because of a worsening bronchial condition she moved from New York City to Seattle, Washington, and became embroiled in women's suffrage, prohibition, and child welfare. Near the end of her life as she lay dying she wrote to her friend Nolan back at the academy, "In my heartsickness I have turned again to my beloved natural sciences for consolation and distraction and am reading J. Henri Fabre, entomologist, and am fascinated." She died on February 23, 1916, after requesting that her ashes be cast on the Puget Sound, because "I have loved this old earth. . . ." W. T. Davis, the Staten Island naturalist and friend of entomologist Annie Trumbull Slosson, said when he heard of all Adele had done in her lifetime, "Just think what she might have accomplished if she had only concentrated on ants."*

*Women drawn into entomology through their husbands are often difficult to ferret out. Usually they are mentioned only as asides in their entomological husbands' biographical accounts and obituaries, if they are mentioned at all. But aside from Anna Comstock, who later developed a career separate from her husband's, at least three other wives emerged as competent entomologists in their own right. Maria E. Fernald was not only the wife of an entomologist but the mother of one as well. Born in 1839 in Monmouth, Maine, Maria was well educated, graduating first in her class at the Maine Wesleyan Seminary and Female College in Kent's Hill and serving afterwards as preceptress there before marrying Charles H. Fernald in 1862. Fernald was a man of many interests, teaching "botany, physical geography, human anatomy and physiology, comparative anatomy, veterinary science and zoology, with special attention to entomology, geology and mineralogy."*

*But first and foremost he was an entomologist, and by the 1870s Maria was also interested in entomology, beginning her compilation of a card catalogue on the* TORTRICIDAE *(small moths). This may explain why, when the gypsy moth was accidentally released in Medford, Massachusetts, in 1869, Maria first identified it. So useful was her card catalogue that she extended it to include all insects, a monumental job that finally led to her publication of one section devoted to* COCCIDAE *(scale-bugs and mealy-bugs) as Bulletin 88 of the Hatch Experimental Station (Massachusetts) entitled A* CATALOGUE OF THE COCCIDAE OF THE WORLD. *According to her son, Henry T. Fernald, his mother also "used to go out in the fields and woods with him [her husband] at Orono, collecting, but a little later restricted her efforts to collecting by lamp in the window at night and by 'sugaring' when moonlight prevented using the light. In these ways she captured a large number of moths, many of them rare, and a few new species. . . ." Her husband claimed she was so skillful that she was able to "put her hand out the window, take the moth, put it in a cage and not disturb a single scale."*

*Elizabeth Gifford Peckham, who married Dr. George Williams Peckham, a teacher of biology in Milwaukee's East Division High School, in 1880, was also an ac-*

*knowledged partner in entomological research. Formerly a librarian and an 1876 graduate of Vassar College, Elizabeth, as a wife and mother of three children, did scientific work with her husband in their free time, specializing in spiders and solitary and social wasps. As the writer of his obituary in* ENTOMOLOGICAL NEWS, *R. A. Muttkowski, later put it, "From the time of their marriage these two are inseparably linked in all phases of their work, in their researches, in their travels, in their very thoughts." They worked on both the psychology of spiders and wasps and on the taxonomy of spiders. They published their definitive work as Bulletin no. 2 of the Wisconsin Geological Survey,* ON THE INSTINCTS AND HABITS OF SOCIAL WASPS. *Later they published a popular version of the same work, called* WASPS SOCIAL AND SOLITARY, *in which they described walking through the woods one day near their summer home not far from Milwaukee and discovering yellow jackets coming out of the ground. They were so intrigued that they sat day after day watching them go about their business, and thus began their interest in wasps.*

*Another husband and wife team similarly intrigued by wasps was Philip and Nellie Rau. As a librarian at the Missouri Botanical Garden and a graduate of the University of Kansas, Nellie S. Harris had been interested in nature. In 1911, she married Philip Rau, who was a Jewish storekeeper. Arnold Mallis, in his comprehensive* AMERICAN ENTOMOLOGISTS, *even maintained "that his wife's interest in natural history stimulated Rau in his investigations." She accompanied him on field excursions and collaborated with him on his published work. Together they wrote* WASP STUDIES AFIELD *published in 1918, the result, they declared, of some four years of outdoor study of wasps in their native haunts. All their observations of over sixty species of wasps had been done within a thirty-mile radius of their home in Saint Louis, Missouri.*

*Near the end of the nineteenth century a few women entomologists started to obtain professional positions. One of the first was Mary E. Murtfeldt, also of Saint Louis, who was an assistant to C. V. Riley, Missouri state entomologist from 1876 to 1878, and then was appointed acting state entomologist from 1888 to 1896.*

*A Fellow of the American Association for the Advance-
ment of Science, she was, in addition, an honorary
member of the Saint Louis Academy of Science. As a
victim of polio, she was, by necessity, a laboratory scientist, but managed to specialize in moths and make an
outstanding moth collection. She also contributed articles on* TORTRICIDAE *to scientific journals, and co-
authored a popular book,* STORIES OF INSECT LIFE, *with
Clarence M. Weed.*

*Doris Holmes Blake, an expert on Central American
beetles, worked at the Smithsonian Institution in an
attic for forty years. She also illustrated the work of
her husband, botanist and taxonomist Sidney Blake,
whom she had met in first grade. Certainly, even as
a little girl, she would have destroyed Quinnett's stereo-
type, since her favorite occupation as a toddler was
catching live grasshoppers. She also refused to play with
dolls asking, "Who would want to play with dead dolls
stuffed with sawdust when you could have all the live
toads for the taking?" Together with her friend, Doris
Cochran, curator of reptiles at the Smithsonian, she
went on many expeditions, including one collecting trip
to South America.*

*Grace Sandhouse, a native of Monticello, Iowa,
worked for the Division of Insect Identification of the
Bureau of Entomology and Plant Quarantine as an expert on bees and sawflies. Educated in zoology under
naturalist T. D. A. Cockerell at the University of Colorado, she shared his interest in bee taxonomy. According to her obituary, she was "industrious, determined
and courageous . . . and blessed with an orderly mind,
a retentive memory for taxonomic characters and a keen
judgment of the significance of such characters." She
identified specimens from all over the world and was
a "scientist among scientists." She also "devoted a considerable portion of her time and income to humanitarian and charitable pursuits," dying prematurely in
1940 at the age of forty-four.*

*Edith Patch, as the best known professional woman
entomologist of her day, was asked to do a paper on
"Entomology as a Vocation for Women" in 1939. She
quickly discovered that fifty members of the Entomological Society of America and the American Associa-*

*tion of Economic Entomologists were women. She also wrote a short history of early women entomologists, mentioning Maria Fernald, Annie Slosson, Mary Murtfeldt, and a lady named Emily Adella Smith, who contributed papers in the 1880s to the TRANSACTIONS of the Illinois Department of Agriculture and to the NORTH AMERICAN ENTOMOLOGIST.*

*Later, in a paper prepared for the Institute of Women's Professional Relations entitled "The Entomologist" she summarized the letters of many professional women entomologists. These included Miriam A. Palmer, an associate in entomology at the Colorado State College and an expert on aphids like Edith herself, and Bessie Broadbent who specialized in California red scale at the Whittier Laboratory in California. Bessie no doubt expressed the feelings of most women entomologists when she wrote, "My work means more to me than living, and I find scientific research utterly absorbing . . . . "*

# Anna Botsford Comstock

DEAN OF AMERICAN NATURE STUDY

HER HUSBAND thought it would lose five thousand dollars, but Anna Comstock's *The Handbook of Nature Study*, first released in 1911, became the all-time best-seller among books published by Cornell University. Schoolteachers all over the United States called it the "Nature Bible," and a generation of schoolchildren were introduced to nature by teachers who had been educated and inspired by Anna's book. That, of course, had been her purpose in writing it, and she had persevered despite discouraging words not only from her husband, Henry, but from other friends as well. After all, she knew her husband would help her financially with her book, even if he thought it would be a total loss. She said "he was kindness and consideration personified in helping me get material and in helping me make up the book." Such support typified the long married life of Anna Botsford and John Henry Comstock; each helped the other succeed in whatever they wanted to do, whether it was writing, teaching, lecturing, or illustrating.

Henry had been raised as a foster child in a series of homes; his father was dead, and his mother was far away trying to earn enough money to support her son. He began making his own hard living by the time he was fifteen, as a cook on a succession of Great Lakes steamers. Anna, on the other hand, was a beloved only child of two wise and loving parents. They raised her without the contemporary prejudices toward women, encouraged her to be a freethinker religiously, and sent her to a number of excellent schools.

Anna was a country girl, born in Cattaraugus County, New York, in 1864. Her first home was a log cabin; even though she and her family moved into a larger frame house in Otto, New York, when Anna was three years old, she described the log cabin in minute detail in her autobiographical *The Comstocks of Cornell.* They were a farm family, the proud owners of a cheese house, a horse barn, and a cow barn.

The heart of her family was her gentle Quaker mother. Rather than singing to put her small daughter to sleep, she recited poetry. And as soon as Anna was old enough to understand, her mother taught her the names of sixty wildflowers and a dozen constellations. Best of all, she gave Anna a "sense of wonder," as Rachel Carson called the feeling over one hundred years later, toward nature, which Anna's mother herself never lost. Even at eighty, she could turn to her daughter with a radiant face after watching a sunset and say, "Anna, heaven may be a happier place than the earth, but it cannot be more beautiful."

Anna was also blessed with male playmates — two cousins and an only child like herself — so amiable that she later said of them, "Blessed is the girl who learns early in life that men are good." The other great influence in her youth was an educated female neighbor, Mrs. Ann French Allen, a former teacher who had married a wealthy widower and whose home overflowed with books, music, and art work. A teenage girl with a reputation as a voracious reader, Anna was a welcome visitor in their home, and Mrs. Allen was quick to suggest that Anna consider a university education.

But first, she had to attend the equivalent of high school. She went to Chamberlain Institute and Female College, a female seminary run by the Methodist Church, eighteen miles from her home. She found the school and its teachers excellent, and she particularly excelled in literary writing and oratory. The one dark cloud was the school's insistence that she "experience religion;" she refused to do this, because she did not agree with their vision of a vengeful God.

For several years Anna had been determined to attend the University of Michigan at Ann Arbor, as her neighbor had suggested, since it had opened its doors to women, but then she heard about Cornell University. It had been in operation for only six years when she entered it in 1874 as a major in modern languages and literature.

John Henry Comstock was already there; he had earned his bachelor of science degree from Cornell the previous June and had then been offered a job teaching entomology. During Anna's first two years in college, both she and Henry were involved with other people. Anna had a way with her that attracted males; she had been popular at the Chamberlain Institute, where the boys' school had been in the same building. In fact, she maintained that she had chosen Cornell because she had understood the men at Cornell did not pay any attention to the female students.

But as soon as she arrived the men came calling, and within a year she was engaged to a fellow student named Will Berry. Henry, on the other hand, was seriously interested in a friend of Anna's who subsequently died of tuberculosis. Anna's own romance "fell by its own weight. It was too emotional to meet the realities of life."

However, she and Henry had become good friends even before she took his zoology course, and he conducted her through his laboratory after class to show her his thousands of insects. To her he was the kindest of men, a good friend, the man she went riding and dining with, and who wrote her letters, when he was visiting his tubercular girlfriend in Florida, about the insects he was collecting — not the kind of courtship most girls dream of. And, as a matter of fact, neither seemed aware such a close friendship might lead to deeper commitments. Only the Cornell students and faculty members wondered about the frequent walks they took together.

The following fall Anna was home again, but the letters from Henry kept coming — long letters describing his entomological research — and an elated letter when he was made an assistant professor of entomology. He spent that Christmas with Anna and her parents, and there, at last, he found the parents he had never had. They called him Harry, and Harry he soon became to everyone who knew him well — a short, restless, energetic, enthusiastic man who could not sit still.

Whether or not he ever formally proposed is not known, but by the next spring he had applied for a building lot on campus with a view of Cayuga Lake and "did not seem to be in doubt as to who would share it with him," Anna wrote, as he planned the house that would be built on the property. A year and a half later, on a beautiful October afternoon, they were married in Anna's parents' home beneath an arch made of hemlock trees and hazel blossoms. Their only concession to a honeymoon was a short stop at Rochester to buy furniture before they returned to Ithaca and their cottage on Fall Creek, Anna installed as a proper housewife, Harry as a professor of the university. But they attended lectures together, and he helped her with the dishes, while she assisted him by keeping his laboratory in order, writing his business letters, making diagrams to illustrate his lectures, and helping him write a scientific report for the U.S. Department of Agriculture on the cotton worm.

Both of them were deeply interested in Harry's students. They began a tradition of entertaining his classes in their home, where

Anna, with her "dazzling complexion, beautiful chestnut hair and sparkling blue eyes," as one male student later described her, provided elegant meals for them. There is no doubt that Anna had a "vibrant spirit, pleasing personality and attractive appearance," as another admiring contemporary said, and that she was the heart of the family just as her own mother had been.

Their life at Cornell was abruptly interrupted a year after their marriage by a call from a former student of Harry's, Leland Howard, who told Harry that C. V. Riley was resigning as chief entomologist at the USDA and that Harry should apply for the position. He was accepted immediately, received a leave of absence from Cornell, and off they went to make a life for themselves in Washington, D.C. For a short time Anna worked with Harry as an unpaid assistant, but to her amazement Harry's boss insisted on giving her a position and paying her a salary. Although her status was that of a clerk, she wrote not only letters for Harry but also entomological notes and answers to agricultural queries, which were checked over and signed by Harry. Then, when his Entomological Department received a five-thousand-dollar grant from Congress, he decided to use it to study the scale insects infesting the citrus fruit trees in California. Anna was his laboratory assistant, while he did all the field work.

She had begun drawing insects for Harry even before they were married. He had given her India ink, pens, a drafting board, and a T square, so she was able not only to care for the insects Harry captured, but to draw those which could not be preserved. Once they returned to Washington, the work continued on the scale insects, which she drew from the microscope, enabling Harry, by her meticulous work, to differentiate between species and to begin a classification of the *Coccidae* of America. Her work, in fact, was so good that when Harry sent one of her drawings to the eminent French scientist M. Signoret, his return letter praised her drawing as "magnificent . . . made by the hand of a master." To Anna, such encouragement was one of the prods that pushed her into her career as a natural history illustrator.

Because Harry's appointment was political, the shooting of President Garfield, who supported Harry, ended their years in Washington, and they were free to return to Ithaca. Together they would now "take up the work at Ithaca with much more confidence, . . . have a happy home, . . . give my students the best facilities for obtaining an entomological training that can be found in the world. And we will do some original scientific work," Harry wrote enthusiastically to Anna.

They returned to Cornell in August of 1881; an Irish maid and a female cousin of Anna's helped with the housework so that Anna could continue her illustrations of *Coccidae* for Harry's report. Anna had her own workshop in her home, its walls hung with her pencil sketches of insects, from butterflies and moths to horned beetles and spotted lady bugs. And while she and Harry worked hard, they also spent hours afield in the Fall Creek Gorge near their home collecting butterflies.

During one expedition, according to Cornell student Edwin Emerson who accompanied them, "she kirtled up her skirt almost to her knees," before she went chasing the butterflies. "At the first sunlit clearing Mrs. Comstock gave a cry of joy and seizing her net from me, darted after a lovely, black-and-white striped swallowtail. 'It's a zebra, a zebra,' she cried, and presently managed to catch the butterfly, as it settled on a tall, waving flower."

The following autumn Anna resumed classes at Cornell as a science student, urged on by Harry, who wanted her to have more formal training and believed she would feel better about herself if she had a degree. They also decided that in order to properly illustrate Harry's next book, *An Introduction to Entomology*, she would have to learn the art of wood engraving. She promptly sent off for a set of wood-engraving tools, saying, "with my usual daring on untried paths I went at it." So that she could accomplish all this, she gave up housekeeping and they ate at the college instead. To get her degree, she wrote her thesis on "The Fine Anatomy of the Interior of the Larva of *Corydalus cornutus*," or the hellgramite, the larval form of the dobson fly. She described the work as "most interesting: I embedded tissues and cut sections and wondered at the beautiful structure of this horrible-looking creature's insides." In June of 1885 she received her bachelor of science degree from Cornell.

One of Anna's best friends was Susanna Phelps Gage, the wife of Harry's colleague Simon Gage. She too had become interested in wood engraving and began taking correspondence courses in the work from John P. Davis of Cooper Union in New York City. Impressed by his letters to Susanna, Anna went to New York to study directly under him, along with eleven other students from all over the United States. Mr. Davis proved to be a gifted, caring teacher, and the six weeks she spent under his instruction were happy ones. Of course, her subjects continued to be insects so that she could use the engravings for Harry's textbook. Two years later she returned for more instruction from Davis with special emphasis on the engraving of insects.

It was also about this time the Comstocks realized they would never be able to have children, and Anna wrote much later that had a child been available to adopt, they would have done so. Instead, they continued as surrogate parents for many Cornell students over the years, giving generously of their time and money to help those who needed it.

Never one to brood over life's reverses, Anna surged ahead in her engraving work. The following spring, with funds from the newly established Cornell Experiment Station, Harry was allowed to have his "Insectary," a greenhouse he had requested where he could grow plants attractive to the injurious insects he wanted to study first-hand. A two-story cottage was built directly behind their home; in addition to the sixty-foot-long glass house attached to it (the insectary itself), it had room for two offices, storage, and janitor rooms. Anna did her engravings in the office with a north window.

Harry had already found a publisher for his textbook on entomology, chosen to get the best possible printing of Anna's engravings. He had also learned how to photograph Anna's drawings and print them on boxwood blocks, which made it easy for an engraver to follow the lines in the photographic print. On November 1, 1888, DeVinne Press of New York, famous for its magazine engravings, published part I of *An Introduction to Entomology.* It sold fifteen copies the first week, and both author and illustrator were thrilled. The following month Anna was one of the first four women to be initiated into Sigma Xi, the national honor society of the sciences.

To finish the second volume of the textbook, Harry insisted he had to learn German, and to do that, he and Anna sailed for Germany in the winter of 1888–89. Probably the highlight of that visit for Anna occurred when they visited the Berlin Art Gallery and saw Anna's own engravings of moths and butterflies on display, which, without her knowledge, had been borrowed from the American Society of Wood Engravers. Anna was definitely getting a reputation as a fine natural history engraver and was only the third woman to be elected into the American Society of Wood Engravers. She modestly explained that she was not a true artist and had been honored only because her work of copying a live insect was original.

Harry decided not to pursue the second volume of his textbook but instead to write a whole new work. This became the monumental *Manual for the Study of Insects,* published by his own newly formed Comstock Publishing Company. Both Anna and Harry spent several years on the comprehensive work. Anna often worked nine hours a day on her engravings. When the book was published in 1895, it was an instant success, and within a month thirty schools had adopted it as a class text.

Anna was listed as the junior author because, as Harry explained in his preface, "Although the chief work of the Junior Author has been with the pencil and graver, many parts of the text are from her pen." Furthermore, he was generous in his praise of Anna's engravings, emphasizing their scientific accuracy and mentioning her high standing in the opinions of the world's best engravers.

Just as the work for the book was completed, Anna was swept up into the recently started Nature Study Movement, which was begun to encourage rural children to stay on the farm rather than leave for the city. The state put the program's funds as well as its functioning into the hands of Cornell's College of Agriculture. For a year Anna, along with four men, did a survey of public schools to see if nature study was being taught. They quickly discovered that, for the most part, it was not, so Anna and several other people were asked to provide instructional leaflets for teachers. One of the persons enticed into the writing was Professor Liberty Hyde Bailey, head of Cornell's Department of Horticulture, and under his inspired leadership the movement began to take off in 1897.

Anna seemed pleased with Bailey's leadership, believing that he had great vision and faith in the Nature Study Movement. A year later she was appointed as an assistant professor of nature study in the Cornell University Division. Her appointment, although not her salary and responsibilities, was quickly withdrawn when Cornell's Board of Trustees objected to giving a woman professorial status. Instead, she was designated a lecturer in nature study.

The work immediately engulfed her; along with Bailey and Professor Roberts, head of the School of Agriculture, she began to teach a full nature study course during the summer of 1899. Anna was responsible for two days of insect life study a week — lecturing, leading field trips, and conducting laboratory work for the 100 students that signed up. Bailey spent an equal amount of time teaching plant study, while Roberts devoted one day a week to instructing the students in general agriculture.

A second summer of the Nature Study School was also successful from the standpoint of the students. Unfortunately, though, they had all come from the city just as the first class had, and it was the country people that the program had been mandated to reach. This forced Anna to take her teaching into summer sessions at state normal schools, which did reach rural teachers. She also became a familiar face on the lecture circuit at teachers' institutes in New York state. Her artwork, regrettably, had to be put aside, but the Nature Study Movement was so important to her that she did not seem to mind. And every summer she lectured about nature at Chautauqua.

The books of fieldwork continued when she and Harry found time, usually during weeks they spent at her old home in Otto. In 1901 they began work on *The Spider Book*, both of them collecting; Harry did the photographing, Anna the drawing. Back in Ithaca that autumn, they snatched more time from Harry's teaching and Anna's — because by then she was teaching a Cornell class in nature study and giving a course of lectures for the teachers of Ithaca — to continue their study of spiders. On October 21, 1901, she wrote, "Went spidering with Harry and saw spiderlings migrating, making a carpet of web over the grass."

In connection with her lecturing that year she also wrote *Trees at Leisure*, which she called, "as good a bit of writing as I ever did." She followed that by collecting several of her periodical articles into a charming book, *Ways of the Six-Footed*, published by Ginn and Company in 1903 and recently reprinted by the Cornell University Press. In her preface she makes it clear that all the insect observations were her own — "I have read chapters of them with mine own eyes, and have been able here and there to add something not before recorded. The complete story of the Ceratina [*Ceratina dupla*, the carpenter bees] was brought to me page by page from the fields by my husband for my daily entertainment while I was prostrated by a tedious illness." That had been back in 1884 when he had nursed her at Otto for most of the summer. At the same time he had been writing an article on *Hymenoptera* and had worked out the life history of the carpenter bee by bringing it in to show Anna — the reason, she continued in her preface, why she called that chapter, "The Story We Love Best." In another chapter, she explained that "the Seine Maker has lured me to various indiscreet excursions to the middle of swift streams."

If there is any question that Anna was a field person, reading this little book and noting its detailed illustrations, most of which were done by her, should dispel all doubts. In "A Little Nomad," the chapter about the maple-leaf cutter, she explains her desire to be alone in the woods, away from "a world of work and care." She "was tired of a world that lectured and talked and argued and did many other noisy things that wore on one's nerves," a confession she did not often make. Her social ideas also creep into these simply written tales for children. In "The Perfect Socialism," a chapter about bees, wasps, ants, and termites, she compares the apparent altruism in social insects to acquisitiveness and competitiveness in human beings. She decides in the insects' favor, concluding that "the generosity of these insect citizens toward each other is an ideal which still lies beyond the horizon of accomplishment in the human world." In her autobiography, Anna never complains about woman's position in the world, but she comments facetiously in "Two Mother Masons" that "it is safe to assert that in the insect world the question of 'woman's rights' is settled permanently in the affirmative."

Slowly Anna's reputation as a teacher and lecturer began to spread beyond the borders of New York state, and one June week in 1903 she taught summer school for teachers at the University of Virginia. The following November she spent lecturing in Washington, D.C., and in that same month she was made a trustee of the incipient Smith College in Geneva, New York. She needed an elementary book on butterflies to use in her Chautauqua lectures, and although Harry thought her summer lecturing was too hard on her health, he agreed to help her with *How to Know the Butterflies* after she signed a contract with the Appleton Publishing Company. The following spring it was published with beautiful color plates.

One of Anna's most interesting projects was a novel she labored over for several years during bouts of insomnia. She called it *Confessions to a Heathen Idol*, and thinking "it would be scandalous for a scientific woman to write a novel," she wrote it pseudonymously as Marian Lee. Doubleday, Page, and Company accepted it within a day, and she confessed herself "breathless with excitement and delight" when it was published in 1906. Since people guessed immediately who the author was, the second edition came out under her own name.

No wonder her identity was apparent. The novel is a thinly veiled account of Anna's inner life. The first-person narrator is named Marian Lee, a woman who is a wood-carver — "I loved the work from the first, and the fact that I really achieved a fair success in it has always been a comfort to me." Her chip-littered room is her refuge; so is nature. To her there is no song as lovely as the bobolink, no light lovelier than starlight. Glowing red is the color she would die for, and she describes herself at forty as "a girl who would not learn to grow old when the gray hairs came creeping into her black locks; a girl who boldly declares the whole world is rose-color because she deliberately chooses to wear pink spectacles . . . a girl stunted in growth by rank optimism and kept in eternal girlhood thereby."

Her chief fault is that she gives too much of her life away to too many people. She despises committees, because she is an unorganized person and likes to do things her own way. So when she is put in charge of a meeting she rushes "business through, right over the prostrate forms of caprices, prejudices and qualms." Her character is to be "calm on the crust" while "seething beneath," "to keep serene when everything around one is seething and bubbling," and

17.   Anna Comstock's engraving of butterflies, 1891. *Courtesy Department of Manuscripts and University Archives, Cornell University Library, Cornell University, Ithaca, New York*

finally, when she is badly hurt, she goes back to the country to stay with her restful, Quaker relatives. But through all her trials, she believes, as Anna does, "that productive labor is the best of all our activities to make the day happy and the night satisfied."

And so Anna's incredible productivity continued, even though, unlike her heroine, she was now fifty-two years old. She had her own nature study department, an assistant, and two rooms in Roberts Hall. In the winter of 1909, she conceived her idea of writing a *Handbook of Nature Study* for teachers. No publisher was interested, but she surged ahead just as her husband continued to slog on through *The Spider Book*. Both books were finished in 1911. The Comstock Publishing Company published Anna's handbook which, before her death, had been translated into eight languages and sold in North and South America, Asia, and Europe.

It was an enormous book — 938 pages — crammed with information on every subject from weather to birds and from rocks and minerals to reptiles. Interspersed throughout was poetry, giving the book beauty as well as factual scientific information. Teachers found all the information they needed along with 232 meticulously planned lessons to follow, complete with suggested field trips, experiments, and questions to ask students. An excellent bibliography and a large section devoted to "The Teaching of Nature-Study" completed the "Nature Bible." Perhaps its eventual best-seller status persuaded the Cornell trustees to finally make Anna an assistant professor in 1913, but Anna suspected that her assistant, Alice McCloskey, had agitated for it once she learned that Martha Van Rensselaer and Flora Rose had been made professors in the home economics department. One thing Anna made clear in *The Comstocks of Cornell* was that *she* had not asked for the promotion.

A year later Harry officially retired from Cornell at the age of sixty-five, happy to spend all his time in research and writing. For Anna, though, work in the form of teaching, writing, and the lecturing circuit continued as usual. She also assumed the editorship of the *Nature Study Review*, first begun by the American Nature Study Society back in 1905.

She turned sixty-five in 1919, and shortly before that Cornell made her a full professor, a promotion considered a tribute to her long service as well as to the Department of Nature Study she had developed. That was also the year women finally received the vote, something Anna believed in but did not actively fight for, because "I had been using all of my strength to fight narrowness, prejudice, and injustice, in the curriculum of the common schools, and I was weary with fighting."

She was not weary of writing though. Both she and Harry loved to write, and while he worked on the second volume of his *An Introduction to Entomology*, she wrote articles for *Compton's Young People's Encyclopedia.* "Our writing was the thread on which our days were strung, despite a thousand interfering activities."

One of those activities ended in January of 1921, when she officially retired from Cornell. She conducted her last class in the now old Insectary, "that place of so much excellent scientific work and of so much of our happiness in teaching and writing."

Two years later she was persuaded to become a candidate for alumni trustee at Cornell. The alumnae believed she was the only woman who had a chance to be elected, but in both 1922 and 1923 she was defeated by electioneering alumni, despite endorsements from various womens' clubs. She claimed she was relieved and had only run because the women had needed her help, but at the same time she admitted that she "was indignant that the men were so unfair toward women." She was also pleased with the men graduates of the College of Agriculture who had supported her.

Anna was not adverse to honors, though, and admitted she was happy to be initiated into the Phi Kappa Phi honorary society that same year. But in 1923 she was completely taken aback by an announcement she read in *The New York Times.* Anna Comstock had been voted one of the twelve greatest women in America by the League of Women Voters. At first she couldn't believe it. Surely they meant some other Comstock woman! But she was thrilled to accept the honor in the company of the other eminent American women who had been chosen, including her good friend Martha Van Rensselaer in the field of domestic science. Anna had been singled out for her contributions to natural science, Annie Jump Cannon for astronomy, and Florence R. Sabine in anatomy. When she protested to Harry that she felt unworthy of the honor, he, as usual, said just the right thing. Her *Handbook of Nature Study* had already sold over forty thousand copies and would affect the lives of many children. For that alone, she deserved the honor. Harry, it seemed, had not minded being wrong about her book and was proud of the wife people called the Dean of American Nature Study.

Harry, on the other hand, finally finished the most important work of his life — *An Introduction to Entomology* — and he was called "the greatest teacher of natural history that America has known," by one notable scientist. They followed their triumphs with a trip to Hawaii, where they became interested in a Chinese boy who helped the steward. In fact, they offered to educate him, the last in a long line of children the childless Comstocks "adopted."

Time, though, had almost run out for the Comstocks. On August 4, 1926, Harry suffered a stroke; to Anna, "this calamity, for us, ended life. All that came after was merely existence." As Harry grew progressively worse, Anna continued to work and to care for him. She ignored her own failing health, in "the struggle on my part to self-control." To her he was "my precious invalid" who never frowned and often smiled even though he was speechless and helpless.

Her indomitable will forced her to keep giving to the world, despite the personal tragedy that had befallen her. She even made a trip to Geneva, New York, in 1930 to receive an honorary Doctor of Humane Letters from Hobart College. She taught her last summer class in her home that August and died of cancer two weeks later; Harry died seven months later.

She was "one of the most deeply loved women in Ithaca," a woman who "could see the good in everybody." But it was her old colleague Liberty Hyde Bailey whose tribute best described her humanity. "Anna Botsford Comstock blessed us all," he wrote. "She leaves a fragrant memory of high achievement, noble service, unselfish co-operation, constructive counsel, inspired teaching, loving kindness and unforgettable companionship. Her life was a poem."

# Annie Trumbull Slosson

## THE OLD BUG WOMAN

"THE OLD BUG WOMAN" was what sightseers on the train up Mount Washington called Annie Trumbull Slosson, and seeing her in action with her butterfly net was as important to the success of their excursion as reaching the summit of the mountain.

"What in the world is that old woman about? What's she got in her hand? Oh, it's a butterfly-net! She must be crazy. Just think of a butterfly up here."

But there were butterflies up there, as well as a wealth of other insects if one knew where to look. And Annie did. Even as late as September 1907 when she was sixty-nine years old, she spent several weeks at Summit House, Mount Washington, creeping under the porch platform, searching beneath chips and boards and among debris for beetles despite persistent rain and fog.

By then she had already published numerous lists of the *Insects Taken in the Alpine Regions of Mt. Washington,* beginning with her first one in 1894. She had also written an account of her early collecting work there for *Entomological News* back in 1893. She explained that the porch of Summit House was painted white and absorbed sunshine during the morning and most of the afternoon, so insects of all orders were attracted to it, making it easy for her to scoop them up. In one sunny week, in fact, she collected six hundred insects. She also turned over stones in search of beetles and looked for grasshoppers on the tough little grasses and sedges growing amid the rocks. To her, it was "wonderful how many forms of animal life exist in this bleak, barren, frigid region. At times the very air seems alive with minute insects, dancing like motes in the sunshine."

Annie, like many women field naturalists, started her scientific work late in life. She began collecting insects one early spring when she was forty-eight years old because, like naturalist Mary Treat, she wanted to know which bugs infested her garden. Previously she had studied botany, even corresponding with Asa Gray about some of her finds, and in 1882 she had reported locating one specimen of a rare plant, *Subularia aquatica,* at Echo Lake in Franconia, New Hampshire. She also authored popular magazine stories and books, mostly on New England village themes, although she later wrote that she believed entomology and literature "work well together in harness, each being a good running mate for the other."

She had been born the ninth child of Gurdon and Sarah A. Trumbull in Stonington, Connecticut, on May 18, 1838, and at least three brothers and two sisters lived to adulthood. The three brothers — James Hammond Trumbull, Henry Clay Trumbull, and Gurdon Trumbull — were all prominent in their chosen fields, and each had some influence on their sister Annie. James had been interested in entomology before he became a philologist and had also catalogued the reptiles, fishes, and shells of Connecticut. Henry became editor of the *Sunday School Times* in Philadelphia and no doubt encouraged Annie's popular writing. Gurdon was the artist who illustrated her first full length book, the *China Hunters' Club,* in 1878.

She married Edward Slosson on June 27, 1867, when she was twenty-nine, but they had no children. Eleven years later she was supporting herself by her own writing, so the marriage was probably short-lived. Her letters to her many entomological friends later in life often lamented the loss of brothers and brothers-in-law, but no mention has been found of her husband.

Her entomological mentor, her "first acquaintance, helper, and adviser" in her new pursuit was Henry Edwards. Edwards, a well-known English actor who also collected insects, with a specialty in butterflies and moths, left a collection of three hundred thousand species when he died in 1891 at the age of sixty-one. Universally loved for his generous and kindly spirit, especially towards amateurs interested in entomology, he helped Annie with insect identifications and put her in contact with other entomologists. He even named a new moth species she had found in Florida after her. Her reaction to the honor was typical of her understated humor. "Without a thought of irreverence I felt like expressing my willingness to 'depart in peace' now that I had seen this greatest of all earthly honors descend upon my humble head. An insect named for unworthy me! And the name so sonorous and delightful in sound. *Inguromorpha slossoni!* Like the proverbial 'Mesopotamia' of the eloquent preacher it stirred one's soul and I think I murmured it even in my sleep." Unfortunately, that particular species was superseded, sinking "into the dread valley of synonymy," she lamented.

Another early influence on her was the Maine lepidopterist Alpheus Spring Packard, Jr., who also named at least one moth species, *Alarodia slossoniae*, after her. Called Slosson's slug, it spends its larval stage in the mangroves of Florida's southern coast. Over the years, one hundred insects were named for her by other entomologists she supplied with her own finds, including *Zethus slossonae*, a wasp that she discovered at Lake Worth, Florida.

The *slossonae* species did not represent all the new insects she discovered. Some she named herself and usually honored the place she had found them. For instance, *Dasylophia puntagorda* was another new moth species she had taken at a light in Punta Gorda, Florida. She enjoyed finding new species, commenting in 1890 about a successful season in Florida, "I have great hopes concerning my unnamed specimens. One large, oddly-marked Sphinx [moth] fills me with visions of a new genus as well as species, and I have already selected its name."

She collected wherever she went, which was usually Florida in the winter and Franconia, New Hampshire, in the summer, with some of that time spent at the summit of Mount Washington. She was one of the first entomologists to collect around Miami, Florida, in the early 1890s, and she made many unusual finds. Since she collected everything from dragonflies to ants, she had to send most of her specimens to experts in their fields for identification — Philip Calvert for dragonflies, William Morton Wheeler for ants — retaining for her own large collection at least one of each species and giving away or selling her duplicates.

With the money she made selling specimens, she helped support the *Journal of the New York Entomological Society*. She had been one of the first elected members of the society when it was started in 1892. The members often met in her home, until she persuaded Morris K. Jessup of the American Museum of Natural History to let them meet there in the museum. For years she was one of the few women members, and she fondly referred to the men as her "boys as I love to style you."

Her first meeting began inauspiciously enough. Escorted there by one of the older gentlemen, she entered to find the men smoking and drinking in what they had thought was an exclusive male enclave. Nonetheless, after she found a seat, they rallied, offered her a cup of coffee, and resumed their meeting. Annie, used to her brothers, had no trouble fitting into male society, and judging by the prominent entomologists who befriended and corresponded with her, she was well liked.

More than a collector, she was also a contributor to most of the entomological journals of the day—the aforementioned *Journal of the New York Entomological Society* and *Entomological News*, as well as the *Bulletin of the Brooklyn Entomological Society*, the *Canadian Entomologist* and *Entomoligica Americana*. *Entomological News*, published in Philadelphia as the organ of the Entomological Society of America (now the American Entomological Society), contained a series of her entertaining pieces in the 1890s about her collecting work in Florida. In "Collecting at Lake Worth, Florida," she explained how she dredged for insects in cultivation ditches using a muslin net "sewed to an awkwardly bent bit of iron wire whose twisted ends made the only handle I could contrive." With this awkward tool she took thirteen beetle species.

"Collecting on Biscayne Bay" involved a variety of approaches to the habitats she found. Many hours were spent along the shore of the bay searching in the sandy beach at low tide. By looking under wet seaweed and pieces of coral rock or wood, she found many beetles, some of them rare. Farther up from the waterline she used her net to chase tiger beetles, flies, and aquatic bugs. Beyond that zone, on higher ground, she hunted bees, wasps, butterflies, and bugs.

She also spent some mornings on a rowboat in the Miami River, rowing close enough to shore to search the leaves of mangrove trees for larvae or cocoons—"an indolent, luxurious way of collecting, not such hard work as grubbing in wet sand or hunting under dark seaweed, and I like it for a change."

An "enthusiastic and strenuous collector," she called herself, and odd-looking besides, tramping "over hill and plain in rough, appropriate costume, butterfly net in hand, poison bottles hanging at my leather belt, with big bag, holding knife, forceps and other essentials. . . ." She walked for miles over rough roads, climbed rugged heights, and often stood in mud or water and blistered her hands as she stripped bark from trees or turned over stones. But her methods were so successful that many years later Herbert Osborn, in his book *Fragments of Entomological History*, praised her unusual ability to discover strange insects.

And nothing, certainly not encroaching old age or continual ill health, kept her from her work. As she wrote to Dr. Henry Skinner, lepidopterist and editor of *Entomological News*, "I have been ill with neuritis all winter and the doctors attribute it to overwork in entomology the past season. They are right too. No one has any idea how steadily and hard I worked, especially in supplying specialists —for love not money!—and correspondence with them."

But she wanted to learn all she could, even though she was sometimes discouraged. Dragonflies, she wrote to Philip Calvert, were "so difficult to distinguish . . . except by slight structure differences which puzzle me. I think I shall give up trying. . . ." Fourteen days later she followed with another letter more characteristic of her spirit—"I am afraid I shall *not* give up the study of the Odonata! It would be wiser for me not to be so diffuse, but to confine myself to a specialty or at least a limited number of families. But it is so hard not to try at least to know a little about everything one takes."

Shortly after the turn of the century Annie's life changed. By the end of 1903 her last two siblings were dead, and her brother-in-law, Dr. William Prime, whose house in New York City she had lived in for many years, was feeble. He apparently had shared her entomological interests too; she mentioned paying his membership as well as her own to the New York Entomological Society. When he died, early in 1905, his home was stripped and sold, and she was forced to move to rented quarters along with her faithful servants. The deaths of all these people in her own generation had saddened and wearied her, yet after a period of mourning, she took up her collecting again and was frequently accompanied by nieces and nephews.

She also changed her collecting grounds. Except for occasional short weeks at Franconia and Mount Washington, her new summer base of operations was the Water Gap House on the Pennsylvania side of the Delaware Water Gap. In the winter, ill health often kept her in New York City, but a couple of early springs and one early summer (1906, 1907, and 1912) were spent in the mountains of North Carolina and four late winters (1908, 1909, 1911, and 1912) in Florida.

Fortunately, Annie had a wonderful facility for making friends— with servants and housekeepers, with guests at the hotels where she stayed, but most of all with younger entomologists who encouraged her work. One of her most treasured relationships was with William T. Davis of Staten Island, the so-called "Cicada Man" who named and described more than one hundred of the approximately 170 species of cicadas known in North America. Like Annie, though, he was a generalist and was interested in all of nature; while still a young man, he wrote a classic in nature literature—*Days Afield on Staten Island.* After a short, late marriage (his wife was dead within a year), he resumed living with his mother and sister and continued to earn his living in New York City as a competent insurance agent. But he was able to retire and become a full-time naturalist at the age of forty-six because of his savings.

By then he had been Annie's friend for at least six years. Their voluminous correspondence first began back on November 24, 1903. Forty to her fifty-five, he was her "dear boy," her "particular chum," and apparently her feelings were reciprocated. "I was more pleased the other day than I showed," she wrote to him in 1910, "when you named me among the close friends you would be sorry to leave. . . . Your friendship has been a comfort and help to me these last lonely years."

He came over on the Staten Island ferry to visit her every other Tuesday afternoon, "our day," as Annie called it, whenever she was in town, and then they would have their "bug chats." When she was away her letters to "Mr. Davis" were frequent and illuminating, recording both her ailments and her attempts to overcome them by continuing to collect.

During her first trip to North Carolina in May of 1906, three letters went out to Davis from Lake Toxaway. "Insects abound especially coleoptera," she rejoiced in her first letter, "and tho I have not gone many yards away from [the] hotel I have taken more each day than I could well attend to." She had already sent off samples to him and asked him to tell William Morton Wheeler that she had found ten species of ants. Three weeks later, despite being restricted to the grounds of the hotel because of poor health, she had taken nearly two hundred species of coleoptera (beetles) and many diptera (flies) as well as thirty species of ants for Wheeler. She had also been busy identifying wildflowers, evidence that her early botanical interests had not faded. And finally, on her return home, she proudly reported over eight hundred insects mounted, all pinned into one large box for Davis to see before she distributed them to entomologists.

The following spring she returned to North Carolina, this time to Hot Springs, and once again her health kept her bedridden for some of the time. "Still," she reported, "I have taken some 500 insects and several very interesting ones. . . . I have had a brood of larvae of the catalpa sphinx since their first moult and enjoyed watching them."

Luckily she recovered enough to enjoy her second stay at Water Gap House in July and early August. She was thrilled to discover many things new to her, particularly the insects she found on the oak trees. At last she would be able to learn still another territory — the "middle-state fauna" and during the next several summers she spent more and more time there, mounting and labeling eight hundred insects the following summer — "a good season's work for an old woman of 70," she told Davis.

That same year she returned to Florida in February, staying in Belleair. There she watched a colony of fungus ants and collected ants for Davis. By mid-March the weather was perfect — "like late June. I have worked off *ten pounds* of flesh in that time. Literally, with the tramping and perspiring and the not resting or eating very much I always wear myself thin in Florida." Best of all, she had made some good finds and was sending along grasshoppers for him.

Thus she went on, year after year, "still more active than many a person forty years younger," as Henry Skinner said in a tribute, "A Loved and Respected Entomologist" published in *Entomological News* in December 1919. He had come upon her with her net collecting at Water Gap when she was eighty-one. It was her fourteenth summer there, and after talking with Annie, he told his wife that he "had loved and respected this entomologist for many, many years. . . ." She "was very good to me in the years gone by and there is many a specimen in my collection taken at Franconia . . . and Biscayne Bay."

Another entomologist who was fond of her was a mutual friend of Annie and W. T. Davis and was often mentioned in her letters to Davis — the librarian-hemipterist Edward Payson Van Duzee. Both she and Davis helped finance Van Duzee's *Checklist of Hemiptera* through the New York Entomological Society in 1915, and as a result Annie was singularly honored. "I have had two long letters from Mr. V. D. one a few days ago telling of the completion of List. . . . He wants to dedicate it to me! . . . Was ever a *Checklist* dedicated to anyone before — a woman too." This seems a fitting conclusion to her life as an entomologist, which began with Henry Edward's *Inguromorpha slossoni* "taken at an electric light in Jacksonville, Florida by Mrs. A. Trumbull Slosson to whom I respectfully dedicate it."

Her last letter to Davis was in 1918, but a letter to his friend Charles Leng in 1920 from the Delaware Water Gap and another to Dr. Skinner in May, 1921, when she was eighty-three, both reported that she was still busy collecting.

She died on October 4, 1926, and Davis wrote an affectionate tribute to her for the *Journal of the New York Entomological Society*. Annie had remained "cheery and vivacious" until the end, "keenly interested in most things," he maintained. "She well understood . . . the meaning of human life. With advancing age she used to observe that she ought not and would not complain, and then with a smile would add, that she 'had had her day.' But to many of us comes the regret that her days were not even longer."

# Edith Patch

## ENTOMOLOGICAL NATURALIST

SHE WAS KNOWN as "Dr. Patch of America" among European, Asian, and African scientists who consulted her about her specialty—the identification and life history of aphids. Lay persons recognized her as Miss Edith Patch, author of over a hundred articles and stories and seventeen books for children about nature. But in her dual career she was first and foremost a field person, watching the creatures she was studying on their home turf in order to write exact accounts of their lives.

As a child she had been angered by a story she had read about a cabbage caterpillar that had changed into a yellow, rather than white, butterfly. Adding insult to injury, the illustration that accompanied the story had pictured a night-flying instead of a day-flying moth. She vowed then that someday she would write accurate nature stories for children.

Edith had been strong-willed and adventurous as a child, the much younger offspring in a family of six children. Born on July 27, 1876, she had spent her first eight years in the family home in Worcester, Massachusetts. Like most naturalists, she had shown her predilection at an early age, keeping toads, green snakes, and caterpillars as pets. Sliding—in a dishpan down a steep gravel bank, down the chute in the hayloft, or on a sled—was a favorite pastime, she later recalled. With such hobbies it is obvious that "woman's role" had not been impressed on her and that she had been free to do as she wished.

Such freedom continued when her family moved to Minnesota in 1884. After two years her father bought ten acres of prairie land between Minneapolis and Anoka. There she was able to continue her study of nature in an environment of lakes, swamps, and woodlands filled with flowers, insects, birds, and mammals. She was especially intrigued by the life cycle of the monarch butterfly, whose "metamorphic fortunes" she followed with fascination — "first a pale egg with reticulated engravings, next a larva ringed with yellow and black and white stripes, gay of garb as a court jester; then a majestic butterfly taking a leisurely flight with wings richly tawny above and bordered with black velvet."

She put her delight with monarch butterflies into a prizewinning essay she wrote about them in her senior year at South High School in Minneapolis. Her teacher was so impressed that she extracted a promise from Edith to spend at least some portion of her life writing nature stories for children.

The twenty-five dollars she won for the essay was spent on the book she had wanted most, John Henry Comstock's *Manual for the Study of Insects*. After reading it she was determined to attend Cornell University one day. But in the meantime, she graduated from high school and immediately enrolled in the University of Minnesota in 1897 as an English major. Her duality, later described as "the mind of a scientist, the soul of an artist," was evident during her college years. She wrote prizewinning sonnets and romantic stories, the latter under a pseudonym, yet at the same time, she was inspired by Professor O. W. Oestlund to study aphids. Apparently, her love of science won out, because as soon as she graduated from college, in 1901, she began applying for jobs in entomology.

She was told over and over that entomology was not a suitable profession for women, so she taught high school English for two years while she sent out letters of inquiry. And then, suddenly, she received an encouraging letter from Dr. Charles D. Woods, director of the Maine Agricultural Experiment Station. He offered her a volunteer assistant position at no pay for a year with the chance that she might be appointed head of the Department of Entomology he wanted her to organize. Against the counseling of friends, she immediately accepted. Realizing that she was serious about her commitment to entomology, Woods arranged for her to teach entomology and agricultural English at the University of Maine on a salaried basis for the first year. At last she had both money and a job in entomology.

Woods took quite a bit of heat, which he ignored, for hiring a woman. According to Edith, "When one of the leading Bureau of Entomology men remarked to Doctor Woods . . . 'I hear you have appointed a woman as entomologist. Why on earth did you do that? A *woman* can't catch grasshoppers,' he received the drawled reply,

'It will take a lively grasshopper to escape Miss Patch.'" She became the head of the Department of Entomology in 1904, and there she stayed for the remainder of her professional career.

Even as she was building a reputation in economic entomology, she continued her formal education. She received a master's degree from the University of Maine in 1910 and then went on to Cornell University for her doctorate, where she fulfilled her dream of working under J. H. Comstock. The Comstocks took her under their wings, as they did so many promising students, giving her, as she later explained it, their "special gift of giving pleasure . . . so that though I went to Cornell to learn and to admire—I remained to love, just as all the Professor's students have . . . and the fact which gave me cause for both pride and pleasure [was] when the Professor, who didn't usually go to commencements, came to mine." The Comstocks continued to keep abreast of Edith's work, and when John Henry wrote *An Introduction to Entomology*, he used material from Edith's doctoral thesis. He also sent her a complimentary copy, inscribed "To Professor Edith M. Patch, with the affectionate regards of her old friend, J. H. Comstock," in 1924. Anna Comstock was just as pleased with Edith's career but was more concerned with her children's books, which Anna thought were excellent. To Edith's delight, Anna offered her her choice of artist's proof engravings, inscribed "With the cordial regards of the artist and engraver, Anna Botsford Comstock."

Edith put most of her energies into the study of aphids for at least a decade after she received her doctorate. Although she wrote eighty technical journal articles, sometimes her artistic side surfaced in titles, such as "Marooned in a Potato Field," a scientific study she did on the potato plant aphid. Of course, she definitely had been confined in the potato fields of Maine's northern Aroostook County for a couple of summers, closely observing the life cycle of the potato plant aphid. Her "technique," as she described it to Mr. C. F. Rainwater at Clemson Agricultural College "is to watch aphids through every generation of their cycle, keeping notes of dates, food habits, idiosyncrasies, and the like. No two species of aphids have the same tricks or manners."

Aphids, or plant lice, those minute insects that feed on plant sap, are also known for their ability to exude excess plant juices in sweetened droplets called honeydew. They reproduce very quickly—often producing thirteen generations in a season—after overwintering as eggs. Ninety percent of all aphid species live on only one species of plant, and such aphid species as woolly apple, melon, and potato lice do great damage to their hosts. After three years of observation,

Edith finally discovered that melon aphids overwintered in the live-for-ever weed worldwide and advised growers to eliminate the weed before raising melons.

Her work with aphids included discovering new species and helping entomologists throughout the world by identifying the aphids they sent to her. Sometimes the aphids arrived in poor condition, and then the sender would be told how to prepare specimens — "Drop alive into *thin* balsam on a slide, clap on a cover glass and transport *whole.*" Sending them in vials of alcohol, as at least one inexperienced collector of aphids did, tore them apart and she did not like "to see perfectly good aphids broken to bits!" Nevertheless, she went on to thank that particular correspondent "for the privilege of seeing this interesting species which is new to me and is apparently undescribed for America at least."

Aphids were, as she told one person, "the insects I study . . . professionally. . . . I shall not desert the aphids while I hold a position as entomologist." Because of her reputation and willingness to help others, she was able to amass one of the most complete collections of aphids in the world for the Maine Agricultural Experiment Station. She had one genus, *Patchia,* and several species of aphids, including *Thecabius patchii* and *Eriosoma patchia,* named for her.

In 1924 she became head of the experiment station, the first woman head in the country. Two years later she was appointed to the Committee for Nomenclature in the American Association of Economic Entomologists, and the following year she was invited as a research guest for six months to the Rothamsted Experimental Station in Harpenden, England, where she studied and wrote about the foxglove aphid on potato plants. But she also indulged in what she called her lifelong habit of visiting the nearest hedgerow. On a glorious day in late May she rose at three in the morning to explore the area and listen to the birds sing, especially the English skylark. She extended her love of field observation to both Scotland and North Wales and altogether recalled her time in Britain as one of the best experiences of her life.

Perhaps the crowning point in her professional life occurred when she was elected president of the Entomological Society of America in 1930. This group, which includes amateurs and professionals, is an affiliate of the American Association for the Advancement of Science, with membership open to everyone interested in insects. She was a fellow of the society, an honor reserved for those who have made important contributions to the science of entomology. Apparently her election as president was a victory a long time coming. Congratulatory letters from both R. W. Harned and Herbert Osborn indicated that they had been trying for several years to get her elected. Osborn merely said her election had "been a wish of mine for several years and very nearly accomplished at least once before." Harned was more blunt. "I am almost certain," he wrote, "that the only reason you were not elected president at least seven or eight years ago was because so many entomologists are *too conservative*. The fact that you are not a man was the only excuse."

Edith never seemed concerned about discrimination, although she always did her best to help professional women. At her inaugural meeting in Cleveland, she invited Ann Haven Morgan of Mount Holyoke College to present her "Notes on the Biology of Burrowing Mayflies." She also did the previously discussed survey of women entomologists. She always believed she had been treated fairly by the Maine Agricultural Experiment Station and that her salary had been on a par with male heads of station departments.

Probably her greatest contribution to entomology was the publication of her mammoth *Food Plant Catalogue of the Aphids of the World*, but she continued to see herself as a dual person — scientist and naturalist, specialist and generalist. In fact, she divided her day in half — mornings for professional entomology, afternoons as a field naturalist. What she learned in both roles was grist for her popular books and magazine articles for children as well as for radio broadcasts. These broadcasts she did in 1936 were part of her work at the station but designed for the lay person. "Aphids, Aphids, Everywhere!" was the title of one talk, and her message was that "in general, aphids are regulated by natural controls."

In her home, Braeside, she had an ideal outdoor laboratory. Her hundred acres included a river ledge, meadow, and woodland, and in her yard she had both a bird feeding station and a garden of wildflowers. Her observations for *Bird Stories* all came from Braeside. Others, such as *Desert Neighbors*, were based on trips farther afield. She did enjoy traveling and managed to visit forty-four states plus Canada and Mexico.

While she liked the company of others, and urged children to form nature clubs, she also counseled them to spend time alone. Such periods might be "some of the very happiest hours of your lives . . . when you take a walk by yourself, along a hill, along a river, or among the trees." Nevertheless, she was definitely a joiner — a member of the American Ornithologists' Union and the Audubon Society, the Museum of Natural History and the Society for the Protection of Native Plants, the American Society of Naturalists and the Bird Conservation Club of Bangor.

Some of her writing for children included chapters on nature in

18.   Edith Patch setting out with her camera. *Courtesy Special Collections, Raymond H. Fogler Library, University of Maine at Orono*

school readers used in the United States and South America. This writing led her to join the National Council of Supervisors of Elementary Science and the American Science Teachers' Association. In Orono she hosted the Women's Club and the American Association of University Women. She was president of still another group, the American Nature Study Society in 1937 and 1938.

By then she had retired because her health was suffering and she wanted to spend more time outdoors. The University of Maine gave her an honorary doctorate at the end of her professional career in 1937, but it was not until 1940 that she was elected to Sigma Delta Epsilon, the women's honorary scientific fraternity. She continued to travel, write for children, observe, and raise flowers, but she stopped working on aphids the day she retired. She did not neglect her entomologist friends, however, and in 1938 she traveled with sixteen other people, four of whom were entomologists, to the International Congress of Entomologists in Berlin.

For years she had shared her home with her older sister Alice, who did the cooking and housework and was supported by Edith. For a time a brother and sister-in-law were also dependent on her. Fortunately, the University of Maine gave her what she considered a fair and adequate pension, and royalties from her popular writing also helped. Over her lifetime two million copies of her books, published primarily by Atlantic Monthly Press and Macmillan, were sold. Edith and Alice were a close pair, entertaining friends, snowshoeing together, and, after Edith's retirement, traveling to Florida by car to spend two winters there in the 1940s.

Alice, who was eight years older than Edith, died in the late 1940s, and Edith could not cope with domestic responsibilities. She had been a professional all her life, and knitting was about the only womanly task she excelled in. Her lovely, outgoing, friendly personality and her generosity to others became almost a caricature as she rode the buses in search of companionship, offering people candy bars, and appeared on the steps of acquaintances, asking if she could share their meal. She also formed an attachment to an osteopathic doctor, who had helped her when she had had pneumonia, and it was he and his wife who inherited her home and belongings when she died in 1954.

Although old age had not been kind to Edith, during her productive years she provided inspiration for women who wanted to become entomologists. Like her friend and mentor, Anna Comstock, Edith had combined entomology and nature study to produce both professional and popular work of lasting value.

# Part V
# *The Ornithologists*

―――――――――――――――――――――――――――――
<br>
❧

Ornithology was harder than botany for women to
break into. Women, after all, were considered too delicate to tramp around in the field and shoot birds, which
is how most ornithological field study was done in the
nineteenth century. The only woman known to have
shot birds as specimens in the nineteenth century was
naturalist Martha Maxwell. Their other professional
alternative was to become systematists who studied bird
skins in a museum setting, such as naturalist Graceanna Lewis at the Academy of Natural Sciences. Indeed, she had discovered one new bird species in that
way — the uni-colored blackbird (AGELAIUS CYANOPUS)
of South America.

Otherwise women came to ornithology as appreci-
ators of birds with a strong desire to convert others to
their way of thinking by writing about their experiences. Examples include Olive Thorne Miller, one of
the earliest popular bird writers, and Mabel Osgood
Wright, who wrote BIRDCRAFT, a book that ornithologist
Frank Chapman considered "one of the first and most
successful of the modern bird manuals." Chapman was
also the editor of BIRD-LORE, the predecessor of AUDU-
BON magazine, for thirty years, and Mabel Osgood
Wright was his indispensable associate editor for eleven
of those years, contributing a steady stream of chatty,
informative columns about bird behavior and conservation.

Still, neither Miller nor Wright devoted all of their professional lives to birds. Both were primarily general writers with a strong interest in birds. Although they joined professional organizations, such as the American Ornithologists' Union (A.O.U.), they and many other women who watched birds and extolled their virtues were considered "dabblers" by serious ornithologists, such as Althea Sherman. Such ornithologists not only spent all their time studying bird behavior but also wrote for professional journals, including A.O.U.'s THE AUK, the Wilson Ornithological Club's WILSON BULLETIN, and the Cooper Ornithological Club's THE CONDOR. Arthur Cleveland Bent utilized their work in his multivolumed LIFE HISTORIES OF NORTH AMERICAN BIRDS. Other male ornithologists also used their observations in their own books, such as Edward Forbush's BIRDS OF MASSACHUSETTS, Ralph Palmer's MAINE BIRDS, and Frank Chapman's HANDBOOK OF BIRDS OF EASTERN NORTH AMERICA.

None of the women ornithologists in this book — Florence Merriam Bailey, Althea Sherman, Margaret Morse Nice, Cordelia Stanwood, and Amelia Laskey — lost sight of the importance of writing for the popular market as well. Florence Merriam Bailey was certainly the best-known woman ornithologist, chiefly because of the several popular books she wrote before the turn of the century. But once she became professional by writing for the bird journals, the public quickly forgot about her. Nice and Sherman confined most of their important writing to the journals, although Nice made two attempts to attract a popular audience by writing THE WATCHER AT THE NEST and her autobiographical RESEARCH IS A PASSION WITH ME. The former was not a commercial success, and she could not find a publisher for the latter. Sherman also longed to reach the popular press with a synthesis of her life work, but she left it until after her death; her posthumous BIRDS OF AN IOWA DOORYARD never sold more than fifteen hundred copies. Stanwood wrote one article for THE AUK on magnolia warblers in 1910, but when she learned that journals did not pay, she switched to the popular magazine market. HOUSE BEAUTIFUL printed her "Six Little Chickadees" photographs as well as many of her stories

*on bird observation. Laskey seemed to be the one or-*
*nithologist who was content to publish only in jour-*
*nals. However, even she made one attempt to write a*
*popular piece, "Watching a Carolina Wren's Nest," which*
*Nice suggested she publish in* THE CHICAGO NATURALIST.

*All of the women ornithologists observed bird be-*
*havior, and three of them — Sherman, Nice, and Laskey*
*— pioneered in life studies of specific bird species. Bailey*
*and Stanwood, on the other hand, specialized in watch-*
*ing all the bird species that lived in or visited their spe-*
*cific areas. Stanwood, the least traveled, confined her*
*studies to her own forty-acre Maine farm with occa-*
*sional forays to the nearby coast. Bailey specialized in*
*the birds of the American West, where she and her hus-*
*band, mammalogist Vernon Bailey, spent large portions*
*of over thirty years camping in tents and studying the*
*wildlife of such hitherto little-explored areas as the Mo-*
*gollon Mountains of New Mexico.*

*All of the women ornithologists knew each other,*
*if only by letter. The Sherman-Nice-Laskey network was*
*particularly strong. Nice originally wrote to Sherman —*
*a much older women — in 1921 to ask her about her*
*article in* THE CONDOR *reporting the unusual length of*
*eighteen and nineteen days for the fledging of two*
*mourning doves she had observed. Nice, at that point,*
*had just begun her work in ornithology and was pleased*
*to receive an enthusiastic reply from Sherman that said,*
*"I am glad there is another woman to join our ranks,*
*who is doing genuine study. Too many women are dab-*
*blers." Although they met only twice, at A.O.U. meet-*
*ings in Chicago (1922) and Detroit (1931), their eleven-*
*year correspondence led to what Nice later called, "a*
*close and inspiring friendship." Sherman's friendship*
*came at just the right time in Nice's career, and the ad-*
*vice of the older woman was what she needed to keep*
*on with her work. Sherman, in turn, used Nice as a*
*sounding board for many of her own ideas about bird*
*study. She also sympathized with Nice's frustration over*
*domestic chores, assuring Nice that, "like you I rebel*
*against spending time on menial tasks."*

*In one letter to Nice, Sherman mentioned another*
*woman ornithologist she had once corresponded*
*with — Cordelia Stanwood. Stanwood, she wrote, "had*

*made some excellent studies of birds but felt unable to give them away to the bird magazines and was selling them where she could get a pittance for them. In 1913 the WILSON BULLETIN was hard up for everything as usual and I thought of a plan to help it out as well as Miss Stanwood."* Sherman then paid Stanwood for her BULLETIN pieces out of her own money, pretending that the BULLETIN paid for articles. She was gratefully thanked by Stanwood, who told Sherman that she had been paid more for articles sent to the BULLETIN than for anything else she had written.

Stanwood, unlike the other five ornithologists, had to depend on her own wits to make a living for herself and her mother, and often that living was precarious. Sherman, whose pen was sometimes sharp, was, in reality, a kindhearted woman known for giving or lending money to anyone who asked. Apparently she recognized Stanwood's proud nature and so devised her plan to help the unsuspecting Stanwood without insulting her.

When Nice received her first letter from Laskey, a housewife from Nashville, Tennessee, sometime in the late 1930s, she undoubtedly remembered Sherman's friendship at a crucial time. Although Laskey was two years older than Nice, she had started her ornithological career nine years later. Unlike Nice, she had neither a college education nor a supportive husband. In addition, she was a shy, retiring person. But her life studies of birds were excellent and her abilities in bird rehabilitation exceptional. Altogether, as Nice told her, "You always write such interesting things." Nice encouraged Laskey to do more than she thought herself capable of, and Laskey protested in 1942 that, "you flatter me that I could write an article on methods of doing field work and analyzing. I feel so incompetent and have had to struggle along alone here." Nice also critiqued Laskey's early attempts at book reviewing, something Nice had specialized in for fifteen years, saying, "You can, with a little practice, write fine reviews." Later, Nice elicited Laskey's support in sending packages to German and Austrian scientists and their families after the war and pulled Laskey into her network of extensive correspondence with such renowned scientists as Konrad Lorenz and Niko Tinbergen. She also enlisted Laskey's aid in her many conservation battles. On March 6, 1955, Laskey dutifully reported, "I have just finished writing several letters about the Dinosaur Dam: protests to each of our three Congressmen, and one each to the three chairmen whose names you sent in your letter."

After six years of steady correspondence, Mrs. Nice and Mrs. Laskey became Margaret and Amelia. When Nice wrote her "Harper Chronicles" (letters to her adult children and close friends about what she was doing), Laskey always received copies. The women had several mutual female friends also studying birds. Their correspondence over thirty years is the best record that exists of the network women in ornithology had established from the 1940s until the early 1970s, when Laskey and Nice died within a year of each other.

By the 1970s it was no longer unusual for women to want to be ornithologists, and many were even getting graduate degrees from prestigious universities. They were also obtaining elective positions in the major ornithological associations and becoming editors of bird journals. Today few people question women's fitness to conduct strenuous field work, especially in the tropics, where much of the original ornithological research is now being done.

# Florence Merriam Bailey

FIRST LADY OF ORNITHOLOGY

IT PROBABLY HELPED that her brother was C. Hart Merriam, chief of the U.S. Biological Survey and a cofounder of the American Ornithologists' Union and her husband was Vernon Bailey, the primary field naturalist for the survey. Although both men did have a profound influence in what she did with her life, there is no doubt that Florence Merriam Bailey deserved the A.O.U.'s most coveted award, the Brewster Medal, when it was presented to her in 1931. She was the first woman to be so honored, just as she had been the first woman elected a fellow in the A.O.U. two years previously. Both honors had been granted ostensibly for her monumental 807-page book, *Birds of New Mexico*, which had been published in 1928. Many years of writing bird books and articles lay behind her by then, however. The youngest child and only surviving daughter of Clinton Levi and Caroline Hart Merriam, Florence began her field experiences in her youth.

She was born on August 8, 1863, in Locust Grove, New York, just west of the Adirondack Mountains. She spent her childhood there at Homewood, her family's country estate. Her father, who had been a successful businessman in New York City, had retired to Locust Grove shortly after Florence's birth, trading city life for the country life he loved. There he pursued his natural history interests while managing his farm. He was also elected to the U.S. Congress for two terms. But when he was home, he encouraged the scientific interests of both Florence and her brother Hart, eight years her senior. By the time she was nine years old, she was even allowed to accompany them on a rugged two-month camping and collecting trip to Florida.

Hart not only tolerated his little sister, he actively encouraged her by answering her questions and sharing his work in ornithology and mammalogy with her. Her mother Caroline, a Rutgers College graduate, was particularly interested in astronomy, which she explained to Florence. Still another early influence on Florence was her father's sister, Helen Bagg, who she called "our family botanist." Small wonder, then, that Florence, while she dutifully studied subjects such as geography, arithmetic, music, and English to prepare for college, was at heart a naturalist.

Her haphazard, mostly informal education at home, supplemented by spates of formal schooling, enabled her to register as a "special student" at Smith College in Northampton, Massachusetts. Being "special" meant that she could choose whatever courses she wanted instead of following the prescribed requirements for a degree. On the other hand, she received only a certificate when she finished her four years.

But by then she had begun her life's work. During her college years of 1882–86, birds were being slaughtered at an unprecedented rate so that women could wear the feathers and even the whole birds atop their stylish hats. Other women, though, were already campaigning against the wanton destruction of bird life, and after George Bird Grinnell launched the first Audubon Society in 1886, Florence almost immediately started an Audubon chapter at Smith College.

Seventy-five students and faculty members attended the meeting she called to propose the formation of the chapter. So effectively did she rally the group that a constitution was drawn up, officers elected, and a field committee appointed by March 17, 1886. Florence, a believer in education, organized the club's first bird walks given by the charismatic and popular naturalist-writer of the day, John Burroughs. He spent three days in Northampton, taking classes of ten to forty students out to observe birds. Despite the dearth of birds in the early spring, "the strong influence of Mr. Burroughs' personality and quiet enthusiasm gave just the inspiration needed," Florence later wrote in her first published article, "Our Smith College Audubon Society" in the *Audubon Magazine* of September 1887. "With gossamers and raised umbrellas we would gather about him under the trees, while he stood leaning against a stump, utterly indifferent to the rain, absorbed in incidents from the life of some goldfinch or sparrow. . . ."

Once Burroughs left, Florence and some of her friends kept the momentum going by running their own field trips, and Florence trained those who were interested in the fine techniques of bird-watching. Although Florence's four years as a special student at Smith ended that June, her club was continued by others for over a decade.

The satisfaction she gained from educating others about birds was transmitted into the beginnings of a writing career back at Homewood, where she continued to write articles about her bird observations for *Audubon Magazine*. Those articles became, in 1889, the crux of her first book, *Birds Through an Opera Glass*. Issued as a volume in Houghton Mifflin's *The Riverside Library for Young People*, it was a popular record of Florence's field work both at Smith College and on her home grounds, where she set out every day accompanied by her dogs to observe birds and their nests.

In her preface she explains that she wrote the book to "furnish hints that will enable not only young observers but also laymen to know the common birds they see about them." She included only the birds she observed for herself and hoped her readers would consist of "not merely those who can go to see for themselves" but also "the careworn indoor workers to whom I would bring a breath of the woods, pictures of sunlit fields, and a hint of the simple, childlike gladness, the peace and comfort that is offered us every day by these blessed winged messengers of nature."

She portrays herself gliding quietly through the woods, standing or sitting motionless for hours at a time, in an attempt to be invisible to the birds she is watching. In the case of the field-loving bobolinks, "I sit down in the grass, pull the timothy stems over my dress, make myself look as much as possible like a meadow, and keep one eye on the bobolinks, while appearing to be absorbed with an object on the other side." She followed a red-eyed vireo "into the edge of the woods where it builds its nest" and hid herself "under the spreading boughs of an old apple-tree in the corner of [a Northampton] orchard and waited to see what would come."

What came that fine May morning was a purple finch gathering nesting materials; the catbird, "who lived across the road by the bank of Mill River"; the singing male rose-breasted grosbeak, a "rainbow of warblers"; and, best of all, the golden-throated vireo—all of which landed above her head. On another day at home she watched an agitated female ovenbird while she sat on a log, trying to ignore the "incorrigible" mosquitoes, and she was finally rewarded by scaring up the hidden youngsters.

Although she talked about her own experiences, she also quoted other well-known naturalists—Henry Thoreau, William Brewster, Robert Ridgway, Thomas Nuttall, and John Burroughs. She even included Mary Treat's account of great-crested flycatchers from her book *Home Studies in Nature*. Florence ended her own book on the beatific notes of the hermit thrush. "Ever since I was a child, in the long summer evenings we have walked through the woods to 'William Miller Hill' to see the sunset and listen to the hermit's vespers. . . . Then from the wooded hillside it would come to us, filling the cool evening air with its tremulous yearning and pathos, and gathering up into short waves of song the silent music of the sunset— nature's benison of peace."

Birds remained Florence's first love, but like her mother and many other women of her day she also had a strong social conscience. Most winters she worked in New York City at one of Grace Dodge's Working Girls' Clubs. In the summer of 1891 she spent a month in Rockford, Illinois, in a summer school started for working girls as a branch of Jane Addams's Hull House, teaching a bird field class to factory workers. But both she and her mother suffered constantly from ill health and took frequent vacations in places with reputedly healthy climates — the West Coast, Lake Placid, New York, and finally Florida, where her mother died of tuberculosis.

Near the breaking point herself, having probably contracted tuberculosis from her mother, Florence headed for Utah, accompanied by her friend, bird author Olive Thorne Miller. There she wrote her charming *My Summer in a Mormon Village*. Although birds do figure in her story, she also describes the kind people she met, including Mormons, whom she portrays in an unusually fair-minded fashion for the times. Every day, Florence and Olive climbed a mountain path in the Wasatch Mountains to look for birds and wildflowers. Once on the mountainside, "the sunshine of the broad heavens, the unbroken horizon, and the great sweep of the landscape lines were a deep rest and a refreshment."

From Utah she went on alone to Palo Alto, California, where she attended Stanford University for six months, taking special interest in Dr. David Starr Jordan's course on evolution.

With the coming of spring in 1894, she left Stanford for Twin Oaks Valley in San Diego County, California, home of her Uncle Gustavus Merriam. There she stayed on his ranch and observed birds. She rode a saddle horse named Canello, and armed with opera glass, notebook, and Robert Ridgway's *Manual of North American Birds*, she set out every morning after breakfast to watch the birds of the valley, arriving back at noon. After eating she would take her campstool and stroll through the oaks at the head of the valley for a longer look at certain nests. This was followed by another short ride on Canello before sunset. The evenings were spent poring over Ridgway, trying to identify what she had seen, and writing up her notes. These eventually became her third book, *A-Birding on a Bronco*, in 1896. "I never spent a happier spring," she wrote. "The freedom and novelty of ranch life and the exhilaration of days spent in the saddle gave added zest to the delights of a new fauna. . . . In my small valley circuit of a mile and a half, I made the acquaintance of about seventy-five birds and without resort to the gun was able to name fifty-six of them."

After a final trip to the San Francisco Mountains near Flagstaff, Arizona, she returned east in the fall of 1895. Apparently cured of tuberculosis, she went to Washington, D.C., to live with her brother Hart. She plunged into writing her book. She followed that up in 1897 by helping to found and work for the Audubon Society of the District of Columbia, where she also conducted bird classes for teachers. In addition, she wrote still another book, *Birds of Village and Field*, for beginners so that they could learn to identify birds without shooting them. She acknowledged help from many people — Robert Ridgway, Frank M. Chapman, T. S. Palmer — as well as others less well known in birding circles. Those were amateurs, such as Mrs. E. B. Davenport of Brattleboro, Vermont, who noted seventy-nine species of birds in her orchard in a year; Mr. John H. Sage, who found ninety-nine nesting bird species within the limits of Portland, Connecticut; and Mr. H. E. Parkhurst, who had seen ninety-four species in Central Park. Obviously Florence had cultivated a wide network of both professional and amateur ornithologists, all of whom contributed their expertise to her book. Her brother Hart had helped her prepare the field color keys, and many of the bird illustrations were done by Ernest Thompson Seton, Louis Agassiz Fuertes, and John L. Ridgway.

Because she wrote the book for amateurs, she disregards scientific classification, arranging the birds according to their commonality, although she begins with the ruby-throated hummingbird (hardly the most common dooryard bird) and ends with the hermit thrush. Like *Birds Through an Opera Glass*, her descriptions are personal and chatty and rely heavily on accounts by other naturalists. In her introduction she explains where to find birds and how to watch them, counseling the reader "to go quietly to a good spot and sit down and wait for them to return and proceed with their business unconscious of spectators." To be a bird-watcher only four things are necessary — "a scrupulous conscience, unlimited patience, a notebook, and an opera glass." She also has a large section on the benefits of birds in insect control, a theme she carries through in her descriptions of individual species. The end of the book discusses the pleasures of feeding birds and providing nesting areas for them. She suggests erecting fences to keep out cats and posting your land against "gunners," birds' two worst enemies, she believed. An instant success with bird lovers from every spectrum of society, *Birds of Village and Field* was one of the first popular American bird guides.

In the last month of the last year of the old century, at age thirty-six, Florence Merriam became Florence Merriam Bailey. She married one of her brother's employees, field agent Vernon Bailey. Hart had known Vernon first as a teenager from pioneer Minnesota. Vernon had written Hart, who had just written and published *Mammals of the Adirondacks*, for help in identifying the animals he was trapping. Hart not only identified them for him but paid Vernon well for every specimen he sent him. When Hart was made head of the Division of Economic Ornithology and Mammalogy, predecessor of the U.S. Biological Survey, in 1887, he appointed Vernon to be a field agent at forty dollars a month. Since Florence had worked with her brother for years, she had known Vernon for a long time.

Florence and Vernon made a perfect team, collaborating together in the field. He specialized in mammals and their life zones, reptiles and plants, while she concentrated on bird life. For the next thirty years they spent most of their springs and summers in the West, camping in tents and collecting data for the Biological Survey, then returning each fall to their permanent home in Washington, D.C., to write up their experiences for books, articles, and government publications.

Their first trip, in April of 1900, was an arduous trek by carriage from Corpus Christi to Brownsville, Texas, a round trip expedition of 260 miles that took them seventeen days. They were accompanied by a "camp man," a local employee who drove the carriage, set up the tents, and cooked the meals, leaving Florence and Vernon free to observe, collect, take notes and most of all, enjoy. "One moonlight night we camped among huisache trees and slept on a bed of daisies, and after the moon set the sky grew fuller and fuller of stars till one could but marvel at their myriad host. Silent night! What infinite peace Nature offers her children," Florence wrote in her later account for *The Condor*, "Meeting Spring Half Way."

In the vicinity of Corpus Christi she was amazed at the abundance of bird species. "Such a cosmopolitan assembly of birds! Resident southerners jostling wings with passing northerners on their way from their southern wintering grounds to their northern breeding grounds." With great excitement she viewed her first scissor-tailed flycatcher — "a little less than astounding . . . with the skill of an acrobat, the dash and fire of a master spirit of the air." She also saw her first Cassin sparrow — "a blithe spirit, an embodiment of the deepest joy of life."

As soon as they stopped to camp, they set traps for small animals that they could catch, kill, and preserve as specimens. In the morning they first checked the traps and then searched for birds, pushing "through the dense cactus and thorn armored thicket, bending low to escape the thorny branches or shoving rigidly through with minds hardened to the pricks of needles, though with eyes out for coiled rattlesnakes." After thoroughly exploring an area, they set out again, wading up to their hubs in flood ponds, since they were no longer following any perceptible road.

On this trip they discovered a new species of air plant related to Spanish moss, which they carefully photographed along with "a solid acre of pink phlox, though alas, we could not reproduce the colors." Florence saw her first white-winged dove, and one day a north wind brought them a flock of forty white pelicans. Large numbers of hawks —Harris, Sennett, and Swainson—sat on telegraph poles. In oak motts (oases of large live oaks set above the sand belt), dozens of bird species congregated. They camped at an oak mott for two nights, spending their days "trapping, skinning and writing up notes among the bird colony of the oak mott."

They named their campsites for their outstanding wild creatures, hence they spent a night at Tarantula Camp, where they found two of the large spiders, one in a sleeping bag. "Perognathus Camp commemorated a little pocket mouse who, when a floor without holes was being selected for the sleeping bags, popped out of a closed door in the ground and ran into the tent, and, who, in searching for his door in the night tramped on our beds and finally got into a trap." They even had a Rattlesnake Camp! It was not an easy life, but one that Florence obviously thrived on.

Although Florence's numerous articles for *The Condor, The Auk*, and *Bird-Lore* continued to have the charm and personal tone of her youthful bird books, after her marriage to Vernon her books became more scientific. In 1902 Houghton Mifflin published her *Handbook of Birds of the Western United States* with thirty-three full-page plates by Louis Agassiz Fuertes and more than six hundred drawings. It was a companion volume to Frank Chapman's *Handbook of Birds of Eastern North America* and remained a standard manual for almost fifty years for western bird enthusiasts. No longer did she eschew scientific nomenclature and precise descriptions of plumages, distribution, and eggs. However, neither she nor Vernon, who wrote parts of it, could resist occasional lively accounts of the birds they were describing. Florence now accepted shooting birds for scientific, taxonomic purposes. "Collecting and Preparing Birds, Nests and Eggs," by Vernon Bailey, was part of the introductory material and included his declaration that "those who collect the birds, study them most deeply, and know them best, are doing the most for their protection." Clearly this was a book for the serious bird student.

She had based her book not only on other ornithologists' information but on her own trips west, both before and after her marriage. One of the least explored areas of the Southwest was New Mexico (not yet a state), and during the first six years of the twentieth century Vernon and Florence made six trips there. They spent their last field season in 1906 at a mountain camp 8,500 feet in the Mogollon Mountains, which Florence wrote about five years later in an article for *The Auk* called "A Drop of Four Thousand Feet." It was the middle of October and chilly, so they pitched their tents "on the warm slope of the canyon under the yellow pines, laying logs against the outside walls of the tent to keep out the wind."

It was an ideal place to camp, because the birds had gathered in the gulch to spend the winter. They collected every subspecies of junco they found — slate-colored, intermediate, Montana, pink-sided, Ridgway's, and gray-headed — representatives of nearly every resident, migrant, or wandering junco in the Mogollons. They also set out a line of mammal traps in that same winding gulch of Willow Creek and one morning had twenty-four specimens, including a shrew and various small mice and wood rats. A pair of spotted owls called every night; large flocks of pine siskins foraged among the spruce and alders by day. At 10,500 feet they discovered an Alpine three-toed woodpecker and at 11,000 feet Vernon shot a Cassin's finch.

The weather grew colder day by day, the water froze in their pails, and one morning they awoke to snow. While Vernon ran a zone line to the top of the 11,000-foot peak, Florence stayed down in camp trying to write up notes in front of a blazing fire. At last a threatening second storm drove them out. They knew that if they were snowed in — a very real possibility at that elevation — they might not get out. They broke camp in a cold rain and made an arduous two-day trek that finally took them down to 5,000 feet at the base of the Mogollons and back into late summer, where grasshoppers still chirped. "We had left the snowy Canadian mountains deserted by all but a few of the hardier birds and by our four thousand foot drop, paralleling the vertical migration, had come down into the warm Sonoran Valley where the weeds were still full of seeds and the trees of berries, and birds were gathered in happy throngs," Florence wrote. As usual, she had delighted in both the snowy mountains and the warm valley, always finding plenty of wildlife to keep her pen busy.

In 1908 Florence was honored when Joseph Grinnell, Annie Alexander's friend, named a subspecies after her — *Parus gambeli baileyae*

19.   Florence Merriam Bailey and Vernon Bailey camping in the Southwest.
*Courtesy Smithsonian Institution*

—a chickadee from the higher mountains of southern California. In her *Handbook*, she calls the subspecies *Parus gambeli Ridgway* "an unsuspicious little friend, most pleasant to meet in the dark coniferous forests, always ready with a cheery word," and she told Grinnell that "*Parus* has always been one of my favorite birds" when thanking him for his recognition of her work.

Year after year the Baileys continued to explore. While in the Pacific Northwest with Vernon in the summer of 1914, Florence stayed in the home of a carpenter, his wife, and small daughter in Oregon for several weeks, following birds through the dense spruce and hemlock forests, sitting in clearings on her campstool watching tree swallows at their nest, or gazing out the windows of the carpenter's home whose open grounds were crowded with nesting species. A large bracken field beyond the garden was also a favorite spot for sitting and observing rufous hummingbirds and russet-backed thrushes and "with the bracken closing me in, the tips of the triangular fronds uncurling over my head, I spent many pleasant hours watching the feathered passers-by. . . . But not until one Sunday morning when I was sitting quietly in the fern field, did I really hear the wonderful song. Then through the clear air, each single, long-swelling note came down from the ridge above like the peal of a golden bell . . . the voice of the varied thrush seems the voice of one who has attained." Florence had finally heard a songster that outdid even her beloved hermit thrush.

In 1918 the Government Printing Office issued *Wild Animals of Glacier National Park—The Mammals* by Vernon Bailey and *The Birds* by Florence Merriam Bailey. Once again Florence combined good, solid, scientific information with poetic descriptions of birds, such as the "gentle upland plover, whose sweet bubbling notes from the sky are heard less and less as the years pass."

Early 1921 found them in the Santa Rita Mountains of Arizona, eager to catch the beginning of spring migration, which started, according to Florence's account in *The Auk*, on March 5, with the arrival of a northern violet-green swallow. Once spring was in full swing, it snowed, driving at least one canyon towhee into their tent. The cold also brought Florence two new birds—the buff-breasted flycatcher and the Coues' flycatcher. Seeing two new birds in one day caused her to walk down the road and think over her blessings, despite temperatures in the range of thirty-five to forty-one degrees Fahrenheit. Although she was then fifty-eight years old, her enthusiasm for camping under arduous circumstances was undiminished. That same year Smith College recognized its distinguished alumna and at last awarded its "special student" a bachelor's degree.

Then came her monumental work, the *Birds of New Mexico*, written, she confided to ornithologist Witmer Stone, to "rouse a nature interest in the state." As always she was concerned with both the "poor student, unable to afford more than one book," for whom she hoped she had included enough technical material, and "the others—sportsmen, men, women and children." For them she had "combed the recent popular material—largely in *The Auk* and *The Condor*—for different angles of interest, throwing in pictures and colored plates to complete the work." She concludes humbly, "My shortcomings are known perhaps best by me. But that is what I have been working for—to help the people of the state."

Apparently the A.O.U. approved of her efforts, since they made her a fellow the following year and awarded her the Brewster Medal at the Forty-ninth Annual Meeting two years later in Michigan. The medal had been established in 1919 by friends of ornithologist William Brewster; since then, it has been awarded biennially to the author of the most important work relating to the birds of the Western Hemisphere published during the preceding six years.

As the years passed, the Baileys continued to travel together—1929 in the Grand Canyon, 1930 on the flood bottom of the Mississippi

Wild Life Refuge—and in 1933 they collaborated on *Cave Life of Kentucky.* But they always returned to the same home on Kalorama Road in Washington, D.C., that they had built shortly after their marriage.

"It was," as one friend put it, "the home of two devoted naturalists—devoted to Nature and to each other—and every room, every nook and corner, was a testimonial to that devotion—the inviting library and living room on the second floor filled with books and pictures, with warmth and welcome." By all accounts their marriage was an idyllic one—working together, yet separately on their individual projects, collaborating when they could, and mutually supporting each other's efforts. This type of egalitarian relationship was so unusual for the times that numerous people commented on it.

Still they kept going—in 1936 they rode across the continent as passengers in one of three cars, well-supplied with cameras, and they camped or slept in automobile camps en route. Although the conditions were not quite as rugged as their early expeditions, they continued to enjoy the places they visited—the fossil forests of New Mexico and Arizona, the prehistoric ruins of Mesa Verde, and Taos. They ended their trip in California in the cabin where forty years ago Florence had written *A-Birding on a Bronco.* For Florence her life had come almost full circle.

She was by then Dr. Florence Merriam Bailey, recipient of an honorary LL.D. degree from the University of New Mexico, again because of her *Birds of New Mexico.* She had one more major work to finish, *Among the Birds in the Grand Canyon Country,* published in 1939 in her seventy-sixth year. She traveled to the North Country with Vernon one summer, sleeping out under the stars again, and they spent their last summer together back in her home country of northern New York state. There they lived outside under the sky day and night, where one night they had a spectacular view of the aurora borealis.

In June 1942 Vernon passed away, and for the last six years of her life Florence lived quietly in her home, taking vitamins and daily walks. The end came in 1948 when she died of myocardial degeneration at the age of eighty-five. By then she had been forgotten by most of the people who had read her books and articles so eagerly. Yet no woman and very few men had ever known so much about all the birds of the United States, and none had tried as hard as Florence to teach everyone—man, woman, and child—about the joys of watching birds and the beauty of the natural world.

# Althea Rosina Sherman

## ORNITHOLOGIST OF AN IOWA DOORYARD

THE ORNITHOLOGIST from National, Iowa, was notorious for her biting wit, her implacable battle against house wrens, and her chimney swift tower. Althea Rosina Sherman, born in 1854 in the first frame house on the Iowa prairie north of Dubuque, had four sisters and one brother. Her parents were pioneers who had trekked west from New York state to Prairie du Chien, Wisconsin, in 1843 and had then moved on across the Mississippi River to Iowa two years later.

Her father, Mark, was a cobbler and investor in farm mortgages, and her mother, Melissa, was a pioneer mother with strong Victorian beliefs. They must have been unusual people for their time and place, since they sent all their surviving children off to college. Their son, Mark, became a lawyer, two daughters were medical doctors, and Althea was an artist-teacher, at least for the first twenty years of her adult life.

She received both a bachelor's and master's degree from Oberlin College and remained a proud and loyal alumna all her life. From there she went on to teach in a country school for a few years, making a deep impression on at least one former student, who remembered her forty years later. "There was never another teacher like her. She took us into the woods . . . showed us how flowers grow; how seeds ripen; how leaves are constructed and how they breathe; how to know trees by the bark."

However, Althea's burning desire, at least as a young woman, was to be an artist, so she gave up her general teaching and went back to school, first at the Art Institute in Chicago and then to the Art Student's League in New York City. From 1882 to 1895 she taught art at a number of places, including Carleton College in Minnesota and in the city schools of Tacoma, Washington, as a supervisor of drawing.

But in 1895 she was called back home to tend her ailing parents. Her father died the following year, her mother in 1902. Dr. Emily Amelia, her older unmarried sister, returned to the homestead that same year to practice rural medicine, horse-and-buggy style. For better or worse, the two sisters lived together there for the rest of their lives. To hear Althea tell it, it was mostly for worse; Amelia, as she preferred to be called, was as tightfisted as her father had been. He had left them both a substantial income, but while Amelia pinched every penny, Althea was known for her generosity to educational, religious, and charitable institutions.

Althea had continued to take art lessons off and on while she had tended her parents, and once she was freed of that responsibility, she began painting more and more. But the landscapes and still lifes were gradually supplanted by charming portraits of the birds she had started to observe. Whenever she had a chance, she would watch the bird life in the acre around her home grounds and in an adjoining pasture and swamp.

Much of her time was taken up with mundane tasks, such as cleaning a smoking stove, baking, picking berries, tending a huge garden, and generally keeping up a large home without running water or an efficient heating system. Amelia, however, "that lazy, shirking, domineering miser," as Althea called her in a letter to ornithologist Margaret Morse Nice, frequently "dons her most charming mood and tongue-lashings in order to *do* nothing" herself.

Apparently Althea never outwardly showed her resentment as housewife to Amelia's more masculine role of chief breadwinner. All Althea's feelings about those she believed had wronged her were revealed in letters and journals. To the world she appeared friendly, optimistic, and enthusiastic, a contrast to the gloomy and doom-saying Amelia. Neighbors and friends respected Amelia for being a wonderful, caring doctor, which she was, and Althea for her artistic talents, bird studies, and housekeeping and cooking abilities. There is no doubt that Amelia often helped Althea, at least with her bird studies, and could identify the various species with an unerring ear as well as eye. Althea, whose hearing diminished rapidly as she grew older, often relied on her sister's sharper ears to pick up the first calls of returning birds each spring.

They lived in a white New England–style home with green shutters. Behind some of those shutters lived bats, which Althea studied for fourteen summers. Vernon Bailey and his wife, Florence, visited Althea one summer; he came to study her little brown bats, while Florence came to see Althea's flicker houses attached to the large old barn. After encouragement from Vernon, Althea wrote about the bats, in her sole article on mammals for the *Journal of Mammalogy*.

Of all the thirty-eight years she spent in bird study and of all the species she observed at great length—screech owls, eastern phoebes, red-winged blackbirds, gray catbirds, brown thrashers, American robins, alder flycatchers, sora rails, house wrens, chimney swifts, ruby-throated hummingbirds, American kestrels—the flickers were her favorites. She called them the "species that afforded me more hours of pleasure than any other bird," in a 1933 letter to Dr. Shaver. To Margaret Morse Nice she said, "If I should have only one family of birds saved from total destruction I should chose [sic] the Woodpecker, since they have given me more pleasure than any other."

In fact, her first long published study on one bird species was devoted to the flicker. It was called "At the Sign of the Northern Flicker," and it appeared in the *Wilson Bulletin* in 1910. Although flickers had been living in a hole in the Sherman barn since 1897, Althea began her detailed studies in 1908, when she took wooden soap boxes and attached them inside the barn wall behind three flicker holes. On the eight-by-twelve-inch floor of each box she spread a covering of excelsior. In the tops of the boxes she drilled an observation hole to let her look down into the eighteen-inch-deep "nest" she had made. Near the bottom of the nests she drilled a large second hole, through which she could reach in to remove nestlings for weighing, painting, and photographing when she needed. A trap door hid that hole from the flickers.

Her many hours of observation and meticulous notes were later appreciated by Arthur Cleveland Bent when he wrote his *Life Histories of North American Birds* series. Using her "very thorough studies," he realized that her statement on the incubation time for flicker eggs, eleven to twelve days, corrected earlier work by other ornithologists stating fourteen to sixteen days. Edward Forbush, whose *Birds of Massachusetts* was considered a classic work in ornithology, was not respected by Althea. His "ignorant trash" regarding flickers, she told one friend, was probably caused by his "Massachusetts complex," which "always prevented him from reading anything printed west of the Alleghany [sic] Mountains. Like many of his neighbors . . . probably he thought . . . none but Indians live there."

Bent, however, did read widely and accepted her incubation figures as well as much of her other original material regarding flickers.

A FLICKER COURTSHIP

20.  A flicker courtship, by Althea Sherman. *Courtesy Fred Pierce*

He used her "very good description of the naked and blind nestlings" verbatim and quoted a number of her careful observations of the young.

Her paintings of young flickers were also attractive and accurate, for she continued her artwork while she observed. A catbird in its nest, four young phoebes roosting, a chimney swift on its nest, three young brown thrashers — year by year her portfolio and her reputation grew. In 1922 she was asked to exhibit her bird paintings at the American Ornithologists' Union's annual meeting in Chicago. How pleased she must have been when America's foremost bird painter, Louis Agassiz Fuertes, told her that her brown thrasher had more life and personality than any bird he had ever painted.

Certainly she had a way of portraying some of her favorite songbirds with great charm and affection. But she was, unfortunately, part of the old, judgmental school of natural history, assessing good and evil in human terms, a not uncommon malady among some ornithologists even today. The "good" birds were prey, the "bad" ones predators or pest species. Her list of those she actively opposed included house sparrows, bronzed grackles, European starlings, house wrens, screech owls, ring-necked pheasants, and American kestrels — all birds that she had carefully observed and found wanting.

The screech owls moved into a box she had built into her blind down by a swampy area, where she had planned to observe migrating birds. Once the owls settled in, she visited the blind several times a day and at least once an hour or two after dusk. She also made long night watches — one until 2:30 A.M., a second lasting until 3:00 A.M., and a third from 12:00 to 1:00 A.M. From these visits, she discovered "verily, a sitting screech owl is not a lively companion for the still watches of the night."

Again Bent respected the "careful observations of Miss Althea R. Sherman," quoting her figures on egg-laying and incubation and her description of nestling plumage and habits. Althea, though, was more concerned about what screech owls ate. To her distress she discovered that song sparrows and juncos were favorite foods, as well as goldfinches, vesper, savannah, white-throated, tree, chipping, field, and swamp sparrows. Twenty percent of their sustenance was gained from songbirds, and so Althea made her decision. "Their ravages were so great that it was decided if we desired a little bird paradise where all good birds were welcome through the summer time there screech owls could not be encouraged to remain." Her solution was to give away the owlets as pets, but after that experience she became judge and jury where screech owls were concerned, killing three of

21.  Catbird on nest, by Althea Sherman. *Courtesy Fred Pierce*

them when she discovered that they had killed a family of northern orioles.

Althea's "Acre of Birds," as she called the area around her home where she did her observing, was definitely managed. House sparrows were killed, dressed and fed to her cats, house wrens were shot by neighbor boys she enlisted and supplied with an air gun, rabbits and woodchucks were trapped and removed, and she urged her neighbors to shoot ring-necked pheasants "that are filling our acres in the township. It is an outrage, a crime to breed this pest on valuable Iowa land, then suffer the rabble to run over us and shoot this game. I have a big fight on hand, but I mean to fight." Even naturalist-writer Aldo Leopold fell under suspicion, "that minion of the diabolical work of the ammunition makers," who "had been in this region" in 1932 "under the guise of restoring the prairie chicken and bobwhite" and was instead "working for the spread of the ring-necked pheasant."

Though unreasonable, judgmental, prejudiced, narrow-minded, and sometimes even vindictive, Althea Sherman did remarkable work, driven to learn all she could about birds. There is no doubt that she loved the outdoors, even though her terms were strict. "The woods," she wrote, "are always alluring and I often spend a day of unalloyed pleasure there."

Althea also loved her Iowa homestead. She believed Iowa a "splendid state to be born in and to study its birds, especially if one sticks to country living." She insisted that her yard was not a garden but an orchard, mostly of plum trees, because birds liked to nest in them. There were apple trees, shade trees, mulberry, gooseberry, raspberry, and elderberry bushes. One visitor called it "a tangle of bushes and native and cultivated trees." Althea admitted that it was run-down, but it was a place the birds liked. She attributed the number of species she had identified over the years (162) to its location near the watershed between the Mississippi and Turkey rivers. As the farmers plowed up the land, even the marshy areas, bird diversity decreased; Althea, by keeping her land as wild as possible and by gradually buying up nearby abandoned lots, created an oasis for birds.

One source of joy was a marshy area three hundred feet from the house, where she built a wooden blind on posts to observe the marsh birds, particularly rails. The blind had a door on its east end and a window on each of its other sides. That forty-six-inch square blind lasted twenty years, and over that time she watched 110 species of birds from it. Althea estimated she had spent two hundred to three hundred hours studying rails—far more time than other people, she asserted. Sora, king, and Virginia rails were all observed, but soras were the common species. In 1909 they nested in her marsh after a courtship that reminded her of boys playing leapfrog. "As one sora stood motionless another one jumped over it; the jumping bird then stood while the other sora leaped over it and took its place about eighteen inches in advance of its partner while another jump was made."

That same blind attracted the screech owl family the following year, and in 1912 American kestrels or sparrow hawks, as they were then called, moved into the box. With agony of mind Althea faced her dilemma. Yet her scientific curiosity, as always, won out over her fears for her "harmless, little feathered friends," and she settled down to make still another outstanding study of a nesting species. She darkened the windows of the blind and observed them through a peephole sixteen inches from where the female kestrel brooded. Day by day she weighed the eggs and then the birds. Long hours were spent "standing noiselessly upon a box with head scraping the roof of the blind." Not an easy task even at first, later "it became almost insupportable with the heat of an afternoon sun beating upon the blind, and with the stench from a nest whose walls were thickly encrusted with excrements."

Facing the question again of what they ate and fed their young, she found one scientific paper that claimed 18 percent of their food consisted of songbirds. Reasoning that the same percentage had applied to screech owls and that despite it, some small birds had survived, she decided to give the kestrels a trial. She also helped them along by feeding the young thirty-three dead house sparrows.

Mostly they ate fledglings just out of the nest, she discovered, along with ground squirrels and meadow mice. And "sparrow hawk" seemed an apt name as far as their favorite birds were concerned. But despite her dislike of the fact that they consumed sparrows, she let them stay around the rest of the season. *The Auk* published her "The Nest Life of the Sparrow Hawk," and once again Bent quoted her account at length in his own work.

Althea's life was not all drudgery in the kitchen and bird observation outside. She was a member of fifteen scientific societies, including the American Association for the Advancement of Science, the Wilson Ornithological Club, the National Audubon Society, the Biological Society of Washington, and the American Ornithologists' Union, although she had only bitter words about the A.O.U. She wrote to Nice, "I have said and believe it, that no woman will ever be made a Fellow of A.O.U. . . . No, man nature must change before a woman is a Fellow."

She also subscribed to twenty-six magazines, many related to her interest in nature, but others, including the *Mississippi Valley Historical Review, Wisconsin Archaeologist,* and the *Journal of History and Politics,* reflected a wider world view. In her notebooks she mentions attending an Equal Suffrage meeting at the schoolhouse in May, 1916. She was the first woman, along with a neighbor who accompanied her, to be entertained at the Explorers Club in New York City in 1919.

Althea also gave talks about her bird work; locally, she spoke on "Our Birds and Ourselves" at a Farmersburg school program and read her "Birds Close at Hand" in Elkader High School, and nationally she was invited to speak on "Birds of an Iowa Dooryard" in front of the esteemed Linnaean Society of New York. Althea was no stay-at-home. Whenever she could get the money she attended meetings as far south as Saint Louis and as far north as Boston. She often went to Chicago, particularly to read and study in the excellent John Crerar Library, which specialized in natural history. When she visited New York City she went to the American Museum of Natural History and observed birds in city parks and on the then-bucolic Staten Island.

Probably the most exciting time in her life occurred from November 7, 1913, until August 26, 1914, when she took her long-anticipated trip around the world. It was unfortunately curtailed by the advent of World War I, but during those ten months she visited twenty countries in Europe, North Africa, and parts of southern Asia. When she returned she wrote four articles about her bird observations there for the *Wilson Bulletin*. The first, "Birds by the Wayside in Europe, Asia, and Africa," mostly recounted her time in India, which she crossed twice by railroad and mail train. Sometimes she used rickshaws as conveyances, although when she reached the village of Mount Abu, she found a better mode of travel. "It suited my purpose better to go afoot and alone in the neighborhood of the village and to confine the rides to two half days. I found the rickshaw as heavy as a buggy, and when empty it was hard to pull up hill, therefore I walked on the upgrades and let the rickshaw boys draw me when the road was level or down hill." She regularly arose each morning at dawn and observed birds for two hours before breakfast.

In Egypt she spent five weeks traveling by train, boat, carriage, hand cart, and donkey, "none of which yielded the satisfaction in bird viewing that was experienced on the few occasions when I could go on foot and alone," she wrote in "Birds by the Wayside in Egypt and Nubia." She finished her accounts in Palestine, where she went from Jaffa to Constantinople, and Greece, which she had been wanting to visit for over forty years. Her articles discussed in detail many of the birds she saw and proved that she was familiar with many foreign species through prior reading on the subject. By then World War I had begun, and her ship was forced to dodge German submarines as it carried her prematurely back to the United States.

Once she reached her Iowa acres, she launched her most impressive and innovative bird study. Hiring a local contractor, she laid out her plans for building a chimney swift tower. Three carpenters

22. Althea Sherman (left) and her sister Amelia show Althea's chimney swift
tower to visiting schoolchildren. *Courtesy Fred Pierce*

constructed the original structure in 1915. Made of white clapboards to match the house, it was nine feet square and twenty-eight feet tall. An artificial chimney of rough pine was built inside, two feet square and extending fourteen feet down into the tower. A door opened into the chimney, and a built-in ladder reached to the top so that the chimney could be opened in the spring before the chimney swifts arrived and closed in fall after they left. Auger holes on two sides served as peepholes, while the other two sides had windows with frames that met in an obtuse angle. This left a space jutting into the chimney where Althea could put her head and have a clear view through glass both to the bottom and the top of the chimney without startling the birds. At night a paper screen was placed over the window with a lamp behind it, so Althea could still watch the birds' activity.

It took three years before chimney swifts discovered the tower, but in the summer of 1918 the first chimney swift nest was built. Luckily the swifts located the nest in a favorable viewing spot just under the right hand corner of the window, fifteen inches from Althea's observing eyes. In her usual thorough way she recorded every facet of the nesting, hatching, and raising of chimney swifts. She was particularly interested in proving that the young chimney swifts were not fed at night, and after many evenings of watching and seeing no feeding activity, she was certain that the noises in the chimney at night were caused by the birds shifting their positions.

She also found that both parents incubated the eggs, and one year she observed a third, unmated bird help out with the domestic chores for the entire season. To her delight, the young swifts were never quarrelsome; in fact, "no evil has been detected in its relations with its own or with other species." Therefore, Althea declared, the chimney swift should be the "bird that properly might be chosen as the emblem of peace."

Year after year her observations continued. In 1928, when she was seventy-four years old, she made four hundred visits to the chimney to observe the longest occupancy the birds had ever made — 130 days. She estimated she had climbed twelve thousand steps throughout the season to reach her observation window. In addition, she had taken 133 visitors to see the swifts and written thirty-two pages of notes.

In 1928 ornithologists T. C. Stephens and William Youngworth made a visit to the Sherman homestead, where they camped outside overnight in their umbrella tent beside the chimney swift tower. Althea had insisted they take an upstairs room, but Stephens, an old friend, knew that she was merely being polite. "The sisters," he informed Youngworth, "did not like to entertain menfolk under their roof for the night." That moral issue settled to the Sherman sisters' satisfaction, they accompanied the men to an ice cream social at the nearby fairgrounds. Later they visited the chimney swift tower and were given a tour of all the other bird nests and nesting boxes in the yard. Then Althea showed them her bird paintings and sketches and told them just how she had discovered her subjects. Despite her obvious pride in her paintings, it was her bird notebooks she was most anxious about. She wanted very much to complete them for publishing.

By then she was suffering from arthritis, although her domestic work load never lightened. When she finally completed her chimney swift studies in 1936, she had filled four hundred notebook pages, which was only a small part of her total output. It proved to be too complex for an eighty-five-year-old woman, who still had to draw fresh water from a windlass well every day, to organize coherently. So the chimney swift notes were not published during her lifetime, and Bent did his chimney swift article without the benefit of her research.

He did, however, make passing reference to her indictment of house wrens, the battle that split bird lovers into factions. In 1925 three articles by Althea on the subject appeared. *Bird-Lore* entitled its piece, "The Problem of the House Wren," and the *Wilson Bulletin* published "Down with the House Wren Boxes," followed by "Additional Evidence Against the House Wren."

It was not the house wren she opposed but the artificially high numbers that were thriving because every backyard bird lover had been erecting house wren boxes. House wrens, she wrote, were far more destructive to songbirds than house sparrows. The males spent much of their time entering the nests of other birds, piercing their eggs, and then throwing them out of the nest. Such depredations had caused a great decline of songbirds in many places.

Furthermore, she cited renowned ornithologist Robert Ridgway and other prominent experts who had observed and commented on the house wren's destructive practices. She exhorted people not to kill house wrens but to tear down all the nesting boxes and let the population dwindle to a reasonable number. But she began poisoning them to redress the balance.

Althea's battle against the well-loved "Jenny Wren," who sings so beautifully, was uphill at best. Even Alfred Otto Gross, who contributed the chapter on house wrens to the Bent series, called her stand against the wren a venomous one and declared that "Miss Sherman's paper stimulated the writing of many of the articles for and against the wren that followed." Naturally, Althea took every attack as a personal affront. "Of course Bighead Baldwin was there running over the sewer spout about his lousy wrens," she wrote to Nice. "Did he attack me in his usual shyster lawyer role in his defense of the wren?"

As part of her scorn toward those she called "bird lovers" as opposed to ornithologists, she wrote a bitter, sarcastic paper, "The Old Ornithology and the New," comparing the scientific work of ornithologists to the "bird talks" of uninformed bird lovers. Undoubtedly her indictment of their ignorance was not exaggerated, because the "nature fakers" were still writing the same incredible "twaddle" that T. R. Roosevelt had objected to several decades earlier, including, in Althea's opinion, Gene Stratton Porter, who wrote "sentimental trash."

But the "scientific approach" Althea advocated appalled the scientists as well as the sentimentalists. Only the good birds were to be "loved and protected." Those not fitting her idea of good – the predators and pests – were to be eliminated. Certainly Althea never saw that her own feelings toward birds were equally sentimental. She was a member of the "old ornithology," along with William Brewster, whose scientific work she admired. Unfortunately, after her house wren articles, she wrote only short bird notes for the rest of her publishing career, and in 1933 even those notes stopped.

Old age and old ideas conspired in the end to stem the outflow of excellent bird studies from her pen. Although she outlived her sister Amelia by five years, dying alone in the old house in 1943, she never accomplished her fondest dream – to write a book about all she had learned and seen over her remarkable lifetime. But she did the next best thing. In her will she left $7,500 to publish "a book as a monument to the memory of Testatrix and as a means of making available to the public some of the literary efforts and scientific accomplishments of Testatrix. . . ."

In 1952 *Birds of an Iowa Dooryard* by Althea R. Sherman was published. Her friend Fred J. Pierce had labored long and hard through her sixty handwritten notebooks to produce the work, and Margaret Morse Nice helped publicize it. However, only fifteen hundred copies were sold of this work by a woman whom Canadian naturalist Louise de Kirilene Lawrence called "a wonderful naturalist and bird student [with an] amazing originality of methods, [a] meticulousness in her research, [and a] grandiose sense of humor!"

And indeed she was all that Lawrence said. Although her old-fashioned Victorian morality toward birds has long been replaced, there is no doubt she was sincerely motivated by her belief that in

23. Althea Sherman in her backyard, National, Iowa. *Courtesy Fred Pierce*

birds "we see reflections of human conduct. It is this mirroring of our own natures in a dim way that awakens our interest in them." For all her scientific studies, it was her emotions that ruled her conduct. The wonder of it all is that even so, what she observed and recorded of bird life has never been contradicted by contemporary ornithologists.

# Cordelia Stanwood

## BIRD WOMAN OF ELLSWORTH

"I LIE UNDER A BIG PINE and listen to the black-throated green warbler that sings and feeds among its branches, to the purple finch that soars in an ecstasy of song. I feel rested, soothed, delighted with the world and myself." Cordelia Stanwood wrote this in her field notebook on May 11, 1913. She was forty-eight years old then and had finally found the peace of mind she had been searching for over the years. She had also rediscovered the delight in the outdoors she had had as a child, and she had made a new career for herself based on it. Her first published article on bird behavior had appeared in *Bird-Lore* the previous year and had already received some notice in the ornithological world.

Cordelia Stanwood was born on August 1, 1865. Her home was a mile and a half from the picturesque town of Ellsworth, Maine, and included forty acres of surrounding fields, woods, and wetlands.

She was the eldest child of a self-sufficient Yankee sea captain and a young woman from Cape Breton Island, Nova Scotia. Her father had originally built their home during his bachelor days to house his widowed mother and an assortment of sisters and their families. By the time he married, in his mid-thirties, only his mother remained to live with his own fast-expanding family of four daughters and one son. Her grandmother Stanwood taught Cordelia the traditional womanly crafts of sewing and knitting, and her mother saw to her instruction in reading. Cordelia was what they called a "delicate" child, and so was not sent to school very often.

However, she must have shown a rare aptitude for learning. When she was fourteen years old, the wealthy and childless aunt she had been named for invited Cordelia to come live with her and her husband, Oliver, in Providence, Rhode Island, so that she could attend good, city schools. Cordelia was ecstatic. "I would have crawled on my hands and knees to go to school if it were necessary," she wrote in her unpublished autobiography over fifty years later.

By all accounts she adjusted quickly to the change in environment. Her Aunt Cordelia and Uncle Oliver moved in the highest social circles of Providence. They belonged to the First Baptist Church, founded by Roger Williams and the oldest church in Rhode Island. Their large house was beautifully furnished with antiques; "everything about the house bespoke intelligence," Cordelia wrote. She was dressed in the latest fashion by her aunt, who not only chose the clothes she wore but also set up the high moral standards Cordelia followed.

Cordelia was enrolled in a grammar school, where she quickly moved to the top of the class. At the Girls' High School of Providence she graduated sixth in a class of sixty, and although her shy nature made it difficult for her to cultivate close friends, she did have at least one, Anna Louise Evans. In addition, she had warm contacts with several teachers whom she admired.

She was twenty-one when she finished obtaining an excellent classical education in high school. A year later she graduated from the Providence Training School for Teachers and began her teaching career at the Messer Street Training School by instructing young children. Cordelia loved children, and apparently the feeling was mutual. School was frequently called off during snowstorms by the blowing of a whistle, but she was always at school before the whistle sounded. Her pupils found out about this and cajoled their parents into packing a lunch for them and hiring a taxi so that they could go and play school with Cordelia.

Such a gifted teacher did not go unremarked, and after four years, Cordelia was asked to be a critic teacher. She spent a summer at Martha's Vineyard attending school, in order to do a good job as a critic. It was Martha's Vineyard where she first heard Henry T. Bailey, the young and talented supervisor of drawing in Massachusetts, give a lecture. Friends, who had heard the charismatic teacher speak, persuaded her to go with them. She too fell under his spell as "he lectured and sketched botanical drawings on the blackboard in such a fascinating [way] that we wished he would never stop."

Thus began a friendship that was to have a number of ramifications in Cordelia's life. She had never, as far as anyone knew, had a romantic attachment. Her sisters later claimed that anyone she brought to her aunt's home would promptly be compared to Uncle

Oliver and found wanting. Henry T. Bailey would probably have passed the most stringent scrutiny except for one thing. He was already married, and in those rigid Victorian days, a highly principled woman like Cordelia would not have dreamed of coveting another woman's husband. He did become a friend, however, who was genuinely impressed by her talents and determined to help and advise her.

By 1892 her yearly salary as a principal and teacher was only $650, and Bailey suggested that she attend Normal Arts School in Boston and attain qualification as a drawing teacher. At that time, drawing teachers were scarce, and as a result they were paid yearly salaries of $1500. Even though Cordelia ranked first in a class of one hundred at art school, there were no jobs available by the time she finished. She had to swallow her pride (and her ambition) and return to teaching in Providence at a salary cut back to $600.

For the next ten years she went restlessly from teaching job to teaching job, always getting good recommendations but very little satisfaction or recompense for her work. Once, after two years as a training teacher in Springfield, Massachusetts, she was fired by a friend, Miss Fraser, who had originally begged her to take the job. No reason was given for the dismissal, although another friend, Henry's sister, told Cordelia that Henry attributed her firing to jealousy on the part of Miss Fraser.

Confused and upset by this reversal, Cordelia returned to Providence and Aunt Cordelia, but Henry quickly arranged a job for her in Greenfield, Massachusetts. She even gained a slight raise, to $750. It was in Greenfield where Cordelia began to rediscover the outdoor world of her childhood. In the company of a school board member, Miss Nims, who had formerly taught botany and English, she made frequent excursions to see the local wildflowers and birds.

Despite her happiness in Greenfield among people whom she called "pure gold," she wanted to continue taking art lessons near Boston, and so she resigned and took another position in the Boston suburb of Brookline. Her next attempt at a change was a job in a private school in Poughkeepsie, New York, where she taught mostly the children of Vassar College professors. The intellectual atmosphere there seemed to appeal to her, and the opportunity to hear both Ernest Thompson Seton and John Burroughs, the two most famous naturalist-writers of their day, was exciting. Despite this, when Henry asked her, in 1901, to take charge of the drawing classes in the Braintree and Plymouth, Massachusetts, schools, she agreed. Then, "while engaged in this work, nervous prostration overcame me and after seventeen years of teaching, I fled to the woods."

She claimed that the job, with its continual traveling from school to school, had been too much for her and that Aunt Cordelia had compelled her to go home to Maine. Unfortunately, except for her rather sketchy and incomplete attempts to write an autobiography, very little is really known about why she broke down. Her biographer, Chandler S. Richmond, believes it was caused by frustration and repression. Whether this was a result of teaching disappointments or something deeper, such as an inadmissable and unrequited love for Bailey, is hard to say. Cordelia kept no diary of her thoughts, and even if she had, a woman with her deeply Victorian beliefs would hardly have confessed to illicit feelings for a married man.

After a short stay in a sanatorium in Jamaica Plain, Massachusetts, she went home to Maine a broken woman. Her youth was gone, sacrificed on the altar of teaching, and the young girl who had hoped to help her family at home with money from her work had become an unemployed, middle-aged woman, forced to accept their help instead. But they didn't know what to do for the distraught stranger she had become. Her favorite sister, Maude, was dead. Her other sisters, Idella and Maria, were married and gone. Only her father, home from the sea, her mother, and her unsympathetic younger brother, Harry, were left.

The males threw up their hands at the hysterical, highly intelligent woman who had invaded the household, but her mother tried to understand and over the years became her closest friend. Whenever Cordelia had screaming fits, her mother called the local doctor, who always came and administered a sedative, but it was Cordelia who slowly cured herself.

It took two long years of home and hearth before Cordelia regained her balance. In 1906 she began her remarkable field notebooks that were to chronicle the next fifty years of her outdoor work. In those notebooks she not only recorded her observations, but also her feelings, at least toward nature and the natural world. At last she had found her real calling—her years of teaching had merely been a prelude.

She began by observing the birds along the path to Boiling Spring, where she went to draw water each day. There at the spring she would often sit and watch the birds that came to drink, to bathe, and sometimes just to sing.

The chorus rallied her spirits, and in the early years of her notebook she spent much of her time attempting to describe individual bird songs and calls. Chickadees had a song "like a paean of victory, sura-suree, sura-suree," and northern juncos "a liquid trill that sounded like water gurgling over hidden pebbles." A purple finch, she said,

24. Cordelia Stanwood sitting in the woods. *Courtesy Stanwood Wildlife Sanctuary, Ellsworth, Maine*

sings "as if in ecstasy, as if it would be a joy to float and float and sing forever, but finally comes down quivering into the treetops," and "the song of the winter wren is high, liquid, wild."

Listening to purple finches "put me in a frame of mind that was almost ecstatic," and it is apparent that the study of birds in general not only saved her mind but her natural affections as well. Her love of birds seemed to be a substitute for the children she never had. She would sit beside a hermit thrush's nest and talk to it, or charm fledgling alder flycatchers into flying on to her finger and snuggling into her lap. She called a black-throated green warbler mother a "delightful thing," telling her, "I never did see anything half so beautiful as you, your nest, and your eggs." One day while in Ellsworth, she caught a young robin, which she stroked and kissed on the "top of his little black head."

Yet what seems like excessive affection and anthropomorphizing did not deter her from the most minute observations of bird behavior. Indeed, her sympathy for birds appeared to yield better results than those of more dispassionate observers. No one ever questioned what she saw. John Burroughs, when told that his ideas about red-breasted nuthatches disagreed with those of Miss Stanwood, deferred instantly to her, saying, "Well, I know Miss Stanwood — she is a real bird woman, and if she has seen this trait [nuthatches excavating their own nesting holes], I believe absolutely what she says must be true. . . ."

So, apparently, did Frank Chapman, editor of *Bird-Lore*. In 1908 she quoted Chapman in her notebook when writing about the call of the hairy woodpecker. By then she had used his *Handbook of Birds of Eastern North America* extensively. She had already begun sending him notes on her observations of bay-breasted warblers; he told her in a letter that these notes "seem to constitute an addition to our knowledge of the life history of this species, well deserving publication."

Thus began her attempts to be a freelance writer. Over the next forty years her work appeared in both scholarly and popular publications, and ornithologists such as Arthur Cleveland Bent, Edward Howe Forbush, and Francis Herrick used her observations in their own work. Bent tried to persuade her to write signed articles on the various life histories of birds, which he edited, but she only sent him her notes. These he quoted liberally, giving her full credit, in his *Life Histories of North American Birds* series. Most of the nest observations of the winter wren, red-breasted nuthatch, brown creeper, golden-crowned kinglet, olive-backed and hermit thrushes, and a wide variety of warbler species, were based on her work.

Bent also used her unique photographs, another attempt on Cordelia's part to record the lives of the birds she loved. Probably the first woman bird photographer, she began with the help of Ellsworth's local photographer, Embert Osgood. Bundling up a nestling in soft cloth, she apologized to the mother bird when she removed the young bird from the nest and carried it carefully into Osgood's studio for a photography session. She hated disrupting the little family, yet she knew how much more valuable her writing would be when accompanied by photographs.

However, when Aunt Cordelia died in 1916, leaving her a small legacy, Cordelia purchased her own camera and telephoto lens. Instructed by Osgood, she learned to take, develop, and print her own photographs. She also built observation blinds. First she cut and hauled poles and brush to construct brush blinds. Then she made a canvas blind. For hours she sat watching and photographing, but although she was rewarded with outstanding pictures, she suffered almost unbearable discomfort as she worked. Her notebook is filled with references to black flies and mosquitoes — those twin biting plagues of a northwoods spring and summer. "The air was alive with mosquitoes. Both mosquitoes and ants were crawling up my sleeves," she wrote one June. In June of 1910, she described "mosquitoes big as cats and the woods dense with them." In her balsam blind she mixed the good with the bad, writing that "the ground inside the fragrant balsam tent was covered with blossoming linnea. The ground was flecked with sunshine. The locust trill for heat. It is a hot sunny day. Mosquitoes extremely plenty and fierce." May 24, 1916, was a particularly unpleasant day. "The black flies are terrible. I never saw such large ones," and in the swamp at twilight on July 2, 1917, "the black flies crawled over my face like so many bees. I could not stand still."

Cordelia suffered for her work, yet the results were amazing. Edward Howe Forbush chose thirty-eight of her photographs for his *Birds of Massachusetts,* and her own articles, such as the one she did for *House Beautiful* on black-capped chickadees, contained superb photographs of young chickadees. Her "Six Little Chickadees" is perhaps her most appealing work, illustrating, as she herself observed, "how birds in the same nest differ."

In addition to sitting in blinds for hours to get pictures, she frequently intervened in nature as well. Today ornithologists would not approve of some of her methods, such as sawing down the nesting tree of a flicker. She also cut down a red-breasted nuthatch nesting tree, sliced it in sections, removed a piece beneath the nest hole so that she could see into the nest, and then tied the trunk back up into its original position. But the photographs she made of young flickers and red-breasted nuthatches seemed worth her interference with nature, especially since she cared so much for the birds that she never injured them in any way. Many bird artists were killing birds to get accurate paintings of individual species.

She also raised a variety of young birds in her home. This kind of work took a good deal of time, as she discovered when she cared for a hermit thrush nestling. She cleaned up after it, carried water to it, and fed it every forty-five minutes from four in the morning until seven at night; she gathered fresh food, such as ants' eggs, earthworms, grasshoppers, strawberries, and mulberries. But she never turned away a bird that needed help. One winter two children she knew trapped a great-horned owl that had been eating rabbits. Cordelia promptly photographed the owl, and then she and the children fed and cared for it for nine days until it was healed and could fly away.

One of her most delightful accounts was the raising of what she

25.   Six little chickadees, photograph by Cordelia Stanwood. *Courtesy Stanwood Wildlife Sanctuary, Ellsworth, Maine*

thought was a pet crow, whom she called Beppo. He was actually a raven, but Cordelia never realized this, since ravens did not frequent her area at the time. She found him in the summer of 1918; she took many photographs of him and filled her notebook with accounts of his clever and sometimes annoying stunts, such as snatching clean clothes from the neighbors' clothesline. But in May, 1919, he disappeared, and days later she found his body in the barn. Someone had shot him.

Her observations, articles, and photographs were not limited to birds. Cordelia had an insatiable interest in all of nature. "Everything in nature is beautiful taken in its supreme moment," she wrote, but "how careful the scientific writer should be to verify all his surmises." Those two statements summed up her approach to all natural life. Nothing escaped her eager eyes as she observed how tree buds developed and earthworms mated, or when wildflowers bloomed and frogs called. She was out on May 19, 1910, to watch Halley's comet, and on May 3, 1916, she spent a half hour recording the ways of a mosquito wiggler.

She also raised cecropia, luna, and polyphemus moths, describing and sketching their metamorphoses from caterpillars to adults. Insects fascinated her, and she often sent off insect specimens that she found in birds' nests to the United States Department of Agriculture or the Maine Experimental Station for identification. She even engaged in such meticulous work as slicing a willow gall open and carefully recording its insect inhabitants.

However, Cordelia's incredible efforts in writing, observing, and photographing natural events were not enough to support her financially. It was her experience that "scientific bird work is intensely interesting, but unless one has a salaried position, it is not remunerative, while writing, unless one is talented, would never keep the scribbler out of the work house." So as the years passed, Cordelia had to scramble harder and harder to earn money.

Her brother, Harry, with whom she had never gotten along, had married and moved away, and her father had died in 1914, leaving her the sole support of her mother and herself. Winters in Maine are long, and although she occasionally alludes to winter in her notebooks, the large bulk of her natural history work was done from April until October. In the winter she lived her other, traditionally feminine life—that of an accomplished craftswoman and seamstress. Even while attending high school in Providence, she had earned pocket money by sewing and darning for relatives, although she did not like the so-called fancy work of embroidering and crocheting. Instead she turned to weaving, dyeing, and basketry during the cold weather. In typical, thorough, Cordelia fashion, she spent one summer at Kezar Lake, North Lovell, Maine, learning how to weave and dye, and she even lived for a short time with the Penobscot Indians to master the art of sweetgrass basket-making. In addition, she hooked and braided rugs, fashioned gloves, and constructed jewelry boxes and picture frames in burned woodwork.

Her life as a writer led to the publication of a wide variety of articles. She wrote instructional pieces for crafts and homemaking magazines, accounts of her various wild bird and animal pets for *The Boy Scouts' Yearbook,* and illustrated articles for *House Beautiful* on the architecture of Castine and Blue Hill, Maine.

She also engaged in some subsistence farming, raising chickens and bees, milking the family cow, and occasionally gardening during the warmer months. This work inspired her to write articles, such as "A Sanitary Poultry Roost" in *Farm Mechanics* and "How to Make a Broody Hen Lay" for *American Poultry Journal.* She once calculated, from careful records she kept, that all her published writing earned her fifteen hundred dollars over her lifetime, hardly a princely sum.

When her mother died in 1932, Cordelia withdrew even more into her own private world with the wild creatures. And, as the neighbors observed, she became a little peculiar. Refusing to take help from anyone, even her sister Idella who tried repeatedly to give her food and money, she retreated to a second story room, which she reached by steep, winding stairs. There she had a wood stove, her bed, and the few belongings remaining to her. She sold or gave away the rest in exchange for food and labor. She even began selling stationery and Christmas cards door-to-door, tramping many miles at the age of seventy-five.

Although she became a misfit in her own community, she continued some intercourse with the outside ornithological world. Her bird photographs occasionally illustrated other writers' work, and *Nature* magazine for December 1939 published "What of the Nest?" a collection of her most exquisite birds' nests photographs supplemented with a few lines of text.

She also kept writing in her field notebooks while she sat outside on her campstool absorbing the sunshine and watching the panorama of wildlife around her. There the tiny, male, ruby-throated hummingbird would perform his mating dance apparently just for her. On another memorable day she discovered a hummingbird in her kitchen. Slowly, cautiously she picked up the bird and took him outside. But before she released him she "kissed the exquisite creature on top of his head," as she recorded in one of her last notebook entries at the age of eighty-seven.

Misunderstood and unheralded by most of her neighbors, nevertheless, a handful of friends remained faithful despite her sometimes irrational acts. Whe she was ninety, though, she had to accept state aid. Even then, however, she managed to save her pride with the help of Sen. Eugene Hale, who arranged for Governor Brann to pay her for bird photographs she sold to the state library. On November 20, 1958, Cordelia died of cancer in a state nursing home.

Although Cordelia had been pitied by many people who did not really know her, she had lived a life far richer and more useful than many women of her day could ever have imagined. Certainly she made that clear in her unpublished book, *Firs and Feathers*, summing up her philosophy in a few words. "One can never tell what delightful surprise is in store for him the moment he loses himself in the big out-of-doors. . . . Interest and attention are keys that unlock new worlds to us."

# Margaret Morse Nice

## ETHOLOGIST OF THE SONG SPARROW

MARGARET MORSE NICE was the real founder of ethology, according to Konrad Lorenz, the well-known Austrian ethologist. "Her paper on the song sparrow was, to the best of my knowledge, the first long-term field investigation of the individual life of any free-living wild animal," Lorenz wrote in the introduction to her posthumously published autobiography, *Research Is a Passion with Me.*

Research was a passion with Margaret, although she had to struggle most of her life to win recognition from professional ornithologists in a field that chiefly honored males with doctoral degrees. Often described as only a housewife with four children, she would tartly retort, "I am *not* a housewife, I am a *trained* zoologist."

She was born on December 6, 1883, at Amherst, Massachusetts, where her father, Anson Daniel Morse, was a professor of history at Amherst College. Both he and his wife, Margaret, who had been educated at Mount Holyoke Seminary, encouraged a love of learning in their six children.

Her father loved the wilderness and was also a devoted gardener. "We learned of nature at first hand, planting and weeding in our own small gardens," she later wrote. Her mother, inspired by a botany course she had taken at Mount Holyoke, taught her children the names of wildflowers, and on Sundays the whole family took walks in the lovely countryside around Amherst.

Margaret showed an early love for nature, especially birds, and was keeping notes on them by the time she was nine years old. When she was twelve she received her most cherished present, the then-popular book *Birdcraft* by Mabel Osgood Wright. It became her bible, along with *Birds of Amherst and Vicinity* by Hubert L. Clark. With those two books she was well on her way to becoming an amateur ornithologist.

But as she neared adulthood, although her father continued to read great works of literature aloud at the breakfast table and encouraged her to write, he made it clear that housewife and mother were to be her ultimate goals. Like her mother, she attended Mount Holyoke, but she had difficulty connecting her college courses with the wild things she loved. Instead, she lived for Wednesdays off, a tradition at Mount Holyoke. While most of the students spent the day studying, she took country excursions with a congenial girlfriend. They explored the woods and later, after purchasing a canoe, the streams. Occasionally she went off alone, which her parents deplored. To quiet their fears, Margaret bought and learned to use a rifle and a revolver. They opposed this even more strongly, but their headstrong daughter continued throughout her lifetime to carry a revolver with her whenever she went hiking.

Margaret graduated from Mount Holyoke in 1906 and was then expected to become a daughter-at-home. Her salvation was a lecture she heard by Dr. Hodge of Clark University about studying live animals. Inspired by his ideas, she enrolled at Clark and began studying for a master's degree in biology. Her research project was the food habits of bobwhites.

She planned to get a doctoral degree despite strong parental objections, but instead she did exactly what they had hoped she would. She married a fellow student, Leonard Blaine Nice, and set up housekeeping while he finished his doctoral work at Clark. Nevertheless, her study, "Food of the Bobwhite," was published in the *Journal of Economic Entomology* in June, 1910. It received quite a bit of scientific attention, especially her claim that one bobwhite ate seventy-five thousand insects and five million weed seeds per season. In 1915, six years after she completed her bobwhite work, Clark University finally awarded her a master's degree in biology.

By then, she was deeply immersed in raising a family. She did not give up her love of research, although while her four daughters were young, her research took a different direction. She studied the mastery of language by her children and published a paper per year on her findings. At Mount Holyoke she had received a splendid liberal arts education and so was able to use her abilities in German, French, arithmetic, and creative thought to formulate her theories.

Her husband received his doctoral degree in physiology, which he taught at Harvard Medical School for two years. They moved, in 1913, to Norman, Oklahoma, where he was made a professor of physiology and pharmacology. Margaret continued her language studies for several more years as her girls matured.

But as year followed year, she became more and more frustrated. Something was missing from her life. "I resented the implication that my husband and the children had brains, and I had none. He taught; they studied; I did housework." And housework, as far as she was concerned, was not important work. She was organized though, with a "technique of housework that was based on efficient preparation of good and simple meals, scalding water instead of dish towels, sending out the washing and ironing, and dispatch in the matter of cleaning. Most of my time was free for activities of more lasting value."

But what were those activities? Her language studies were not receiving the attention she had hoped for. Suddenly, on August 20, 1919, she changed her direction. A long walk on a beautiful day observing nature made her resolve to return to her childhood "vision of studying nature and trying to protect the wild things of the earth." She wanted to open the eyes of people to the wonders around them, to become "a sort of John Burroughs for Oklahoma." Margaret Morse Nice, at the age of thirty-six, had begun her real life's work.

She started by learning to identify all the birds, using Florence Merriam Bailey's *Handbook of Birds of the Western United States* as a guide. Then she took up the mourning dove cause. Oklahoma wanted to open the dove hunting season in August, claiming that doves were finished nesting by then. Margaret did not agree. She marshaled her girls together, and they climbed trees on the University of Oklahoma campus to report nest contents. They discovered that mourning doves nested not only in August but also September and even, in some cases, into October. With that information, Margaret was able to defeat the August mourning dove season.

In addition to her daughters, Margaret had the help of her husband in her studies, who, it turned out, was the most amiable of men. He encouraged her in all she attempted, took care of the girls when she was pursuing research, and was always happy to finance her work. In her article, "A Study of the Nesting of Mourning Doves," which was published in *The Auk*, she had a footnote to the title: "I wish to acknowledge my indebtedness to my husband, Dr. L. B. Nice, who went on many searches for Dove nests and to my daughter, Constance, who with her unquenchable zeal for climbing the trees, was of indispensable assistance to me."

They were an unusually close family. In 1920, when they decided

26.   Margaret Morse Nice with daughters Janet (left) and Constance (right) in the field. *Courtesy Smithsonian Institution*

to contribute a Christmas census to *Bird-Lore* magazine, "Constance and I went south in the morning, finding twenty-five species and two hundred and eighty-six individuals; Blaine went west in the afternoon recording twenty-one species and two hundred eighty-six individuals." They raised two juvenile mourning doves, Bewick's wrens nested in the children's play house, and the bluebird boxes and purple martin houses Blaine erected were occupied by the birds they were intended for. Many years later, one friend commented, "As had been her custom in Oklahoma, she had birds of several kinds flying about the house. I found it difficult to concentrate upon the subject at hand, especially when a nuthatch alighted on my head or a song sparrow hopped across my dinner plate."

They also bought a car and started camping out in the summers so that Margaret and Blaine could work on a bird list of Oklahoma for the State Department of Geological and Natural History. As a result of this, a small, paperbound book called *The Birds of Oklahoma* by Margaret Morse Nice and Leonard Blaine Nice was published in 1924 as a University of Oklahoma *Bulletin*.

Shortly thereafter, Blaine had a sabbatical leave that he planned to take in Europe. Margaret and her daughters, meanwhile, stayed in Massachusetts visiting friends and relatives during the winter, but with the arrival of spring, she began her first study of a nesting species there.

She chose the magnolia warbler. Encouraged by her friend, Edward H. Forbush, who was the state ornithologist of Massachusetts, she started watching a magnolia warbler nest built in a juniper bush rather than in its customary spruce tree. Later, in her classic book, *The Watcher at the Nest*, she wrote about her experience of watching the three nestlings from a distance of five feet during seventeen sessions over a nine day period. Altogether she spent twenty-six hours at this solitary pursuit and made an original discovery. The male actually fed the nestlings more meals than the female did. This experience watching the magnolia warblers was "never-to-be-forgotten. . . . The magnolia warblers gave me my initiation into bird watching, and although later I was to spend far more time at warbler nests, yet none held quite the same enchantment for me as this little family nesting in the juniper."

In September of 1926, the reunited family returned to Oklahoma, and for the next twenty-one months Margaret spent many hours afield. One day a month she took an all-day walk to observe birds over a variety of habitats. "It is," she maintained, "an inspiring experience to have a day for wandering—to be free and alone with nature for a whole long day; to feel unhurried, to be able to search carefully for birds, to be unmolested by considerations for other people."

Her bird work, begun in Oklahoma and carried on during summers visiting her family in Massachusetts, reached its culmination when they moved to Columbus, Ohio, in 1928. Blaine had been appointed as a professor at the Ohio State University Medical School, and they were able to find a home on a bluff above the Olentangy River. Their home was surrounded by woods, a large stream, and a weed patch. The weed patch was actually a flood plain, which she called Interpont (meaning between the bridges). The tangle of vines, trees, weeds, and bushes on Interpont, the jungle of burdock in their garden, and the fields crowded with goldenrod and asters, made ideal bird habitat. Best of all, though, was an avenue of giant ragweeds near an ancient sycamore tree along the river, which in autumn was filled with migrating warblers. In such a congenial setting she began her classic song sparrow study.

She also enjoyed the Columbus area because its central locality made it easy to attend the annual meetings of the American Ornithologists' Union, the Wilson Ornithological Club, and other bird associations. At those meetings she met prestigious ornithologists who encouraged her in her work. For instance, at the 1924 A.O.U. meeting she was greeted by Florence Merriam Bailey as "Mrs. Mourning Dove Nice," and she and Blaine were invited to the Baileys' home for dinner. At the same meeting Margaret read her paper on the yellow-crowned night herons she had watched one spring back in Oklahoma, and she found that unlike her papers in child psychology, which had brought almost no reaction, her bird work not only aroused interest but led to many lasting friendships with American as well as European ornithologists.

During the winter of 1927–28, the Nices' lost their third child, nine-year-old Eleanor. Her death was a sudden blow that was only alleviated the following March when Margaret was able to launch her song sparrow study by banding a male whom she later named Uno. She spent hours watching the nests his mate built and keeping an eye on nesting blue-gray gnatcatchers and black-throated blue warblers.

To her delight, Uno returned the following spring, so Margaret began piling up data about the lives of song sparrows. Over the next eight years she made several original discoveries about this common bird. She learned that male song sparrows begin singing in mid-February and that each male has a different song, which clearly defines his territory. But when the females arrive, the males stop singing and begin courting. She also observed their mating, which begins when the female calls "eee eee eee." The male responds by rushing up, pouncing on her, and making a quick exit. In child care, male song sparrows are exemplary. They are the sole incubators of the eggs, and after the nestlings hatch, they help care for the young. On the other hand, females vary in their abilities as mothers — one she named Xantippe was a "cold, old-maidish creature, tyrannizing over her fine husband. She is the most shrewish female I ever studied." The pair Una and Uno, however, were "affectionate, vocal and responsive to each other."

But of all the song sparrows she banded and studied, it was 4M who became a legend. Margaret estimated that he was in his second year of life when he first came to them. He returned faithfully to raise new families each spring for eight years, reaching the venerable age, for a song sparrow, of nine and a half years. During his youth he was quarrelsome and overbearing, but later he seemed to temper his personality. He sang more than any bird she ever observed, starting in late January or early February and continuing into July. Then he resumed on the last day of September and sang through the "pleasant days in October, the picture of abounding energy and joy in living." On May 11, 1935, Margaret arose at dawn to record the total number of songs 4M could give in a day. Then over eight years old, 4M produced 2,305 songs, much to Margaret's amazement and delight.

Margaret worked alone on her study, because the Wheaton Ornithological Club of Columbus excluded women. Although they eagerly accepted Blaine, she was ignored. In contrast to their attitude, the national bird groups began to recognize her. She was made a member of the A.O.U. in 1931, only the fifth woman to be elected in its history. With her abilities in foreign languages, she was able to write reviews of foreign ornithological studies for *Bird-Banding* magazine. When she went to Europe in 1932 with Blaine and her two oldest daughters, she spent her time working and studying with ornithologists in Germany, Switzerland, France, Italy, and England. In fact, it was the German *Journal für Ornithologie* that first printed her full-length study of song sparrows; American journals would not publish any paper over twenty pages long.

Her commitment to *Bird-Banding* was increased when she became its associate editor in 1934. The A.O.U. honored her as a fellow three years later. The only other woman who had achieved that position was Florence Merriam Bailey. In 1937 Margaret was made president of the Wilson Ornithological Club. Blaine, in the meantime, became head of the physiological and pharmaceutical Departments in the Chicago Medical School, so they moved to Chicago in 1936. Gone were the wonderful shrubby areas to explore, and, as she wrote to her daughter Marjorie, "a great city is no proper home for me. We have no birds around our home but English sparrows."

Chicago ornithologists appreciated her, though. She was made vice president of the Chicago Ornithological Society and director of the Illinois Audubon Society. She also found solace in the forest preserves and parks in and near Chicago, where the bird life was rich and varied.

When her *Population Study of the Song Sparrow* was published in 1937, the praise both at home and abroad was overwhelming. "Perhaps the most important contribution yet published to our knowledge of the life of a species," French ornithologist Jean Delacour wrote. For the song sparrow study, she received the Brewster Medal in 1942. Margaret Morse Nice had truly arrived in the ornithological world.

She was persuaded, after twenty-one years of writing for professional journals, to attempt a popularization of her nest studies. She called her book *The Watcher at the Nest*, and it was published by Macmillan in 1939. A charming, chatty book, it covered her major finds about song sparrows, but it also related studies she had done of cowbirds, magnolia and black-throated green warblers, ovenbirds, and mourning doves. In addition, she began to air some of her ideas about conservation, pleading that weeds, shrubs and vines should be left along roadsides and fence rows to provide bird habitat. She spoke out against logging cypresses and poisoning prairie dogs. She also spoke out in favor of dogwood, decrying the concept of scientifically managed forests where dogwood was cut out as a weed tree. Highways, too, she maintained, were often a blight on natural beauty. Her book ends with a plea to leave space for wild creatures, forests for beasts and birds, swamps for wild fowl, and prairie for wildflowers. From then on, she became an activist in conservation fights, speaking out, as early as 1944, against the use of lead shot in waterfowl hunting.

Unfortunately *The Watcher at the Nest* was not a commercial success. Only 1,006 books were sold, for which she received $206. Yet the book has become a classic in bird-watching circles and was later reissued in paperback form. Margaret never did have much success in the popular literary world. Near the end of her life she completed her autobiography, which was rejected by several presses and was finally published posthumously by a women's ornithological club in Canada. That group, the Margaret Morse Nice Ornithological Club, was founded in Toronto in 1952 by Doris Spiers, who later became the editor of Nice's autobiography, *Research Is a Passion with*

*Me.* The Toronto Ornithological Club, like the one in Columbus, was for men only, and Doris, an excellent ornithologist in her own right, decided to form a counter club for women only. She received the blessing of Margaret, who was pleased to have the club named after her. Doris recalled that Margaret had treated her, a young amateur back in 1938, with a sincere and keen interest.

Indeed, Margaret was loved by everyone who met her. "A person of contrasts, she was usually demure, soft-spoken, and reserved, but could become assertive and somewhat opinionated when convinced that she was in the right or had been misunderstood," Milton Traut-man wrote in her obituary for *The Auk.* Trautman also praised her "tremendous ability for concentration during long periods of time, [her] patience in observing and recording data, including minute details, [her] consuming interest in behavior," and her "determina-tion to publish as much as possible of what she observed."

She continued her extraordinary activity throughout her long life, publishing more than 250 articles on birds in scientific journals, as well as 3,313 reviews of the works of others. As she grew older, she increasingly turned her attention to educating the public about con-servation and nature. She gave nature talks to small groups, and she also gave radio talks "to help listeners to get more joy out of life" and "to raise a host of friends for wildlife — to love and protect nature." She battled to save the Wichita Mountains Wildlife Refuge in Oklahoma, the Dinosaur National Monument, the redwood trees in California, and the Indiana dunes. She protested against roadside spraying and spraying for fire ants, and she campaigned in favor of saving prairie reserves along railroad rights-of-way.

In 1955 she received an honorary Doctor of Science degree from her alma mater Mount Holyoke, and another in 1962 from Elmira College. A subspecies of song sparrow in Mexico, *Melospiza melo-dia niceae,* was named for her, and the Wilson Ornithological Club started the Margaret Morse Nice grant-in-aid for self-trained, ama-teur researchers.

Her home circle remained close through all of her honors. Con-stance, her oldest daughter, was also interested in ornithology and often accompanied her on her research trips. Her husband remained her staunchest admirer and dearest friend. "It was apparent to those who knew him that he was willing to sacrifice his free time so she could pursue her researches," Trautman wrote.

Doris Spiers also maintained that "the Nices were a very happy couple. Dr. Nice accompanied his wife to the bird meetings when-ever it was possible for him to do so, and I would observe the pleasure in his face when he saw his Margaret surrounded by admiring friends. She loved her friends and he liked her to be loved."

Both of the Nices lived to be ninety years of age. Blaine died early in 1974 and she followed him a few months later. She had had a wonderfully satisfying life as a wife and mother, but she had managed to combine it with a career she designed for herself. Her career brought her deep fulfillment, for she believed that "the study of nature is a limitless field, the most fascinating adventure in the world. . . . We who love nature, who see and try to understand and interpret, are following the true goal. We have a talisman against the futility of the lives of many people."

# *Amelia Laskey*

## PATRON SAINT TO THE BIRDS

NOTHING in Amelia Laskey's childhood or young adulthood suggested she had had any interest in birds. She attended her first Bird Club meeting in Nashville, Tennessee, when she was forty-three years old. Before then her interests had been the same as many married women of her day—she played bridge, joined a garden club, and read papers before a literary society. Although she had been married for seventeen years, she had had no children, and much of her energy, instead, was invested in gardening just as her mother's had been.

Born in Bloomington, Indiana, on December 12, 1885, to recent German immigrants, Susan and Frank Rudolph, Amelia's family moved to Chicago when she was only an infant. Apparently even then Amelia preferred the country to the city; she later wrote to her friend and mentor, Margaret Morse Nice: "You have my sympathy living in a big city [Chicago] when you have such strong attachment for the country and its bird life. I almost hated it when I lived there."

As a child, however, the environs of Chicago were still bucolic enough for her to "have memories of the waving grasses, the pink shooting stars, wild phlox, yellow star grass and even an occasional dark blue dwarf iris, all of which were soon covered with myriads of houses as Chicago gobbled up everything." Nevertheless, Chicago remained her home for thirty-six years. There she attended school, worked as a stenographer at the Oliver Typewriter Company, met and married Fredrick C. Laskey in 1911, and was active in church work.

Then, in 1921, Fred and Amelia moved to Nashville, Tennessee, where they bought a new home in the outskirts of the small city.

Amelia named it Blossomdell and immediately turned her considerable energies into making a wild garden in her four-acre backyard.

No one knows who first invited her to a Bird Club meeting, but
whoever it was changed her life. That same year Amelia joined the
Tennessee Ornithological Society, and on April 21, 1928, she wrote
that she "had the first hummingbird of the year." The following year
she began her thirty-year study of mockingbirds.

Two years later she started writing for the Tennessee Ornithological Society's journal, *The Migrant*, entitling the first of the 153 papers
she wrote for journals over the next forty-two years, "Attracting Birds
to the Home." That was also the year she applied to the United States
Fish and Wildlife Service for a banding permit and began at least
three long-range bird life history studies — on the bluebird, the tufted
titmouse, and the cardinal.

The banding was absolutely essential, she believed, in order to
study bird life adequately, and from 1931 until 1934 she banded 3,734
birds of 69 species. Of those, 300 returned or their bands were recovered. "Bird banding," she wrote in the *Journal of the Tennessee
Academy of Science* in 1934, "is one of the most fascinating and en-
grossing [of] hobbies . . . being not only a healthful outdoor diver-
sion but affording opportunity for discoveries of scientific and economic value." Originally she had banded only to find out where the
birds went when they left Nashville, but she quickly discovered other
uses of banding. By the systematic, daily trapping of field sparrows,
for instance, she learned that although field sparrows were year-round
residents, the winter and summer residents were different. The cardinal population also changed constantly though their numbers remained the same. In just three years of work, she caught a rare (to
Nashville) species, the tree sparrow; another species, the Harris' sparrow; and a subspecies, the Gambel's sparrow, never before recorded
from Tennessee. In 1940 she added a subspecies to the list, a Bick-
nell's thrush.

Her banding station quickly became an "avian infirmary and home
for feathered foundlings," and to the local children she was known
as "the lady that fixes birds." To her they brought sick and stunned
birds, those with broken bones, orphaned nestlings, and baby birds
that had fallen from nests. The sick ones she could not help but the
stunned ones recovered quickly after a rest. Those with broken bones
she put in a large flying cage with food, and usually they too recovered even though she did not believe in splints or tapes. "Nature's
way of healing," she maintained, "is far superior to my inexperienced
surgery."

She had remarkable success in getting other species of nesting birds to adopt orphaned nestlings — robins took in a cardinal and cardinals tended mockingbirds, bluebirds, and robins. Amelia also raised many nestlings and fledglings by hand. In 1940 she recorded success with chimney swifts, a purple martin, cliff swallows, two bronzed grackles named Bertram and Dusky, Amos the crow, a mallard, chipping sparrows, a cardinal, bluebirds, a robin, a red-winged blackbird, a brown thrasher, and a starling.

She was partial to the species "most persecuted by man, the crow, the grackle and the owls," because she discovered that those species "responded best to human companionship." Once she kept an injured barred owl in her basement, and when it partially recovered she put it in a large flying cage in a protected corner near her house. It stayed there until the end of its life, since its amputated pinion had destroyed its ability to fly. An American bittern, on the other hand, with an injured wing, spent the winter in her garage perched on the top step of an eight-foot ladder and in the spring was able to fly away and resume a natural life.

Probably her favorite bird, though, was "Honey Child," a male mockingbird she got at the age of nine days on August 1, 1939, and kept until his death fifteen years and four months later. She had made the conscious decision to keep him as an "experimental mockingbird," supplementing her wild mockingbird study. She wanted to learn specifically if song imitation in mockingbirds was inherited or learned. It was learned, she discovered, as Honey Child added songs to his repertoire based on those he heard from nearby birds. Although kept in the house, he responded to the seasons with appropriate behavior, defending his "territory" in winter by flying to a certain window where he met an outdoor mockingbird. Both birds would "chuck" through the window at each other and "dance" up and down the window pane for as long as an hour at a time. His courtship behavior in spring he directed at Amelia, going through copulation movements both on Amelia's hand and with objects in his cage. Then he would place nesting material on a ledge. Later, he molted at the same time his wild brethren did.

For twelve years his cycle continued until he fell twice from his perch. After that, all mating behavior ended, although he continued singing and courting behavior until four months before his death of natural causes, outliving by three years the oldest mockingbird record in the wild at that time.

Until 1936 Amelia's bird study had been done in her backyard and nearby open environs, but in that year, she expanded her bluebird study into the two-thousand-acre Warner Park, which became her outdoor laboratory and the place where she began erecting large

27.  Amelia Laskey repairing a bluebird box. *Courtesy Katherine Goodpasture, Archivist, National Chapter, Tennessee Ornithological Society*

numbers of bluebird nesting boxes. Starting with twenty-six boxes in 1936, she expanded to thirty-seven in 1938, fifty-six in 1939 and, at the height of her study, close to a hundred boxes. She kept meticulous records of every box, and over the years had data on as many as three generations of the same family. It wasn't easy work; she always had to contend with vandalism — destroyed or mutilated boxes — as well as park workmen who mowed down and broke the boxes with large mowing machines, even though she carefully weeded for a yard around every box in an effort to forestall destruction.

Amelia, it must be said, was no sluggard. She kept an immaculate home and yard and was "always overworked and dead tired" during the spring and summer. Her inside birds were confined to

235

the screened porch and kitchen and she followed them around to pick up any "packages" they dropped. Although Margaret Morse Nice often urged her to neglect her cleaning and get on with her bird work, she continued to "have long sessions with dandelions, chickweed and their ilk and more of the same indoors on my knees cleaning with steel wool, mineral spirits, waxing and polishing floors."

Amelia was also an omnivorous reader, and evidently her husband Fred's salary as the manager of Swift and Company was ample enough to support her appetite in books. She subscribed to most of the bird journals and purchased all of the important books on birds, those long out-of-print as well as the current studies. No doubt it was Amelia's reading that first acquainted her with the work of Margaret Morse Nice. Although Amelia was two years older than Margaret, Margaret was definitely the adviser and teacher and Amelia the pupil, but each freely used the other's material in their writing. It was Margaret who encouraged her to write for *The Auk,* to publish saw-whet owl photographs she had taken, and to try her hand at book reviewing.

Amelia needed encouragement. She did not have a college education, and she was a very shy person. Margaret plied Amelia with questions about her birds and complimented her work. Unlike Margaret's husband, Amelia's husband did not encourage her. He did, however, drive her around to her bluebird boxes and help her to repair the broken ones. Still, in later years, when Amelia began traveling to ornithological meetings, she always went with female friends or alone, because Fred did not like to travel.

Gradually, though, she gathered her own coterie of bird friends and youthful assistants in the Nashville area and even led a children's Nature Club at the Nashville Children's Museum, where she had been made a trustee. Volunteers had been particularly helpful during her study of chimney swifts. She described her travels over many miles around Nashville and its suburbs: "evening after evening, hunting roosting flocks, . . . seeking permission to work at various places, then preparation for the actual work which often kept me busy until midnight, only to rise at 3 A.M. to get the volunteer workers to the roost by daylight. The work is dangerous as many chimneys were high. My 40 foot extension ladders on the roof set the height limit. We banded on roofs of buildings, in alleys, on fire escapes, and other unconventional places, often spending the entire day working with one flock."

For this work, though, she was finally rewarded. On October 13, 1940, she banded a chimney swift, with the help of young men, in a nineteen-foot-high chimney in a three-story Y.M.C.A. building in downtown Nashville. Three years later, in December of 1943, that swift, along with twelve other banded swifts, was killed on the Yanayaco River in Peru; this was the first record of the chimney swifts' winter destination.

Despite Amelia's use of assistants in both her chimney swift studies and her bluebird work, for the most part she gathered data based on long, solitary hours of watching her chosen species. Early in 1943 she began color-banding cowbirds preparatory to three intensive seasons of watching the little-studied species. From 1944 until 1946 she started her observations each year when the first birds arrived for the year in Nashville in early March and continued on a daily basis until their disappearance in July. The following two years she only watched intermittently, but in all she spent several hundred hours trying to make sense of cowbird behavior. Some of her conclusions directly contradicted other observers, such as her statement that cowbirds, for the most part, were monogamous and that both males and females did fight with each other on several occasions. But her best observations were her descriptions of two new behavior patterns never before described. The first she called "intimidation bows" in which the dominant male cowbird challenged other comers by toppling forward with his wings and tail spread out and his bill or head touching the ground. The second was the guarding of its mate by a dominant male or female, which stepped between its mate and others of the opposite sex. According to her younger friend and fellow bird bander, Katharine Goodpasture, Amelia's cowbird studies were probably the most significant published work she contributed to the ornithological world.

She published her results in the *Wilson Bulletin* in an article called "Cowbird Behavior," which was written in the same scholarly style as the later results of her tufted titmouse, cardinal, and mockingbird studies. She allowed Margaret Morse Nice to send off her more popularly written study of watching a Carolina wren's nest to *The Chicago Naturalist*. In it Amelia revealed much of the joy as well as the discomfort of nest watching, writing about the myriad wildflowers in bloom around her that hot, humid July morning and the various species of butterflies. "Life is buzzing all about me. Birds are singing and calling. . . . Close to me came insects of many varieties. . . . A June bug zoomed past on its way to the peaches, a fly persistently landed on my hand to crawl about. . . . Wasps had to be brushed off. Once something landed on my collar to crawl to my neck. Without thinking, up went my hand to brush it off, but *wow!* a painful sting on a finger cushion sent pains into my hand and arm."

Singing birds were a temptation to take her eyes off the Carolina wren nesting box she was watching in Warner Park, but instead she contented herself with identifying them by their songs, counting almost twenty species as she sat for three and a half hours with her eyes "almost glued to that box, trying to relax a bit by using one eye at a time, and other devices to relieve the tension." Dressed to shade her face from the sun, she was still spotted by the female Carolina wren, who scolded for five minutes before going into the nesting box to sit on her five eggs. During Amelia's morning watch, the female spent 73 minutes on the nest and 126 minutes off, according to her statistical summary at the conclusion of what was one of the most entertaining pieces she ever wrote.

In addition to bird banding, nest watching, and bird rehabilitation, Amelia also enjoyed participating in the annual Christmas Bird Count sponsored by the National Audubon Society each year during the Christmas season. Assigned to cover Warner Park, she spent six hours in 1943 "alternately tramping and driving — all by myself. I really enjoyed it as my field jaunts are so limited these days" (this was during the Second World War when gas rationing hindered many field workers). "I was a sight to behold but I was dressed for the weather with sinus disability in mind: corduroy slacks, wool sweater, leather jacket, long cotton hose, husband's wool socks, rubber boots, a tam with a scarf tied over it. My list was only thirty-four species but I brought in three that no other group found — a shrike, a fox sparrow, and some purple finches."

As the years passed Amelia's bird-watching even continued at night with her enthusiastic participation in "moon watching." On full moon nights in September, October, and November she and a companion would sit on top of a high building all night long. Equipped with her own telescope, flashlights, and record-sheets, she counted the silhouettes of migrating birds, following the directions of George Lowery and Robert Newman of Louisiana State University.

On an evening in September, 1948, the first birds were observed crashing into an airport ceilometer light, an event that started Amelia on still another project — watching for bird casualties at both those lights and at television towers for over twenty years. Her pioneering work led to the establishment of many new early and late fall migration dates as well as to awareness of just how many birds were being killed by man-made structures during fall migrations.

She continued to write up her bird data for prestigious journals during the 1950s and early 1960s. In "Some Tufted Titmouse Life History," for *Bird-Banding* in July of 1957, she summarized ninety-eight hours of titmouse watching between 1931 and 1956, when she

238

banded 327 individuals. Titmice, she had learned, associate with other family members in the fall and winter. During that period they also hide seed in tree crevices or in the ground. In the breeding season the female alone incubates the eggs, while both parents later feed the nestlings.

Another important piece was Amelia's "Breeding Biology of Mockingbirds" for *The Auk* in October of 1962. After examining 250 mockingbird nests and banding over 900 nestlings in twenty-nine years, she discovered that mockingbirds in her area prefer to nest in evergreens 33 percent of the time. She also found that the female determines the nest site, a pair remains together for a season and sometimes for several years, the female incubates the eggs, and the nestlings are fed by both parents.

It may have been for the mockingbird study that Amelia was finally elected a fellow of the A.O.U. in 1966. Certainly the greatest honor she received over the years, it came seven years before her sudden death in December, 1973, after attending her last A.O.U. meeting in the fall at Provincetown, Massachusetts. At her death, she had left undone the final summarizing of her immense bluebird data. But to Amelia, "the most enjoyable part of a study is gathering the material first hand — the joy of watching the birds and trying to understand them."

# Part VI

# *The Ecologists*

---

*The battle cry to save specific areas and wild creatures began late in the nineteenth century with the establishment of the first U.S. national parks and the crusade, by the Audubon Society and other fledgling conservation groups, against the killing of birds. Elizabeth G. K. Britton, who helped found the Wild Flower Preservation Society of America in 1902, and Margaret Morse Nice and Amelia Laskey, who wrote protest letters to save specific areas, reflected women naturalists' awakening concern about threats to the habitats they explored.*

*Although women naturalists, like their male counterparts, continued to become more specialized in their fields of study, they also began to use their specialties to understand how the natural world functions. A new word, ecology, was coined to describe the new concept of the study of the mutual relations between organisms and their environment, and those who studied ecology were called ecologists. Armed with knowledge about their specialties that reflected on the entire web of life, ecologists were able to join the battle to save at least some of the natural environment from the rampages of humanity.*

*Most of the women ecologists were full-fledged scientists with advanced degrees, such as Ann Haven Morgan, E. Lucy Braun, and Rachel Carson. Carrie Dormon had only a bachelor of arts degree and was self-trained in her scientific specialties, but so thorough was she* in her work that professional foresters, botanists, archaeologists, and ornithologists recognized and accepted her expertise.

The lives of Morgan, Dormon, and Carson will be covered in the following chapters, but since the Braun papers are not available to researchers, only a small part of her life has been pieced together by reading scanty secondary sources. Nevertheless, as one of the pioneer women ecologists specializing in plant ecology, E. Lucy Braun of Cincinnati, Ohio, played a pivotal role in the new discipline of ecology from 1910 until her death in 1971. Like Carrie Dormon, she never married, lived in harmony with an older sister Annette, who was an entomologist and accompanied E. Lucy on all her field trips, and had a strong sense of place, namely the flora of Ohio and surrounding regions. She fought to save unique habitats, particularly the prairie remnants in Adams County, Ohio. Eventually she persuaded the Nature Conservancy to preserve two dry prairies in the area, which were later deeded to the Cincinnati Museum of Natural History — the 386-acre Buzzardroost Rock and the 53-acre Lynx Prairie E. Lucy Braun Preserve. She had been taking her students at the University of Cincinnati to the latter preserve for years and had identified and catalogued the unique mix of southern, Appalachian, and western plants that grow there. Other explorations by her in that area led to the acquisition of the Wilderness (now called the Charles A. Eulett Preserve), Red Rock, and another prairie at Lake Adams. All three are still being gradually expanded due to the Dr. Lucy Braun Memorial Fund, established by the Cincinnati Museum of Natural History.

In concert with her belief in land preservation and plant conservation, she joined the Wild Flower Preservation Society of America in 1917. She went on to form a Cincinnati chapter, serving as director for twenty years and as editor of their publication WILD FLOWER, which became the magazine for the national society in 1925, from 1928 until 1933. In addition, she was the first woman president of both the Ohio Academy in Science, in 1933–34, and the Ecological Society of America, in 1950.

She and her sister lived in a house on a two-acre

*wooded lot in suburban Cincinnati; they dedicated por-
tions both inside and out to their naturalist studies, calling the entire area the "science wing." Their garden was
an experimental one, featuring rare and unusual wild
plants, such as the box huckleberry (GAYLUSSACIA
BRACHYCERA), Cumberland azalea (RHODODENDRON CUM-
BERLANDENSE), nodding mandarin (DISPORUM MACULA-
TUM), Allegheny-spurge (PACHYSANDRA PROCUMBENS),
and stoneroot (MICHELIELLA VERTICILLATA).*

*E. Lucy Braun, accompanied by her sister, was a dedi-
cated field person, making thirteen trips to the western
United States between 1915 and 1963. She also covered
sixty-five thousand miles over twenty-five years in eastern North America in order to write her monumental
DECIDUOUS FORESTS OF EASTERN NORTH AMERICA, which
she finally published in 1950. The book, she explained
in her preface, was based "on many years of familiarity
with the deciduous forest as a whole, and on intimate
association with the study of parts of this forest." She
wanted "to give a broad and coordinated account of
the entire deciduous forest—a comprehensive view
which may make possible the better understanding of
fragments of forest and give a setting for past and future local and detailed studies," and, in the words of
researcher Donald L. Stuckey, the book "lays the foundation for the measurement and evaluation of all future ecological changes in the hardwood forest and
remains her most remembered and lasting scholarly
achievement."*

*In the course of her field trips she made numerous
botanical discoveries, finding and naming nine new
plants from Kentucky. Two of these (EUPATORIUM LU-
CIAE-BRAUNIAE and ERIGERON PULCHELLUS MICHX. VAR.
BRAUNIAE) were named for her by Kate Furbish's friend
Merritt Fernald, and a third (SILPHIUM TEREBINTHINA-
CERUM JACQ. VAR. LUCY-BRAUNIAE) was named by bota-
nist Julian Steyermark.*

*Braun believed that to be an ecologist, one must
understand one group of organisms. In her case the organisms were plants. Ann Haven Morgan, however,
specialized in all pond life, and Rachel Carson, first a
specialist in marine life, finally embraced the entire web
of life with her pivotal SILENT SPRING.*

But no matter what their specialties, all women ecologists, past and present, would have agreed with Dr. Ruth Patrick, at the Academy of Natural Sciences, whose specialty has been diatoms — single-celled algae that feed many kinds of marine life. Patrick, at the age of seventy, told one journalist: "I have the greatest appetite for understanding how the natural world functions together and what are the patterns that ensure this function. And I'm still hungry to understand the natural world."

# Ann Haven Morgan

ECOLOGIST OF PONDS AND STREAMS

EVERYONE had a different nickname for Ann Haven Morgan. Freshmen in her class at Cornell University called her Mayfly Morgan, because of her intense interest in her Ph.D. dissertation on the biology of mayflies. When she spent two summers studying landlocked salmon in the Connecticut Lakes of New Hampshire, her guides knew her as the Big Fish Lady. And trolley car crews, who took her from South Hadley to Northampton, Massachusetts, so she could hike to a pond on Mount Tom to study water bugs, referred to her as the Water Bug Lady.

Certainly her favorite pursuit was wading in fresh water in search of the aquatic insects, newts, fish, and plants that lived there. All the information she gathered was grist for her best-known and most popular book, *A Field Book of Ponds and Streams: An Introduction to the Life of Fresh Water.* "An angler's favorite," as she later referred to it, the book was also useful for amateur naturalists because of its ecological focus. To Ann every creature had its place and function within the natural world. She no doubt had absorbed this idea from her professor and mentor at Cornell University, James George Needham, who wrote the introduction to her book.

Born Anna Haven Morgan on May 6, 1882, she did not become Ann until she received her doctoral degree in 1912. She was the oldest of three children and spent her childhood exploring the woods and fields around her home in Waterford, Connecticut. After finishing her secondary education at Williams Memorial Institute in New London, she enrolled at Wellesley College in 1902. But she found the atmosphere too restrictive there and transferred to Cornell University, where she received her A.B. degree in 1906.

That year she began her lifelong association with Mount Holyoke College in South Hadley, Massachusetts, as an assistant and then instructor in zoology. After returning as a graduate assistant to Cornell for three years to get her doctorate, she resumed her position at Mount Holyoke. She was rapidly promoted to associate professor in 1914, chairman of the zoology department in 1916, and full professor in 1918. In addition to teaching general zoology, she also specialized in a water biology course with field trips and started a winter biology course, which led to another book, *Animals in Winter.*

Most of her field work was restricted to the northeastern United States, and during the academic year she focused on that little pond toward the top of Mount Tom. After alighting from the trolley in the winter, she would walk up the car tracks through snow and ice to reach the frozen pond. Once there she would chop holes in the ice in search of the water bug traps she had set out. All this effort was expended to find out when they began their annual cycle.

Beginning in 1918, when she taught about echinoderms at the Marine Biological Laboratory in Woods Hole, Massachusetts, she spent several summers (1918, 1919, 1921, and 1923) on the teaching staff there. The summer of 1926 was spent doing research at William Beebe's preserve, the Tropical Laboratory in Kartabo, British Guiana.

But all the while she was also accumulating material for her *A Field Book of Ponds and Streams.* In addition to writing the book, she illustrated it with her photographs and line drawings. The book was published in 1930 to instant acclaim, and in its preface, she set out her reasons for writing it. "It originated where water plants and animals live and I hope that it may be a guide into the vividness and variety of their ways. Most of all I hope that it may help toward wider enjoyment and further acquaintance in the field of water biology that offers abundant opportunity to all explorers, both beginners and seasoned investigators."

James G. Needham further elaborated the purposes of the book in his foreword, hoping that if readers learned more about the life of ponds and streams, they would try to keep them free of pollution. Ann also paid tribute to Needham in her book, giving him the credit for first showing her "how to look for things in the water" and continuing his "help and encouragement for finding more." Needham had apparently supported her even before she became his doctoral student in 1910, since it was he who had first proposed her name for membership in the Entomological Society of America back in 1908.

The other strong professional influence on her career was Dr. Cor-

28.   Ann Haven Morgan with student Eileen B. Hines dredging for stream creatures. *Courtesy Mount Holyoke College Library/Archives, South Hadley, Massachusetts*

nelia Clapp, a zoology professor at Mount Holyoke for forty-four years. Clapp looked on Ann as her inheritor and friend, and it was probably her influence as a member of the board of trustees at Woods Hole that encouraged Ann to go there. The letters Cornelia wrote to Ann had the tenor of a much older sister writing to a beloved younger sibling. In fact, strong female relationships were important to Ann, and just as she had formed a friendship with the much older Cornelia, so too did she with the younger Professor A. Elizabeth Adams, also a teacher of zoology at Mount Holyoke, with whom she shared a home.

Otherwise, though, Ann was characterized as a loner from the time she was a small child. "Complex," one friend called her, but "consistently kind, helpful, cordial." Students found her exacting but memorable — a short, trim woman with bobbed hair and blue eyes who always wore a tailored skirt, shirtwaist, tie, and white physician's coat, she lectured in clear, crisp tones.

But out in the field she was more approachable. One reporter followed her while she did a conservation workshop at Goddard Park in Rhode Island for teachers in July of 1945 — "a gray-haired lady knee-deep in muck and water ferociously pursuing nasty little herbivora and carnivora with a net." To the reporter she said that she didn't "'ever want to come out' of some particularly oozy mudhole, where she happily captures nymphs, sponges and other creatures and encourages her students to do the same."

She apparently derived great satisfaction from teaching a wide variety of people about the outdoors, in the classroom as well as in the books she wrote. She told one *Time* writer it was "great fun" to read fan letters about her field book on ponds and streams. That was in 1933 when she was 1 of 3 women in a group of 250 leading scientists featured in the fifth edition of *American Men of Science.* To that same writer she also maintained that "her favorite preoccupation has been and . . . will always be mayflies, because mayflies are fine for small boys to fish with."

Other honors also came her way. She was a Schuyler Fellow at Cornell, a visiting fellow at both Harvard and Yale, and a fellow in the American Association for the Advancement of Science. She held memberships in a wide variety of organizations that illustrated her diversity of interests — the Entomological Society of America, the American Society of Naturalists, the American Society of Zoologists, the American Association of Museums, the Association of Social Hygiene, the National Advisory Board of Eugenics, and Sigma Xi Society.

After her retirement from Mount Holyoke in 1947, Ann became

heavily involved in conservation efforts. As a member of the newly formed National Committee on Policies in Conservation Education sponsored by the Izaak Walton League, she and her friend Elizabeth Adams took a trip to the western United States to observe the West's approach to conservation projects. They went by way of the Canadian Railroad to Alberta, where they hiked in Jaspar National Park, then on to British Columbia. From there they took a boat south to Washington State and visited Friday Harbor, the University of Washington's Marine Laboratory in the San Juan Islands, which they enjoyed very much. In fact, the trip west convinced Ann that the West was far ahead of the East in its conservation efforts. This inspired her to support conservation efforts in her own Connecticut River Valley.

To Ann, though, conservation was only possible if people understood the importance of it. As part of that effort, she worked hard to reform the science curriculum in schools and colleges. She also gave summer workshops for teachers, with the hope that ecology and conservation would become an acceptable part of school curricula.

And, of course, she continued writing. In 1955 she published her third and last book, *Kinships of Animals and Man: A Textbook of Animal Biology.* Ostensibly it was an introductory zoology text, but its real message was embodied in one of Ann's statements in the book. "Now that the wilderness is almost gone, we are beginning to be lonesome for it. We shall keep a refuge in our minds if we conserve the remnants."

Ann Haven Morgan lived long enough to see the strong beginnings of an ecological movement in America as well as the publication of the book most people consider the pivotal ecology book of the twentieth century, Rachel Carson's *Silent Spring.* Both she and Rachel died in 1966, and both of them died of cancer.

# Carrie Dormon

QUEEN OF THE FOREST KINGDOM

"I WAS BORN with something—I call it the gift of the wild things—
and because I am simple myself, and have a sympathetic heart, I
can understand animals and simple people to an unusual degree.
I see, too, so much that others miss. When I know so many lovely
things, I feel greedy in keeping them all to myself." Thus Caroline
Dormon described herself to Henry Allen Moe, secretary-general of
the Guggenheim Fellowship in 1942. She had applied for a fellowship, hoping to have one year of freedom to write about the wild
things with which she empathized. But they turned her down. Was
it her age, she wondered? She was then fifty-four years old—a vigorous, red-haired woman with blue-green eyes who still climbed trees
in search of birds' nests.

Climbing trees had been something she had done almost as soon
as she could walk, especially in March, when she was seized with
"March madness." On a windy day she would scale the big white
hickory tree in her family's yard in Arcadia, Louisiana, and, singing
at the top of her voice, "sway back and forth in great arcs. I *was*
the March wind—the very heart of wildness."

However, nothing but the strength of her lungs suggested that the
frail little infant born to Jim and Caroline Dormon at their summer
home, Briarwood, on July 19, 1888, would survive. This sixth child
and second daughter was determined to keep up with two of her
older brothers, Ben and George, and tramped doggedly after them
as they searched for birds' nests. Because she was so light, she was
able to climb out on the thinnest tree branches to collect eggs that
Ben preserved and mounted on carefully labeled cards. Although
the boys and Carrie, as she was nicknamed, also killed, plucked,

and ate songbirds roasted over a fire on their wilderness forays, they knew enough about conservation to take only one egg from each bird species for their collection.

The "wild" Dormon children were tolerated in Arcadia, but Carrie and her brothers eagerly looked forward to the six weeks the family spent each summer at Briarwood, a 135-acre estate in the sandhills of northwestern Louisiana. To Carrie, Briarwood was heaven on earth and remained her spiritual home throughout her lifetime.

As a child she also looked forward to her frequent outings with her beloved "papa"—a lawyer, quail hunter, and amateur naturalist. Carrie was his favorite child, and he rarely went anywhere without her. "How green were the roadsides when, as a child, I rode in a buggy with my father. Wide paths of white sand wound in and out among tall brown trunks of longleaf pine, and dipped down into little valleys where clear streams dashed across the road! . . . If it were spring I could hear the bees, busy in the masses of pink azaleas, and see the brownish coils of giant ferns unfolding. At nearly every ford at least one magnolia leant lovingly over the road, fragrant creamy buds nestled among the shining leaves." In addition to buggy rides, she accompanied her father on his quail hunts, riding behind him on his "bird mule" (a mule specially trained to stop whenever it saw a quail), and as they rode, he gave her impromptu nature lessons.

Her interest in wildflowers was kindled at the age of five, when she discovered several clumps of white bluets. That same year she started a little wild garden in a shady corner of the Arcadia yard, filling it with Jack-in-the-pulpits, closed gentians, pink root (spigelia), and several species of violets and ferns. The following summer she found an albino partridge pea, and the discovery of two albino species in two years gave her a partiality toward white flowers that she never lost.

When Carrie was not outdoors she was either writing, a skill she developed at the age of three, or reading books from the extensive collection in her parents' comfortable home. The Dormons were cultured people, and both parents had been well educated. Carrie's mother wrote poems, songs, and short stories, mostly for Baptist periodicals. She too loved nature, especially her paternal inheritance of a portion of the former six-hundred-acre Briarwood plantation, and, unlike her siblings, she held on to her land during hard times and high taxes.

Carrie's idyllic childhood came to an end. Her father, a little perturbed by the tomboy he had raised, decided to send her off to an elite Baptist girls' school, Judson College at Marion, in north-central

Alabama, when she was sixteen. Her first year was difficult and she was very homesick, but during her second year she discovered that her wittiness helped her socially. Then one day a teacher found out she could identify bird species by their calls, after which Carrie quickly found herself in demand as a teacher of birdcalls to both students and teachers. Gradually, too, she was socialized, but it was just a veneer. "I still belonged to the wild," she declared. Rambling in the nearby woods of Grey's Hollow, she discovered *Iris cristata* for the first time, as well as *Iris verna*, bloodroot, hepatica, and yellow violets.

She graduated with an A.B. in literature and art in 1907, the same year her mother died, and the following year she taught first grade in nearby Bienville Parish. When her father died in 1909 Carrie was devastated. "Papa possessed magic," she later wrote, and with his death the magic was gone. Three months later their Arcadia home, with its large library, burned to the ground. Only Briarwood was left. There she and her older sister Virginia went during vacations from their teaching careers, moving in permanently in 1918 after having a log home built from trees on the property.

Virginia had always been part of her life — the older sister who had obligingly acted like a real daughter should — learning needlework when Carrie refused, becoming an excellent manager and competent cook, and acquiring a social grace that was not a veneer. Twelve years Carrie's senior, Virginia was a second mother as well as a loving sister to Carrie. Virginia's marriage in the late 1920s was over in less than a year. Virginia's chiropractor husband had taken her to live in Nebraska after a long honeymoon in the West, and it is entirely plausible that the sisters could not tolerate the separation. Whatever may have caused the rift, Miss Dormon returned as the divorced Mrs. Miller and resumed her protective older sister role.

Carrie, too, had had a brief fling with romance, judging by the several love letters written to her by "Jamie," in 1913 and 1914, but he, like other suitors, could not compete with her passion for the outdoors. Carrie's only recorded comment about marriage, made to a friend, was negative — she didn't want men digging in her flowers. Nevertheless, she did establish many enduring friendships with male writers and botanists and, during her teaching years, she often concentrated on saving the "bad boys." Miss Carrie, as her neighbors called her, was partial to boys, especially if they showed any interest in nature.

She was a natural teacher, but she found classroom teaching too confining and in 1918, after she and Virginia had settled permanently at Briarwood, she began looking around for an outdoor job. That was the year she attended her first Southern Forestry Congress at New Orleans. She pleaded so eloquently for the conservation of long-leaf pine virgin forests that she was appointed state chairman of conservation for the Louisiana Federation of Women's Clubs. Still, what she really wanted to be was a forester, but she was told that was not a career for women. Women were teachers, and Carrie continued reluctantly in that role.

In 1919, though, she became ill and asked the school superintendent to give her a job in the pine woods. He sent her to the forested sand hills of Kisatchie in Natchitoches Parish. In those days only rough dirt roads penetrated the still wild area, and her school was twenty miles from the nearest town, Provencal. Transportation was by wagon "through mile after mile of majestic longleaf pine forests. It was heaven. . . . Immediately I began exploring this fascinating country! . . . The great pines came right to the water's edge on those lovely clear creeks, with only an occasional magnolia and dainty wild azalea and ferns. There the idea was born — this unspoiled beauty must be preserved for future generations to enjoy."

Carrie had two objectives — to save a virgin tract of the Kisatchie, called Odom's Falls, and to persuade the federal government to buy up cutover areas for a national forest. She moved ahead energetically on both counts, giving lectures and writing newspaper articles about her ideas. Despite her gender, the Louisiana Department of Conservation and specifically the commissioner of conservation, M. L. Alexander, took notice. In September of 1921 Carrie was hired by the department to do publicity for them. She lectured all over the state and prepared posters and bulletins about the value of trees to Louisiana. The following year she met Colonel W. B. Greeley, chief forester with the United States Forest Service, at a meeting of the Southern Forestry Congress in Jackson, Mississippi. She told him of her plans for a national forest and initially persuaded him that her idea was a good one, but first he sent W. W. Ashe, land acquisitions official for the U.S. Forest Service, to look over the proposed lands. Carrie was his guide on many trips into the Kisatchie, and the two quickly grew to respect each other. To Carrie he was simply the finest botanist she had ever known and when she discovered a hawthorn tree that bloomed two months later than the common *Craetaegus aestivales*, Ashe named the variety *Craetaegus aestivales dormonae* for her. Together they discovered the first incidence of the *Lilium michauxi* in Louisiana.

In addition to persuading Ashe of the importance of preserving the Kisatchie, she and Virginia took other interested people into the area. Carrie studied local maps and plotted the virgin area she wanted saved, and when Greeley decided she was right, he learned that Louisiana did not have an enabling act to permit the Forest Service to purchase lands in the state. Undaunted, she asked her lawyer brother to draft such an act; after he did, she talked Henry Hardtner, a state senator, into making certain it was passed by the state legislature.

Finally, after nearly eight years of negotiations, the government was prepared to buy the virgin tract between Sandy and Odom creeks from its owner, Crowell-Spencer, at eighty dollars an acre. But the forester from the New Orleans office of the U.S. Forest Experiment Station who was to make the purchase decided to save the government money and make a name for himself. He offered Crowell-Spencer twelve dollars an acre. So incensed was the company by the insult that it immediately sent men and machines into the area and clear cut the land. "This beautiful forest lost to posterity," Carrie later mourned. In June of 1930, however, when the government purchased 75,589 acres of cutover land for a national forest, she did have the satisfaction of naming it Kisatchie after the Kisatchie Wold she had first seen back in 1919.

Her work for the Louisiana Department of Conservation was similarly frustrating. With no job description to follow, she charted her own course, including the planning of a forestry education program for schoolchildren that other states emulated. She was also a prolific letter writer and talented lecturer. Her supervisor, V. H. Sonderegger, seemed to take an instant dislike to her, badgering her about petty details, such as her habit of staying with friends overnight instead of at the state's expense during out-of-town assignments. Finally, harassed beyond her limit, she resigned on September 1, 1923, after two years as Louisiana's first woman working in forestry.

In January of 1927 she was persuaded to return to the department, this time as an extension forester under W. R. Hine. She continued with her plans for teaching forestry in public schools and wrote the bulletin "Forest Trees of Louisiana," thirty thousand copies of which were distributed free to schools, clubs and other interested groups. And with the help of W. W. Ashe, who wrote a glowing letter about her qualifications, she was one of the first three women in the country to be elected an associate member of the Society of American Foresters in 1930.

Once again her stint with the department lasted only two years. Outspoken in her liberal political beliefs, her disgust at Huey Long's election as governor forced her to resign from a state position. But she did not stop lecturing on conservation issues and over the years continued to campaign for such things as a state park system and a state arboretum. Both of these eventually transpired, the latter a

301-acre tract in Chico State Park near Ville Platte. She also had two more jobs with the state government. First she worked as a landscape architect with the Louisiana Department of Public Welfare from February 1938 to August 1940. While there, she helped landscape the Huey P. Long Charity Hospital grounds at Pineville. She served as a Highway Beautification Consultant to the Louisiana Department of Highways in 1941. Although she was successful in her landscaping job, she was not able to persuade the highway department to preserve the native trees and shrubs already growing beside state highways. Instead, at the behest of nurserymen, the native species were eliminated in favor of exotics.

Although Carrie threw herself into every job she ever had, her real life centered on Briarwood. "All I ask of life is to be able to stay in the woods, fooling with plants and birds," she once wrote to writer Lyle Saxton. She also wanted to write about what she learned, and in 1922 *Holland's* magazine paid her sixteen dollars for her first article "Highways Plus Trees." Most of her magazine writing over the years was for southern gardening periodicals, such as *Home Gardening*, because of her firsthand knowledge of southern wildflowers and their cultivated varieties.

As soon as she moved to Briarwood, she determined to make it a sanctuary for as many southern trees and wildflowers as she could obtain, specializing in magnolias, quinces, native azaleas, and mountain laurel. Her real specialty, though, was the famed Louisiana iris, which she discovered long before Dr. J. K. Small of the New York Botanical Garden began naming the large luxuriant varieties he found thriving in the swamps of southern Louisiana.

In 1920 she had been driving near Morgan City, in the coastal region of Louisiana, when she spotted masses of giant iris growing on the banks of ditches. She quickly consulted her botany books and found no such flowers in them. In fact, only three small species of wild iris were listed for the state. That was the beginning of her life as an "irisiac."

The following year, when she learned of Small's interest in wild Louisiana iris, she offered to collect for him. From all over the state she collected not only for Small but for Briarwood, and her discoveries frequently extended the known range of many iris species and varieties. At Briarwood she planted iris in natural bogs, not to make a "show place," she wrote to a correspondent from California, but "primarily to learn something about them. They constitute one of the great botanical mysteries — the unbelievable variations in size, form and color make classifying extremely difficult. But I am also testing them out for horticultural purposes and hybridizing."

Her work with iris consumed a lot of Carrie's time over the years, especially during the 1940s, when she and Virginia encouraged their widowed sister-in-law, Ruth Dormon, to sell iris as a business. They called the enterprise Wild Garden and helped supply Ruth with hybrid species they had developed at Briarwood. When Ruth died, her customers persuaded Carrie and Virginia to sell them the many varieties they had that were not obtainable elsewhere. Although the business was lucrative, it did require hours of correspondence, often with unappreciative bulb suppliers in the northeast, and near the end of the decade Carrie went back to exchanging only with friends. In the early 1940s, though, she helped form the Mary Swords DeBaillon Louisiana Iris Society, named for a friend she had collected with in the hills of Louisiana as well as in the prairies and bogs of the southern part of the state during the 1930s.

In addition to collecting, growing, and writing about wildflowers from Louisiana, Carrie also began painting them. She believed Louisiana had great botanical diversity that scientists were unaware of, and by writing and painting, she was determined to bring Louisiana renown in the botanical world. Her persistence in sending specimens to Professor R. S. Cocks of Tulane University, for instance, finally convinced him to visit her, and together they made several collecting trips in the Natchitoches Parish area southwest of Briarwood.

Word spread in the botanical world of the gifted Louisiana woman who was always willing to take botanists on collecting trips, and over the years she hosted such botanical luminaries as Edgar Wherry, Joseph Ewan, Edgar Anderson, E. J. Alexander, and Eula Whitehouse. She also went on collecting trips with her sister and other female friends. Her most exciting find was a *Magnolia pyramidata*, which she discovered in Sabine Parish during a camping trip with two nephews. That discovery extended the known range of the attractive small tree, with its rose-red fruits, 350 miles farther west. In fact, it was when she took W. W. Ashe to see the *Magnolia pyramidata* in western Louisiana that she also spotted *Lilium michauxii*, the Carolina lily.

She discovered a new species of wildflower — a *Hymenocallis*, or spider-lily, but when she reported it to the experts they dismissed it as the common *occidentalis* species. Nevertheless, she planted specimens at Briarwood, and many years later, when the same species was discovered in eastern Texas by Dr. Lloyd Shinners, it was declared a new species and named in honor of Texas botanist Eula Whitehouse, *Hymenocallis eulae*. Carrie never did have a wildflower species named for her, but in 1941 her sister-in-law Ruth named a hybrid Louisiana iris "Caroline Dormon."

29.   Caroline Dormon painting irises on site. *Courtesy Archives, Eugene P. Watson Memorial Library, Northwestern State University of Louisiana, Natchitoches, Louisiana*

Year after year Carrie collected, studied, and painted the wild-flowers of Louisiana, and in 1934, she published her first book, *Wild Flowers of Louisiana*. Written for amateurs like herself, with simple, nontechnical information, it was replete with warnings of what plants to pick "freely," "sparingly," or "never."

Except for *Forest Trees of Louisiana*, published by the Louisiana Department of Conservation in 1941, Carrie's other books all came in a rush during the last decade and a half of her life, after Virginia had died and it was no longer possible for her to go far afield. By then she had angina problems and a crippled hip, and most of her nature observations took place from her living room window, where she sat and watched the birds and squirrels.

*Flowers Native to the Deep South* was published in 1958, in part to update the botanical names in *Wild Flowers of Louisiana*. In Carrie's words it had been written for "those to whom the finding of a new flower is a real adventure and who cannot be content until they learn its name." Like her first flower book, it was aimed at the amateur and was filled with her line drawings as well as paintings of many species, almost all of which had been done from the "fresh living flower." "Having lived with most of these flowers and observed them day by day, I hope that I may be able to tell something of new interest to nature lovers." She also hoped to arouse renewed interest in preserving native wildflowers.

Her acknowledgments of help from well-known botanists and friends indicated just how widely her botanical net had been spread and how authoritative her work was. Its scope included all of the Deep South except for subtropical Florida, so it was a far more comprehensive book than *Wild Flowers of Louisiana*. Despite Carrie's championship of her state, she had frequently collected in other southern states as well, particularly in central Alabama, where one of her brothers lived. Once, in fact, she and Virginia had driven to Appalachicola, Florida, just to obtain cuttings of the rare evergreen tree — *Torreya taxifolia* — for Briarwood, where it still grows today.

Carrie continued her championship of native wild plants in the next book she published in 1965, *Natives Preferred*, written "for those who love the informality of Nature, with softly rounded masses of foliage, and flowers scattered freely by her hand." Written in a chatty, informative manner, the book tells a great deal about Carrie's life as a naturalist and the botanical friends she has made and is the most interesting of her books to read.

Her next book, *Southern Indian Boy*, published in 1967, reflected Carrie's interest in the native Indians of Louisiana. During the decades when she collected plants, she frequently found Indian mounds, which she mapped. She also discovered remnant populations of five distinct Louisiana tribes and visited all of them, gathering their lore and legends. She shared much of the information with ethnologist Dr. John R. Swanton of the Smithsonian Institution. After reading her collection of Indian stories, he declared them "the best for popular usage for the region covered with which I am acquainted."

During the depression, Carrie had been instrumental in getting Red Cross and government loans for the desperately poor Tunica Indians to grow food. In return they had become her friends and had helped her when she assisted the Smithsonian in their Indian site surveys and excavations in Louisiana. *Southern Indian Boy,* dedicated "to my Indian friends, who shared their knowledge with me," includes two Indian tales written for young people.

Her last book, *Bird Talk,* came out in 1969. A compilation of articles she had written over the years for the *Sunday Magazine* of the *Shreveport Times,* they reflected her other lifelong nature interest — bird-watching. In the haphazard diary she kept during her later years, she often mentioned her pleasure in both handfeeding such birds as golden-crowned kinglets and pine warblers and watching birds as she lay in bed. On Christmas Day, 1965, she thanked God for "my gift of happiness in my world of trees, birds, and flowers." "My birds are my life," she wrote to a friend two years later. "I put feed on the flat rocks right below my window and can barely get any work done for watching them." She also made new discoveries, such as the six Cassin's finches she saw on April 13, 1969, feeding on the flat rocks. They had never been reported in Louisiana before.

She had learned the common names of birds from her father, and she recalled "inching out on a mossy limb of an old sweetgum to look into my first blue-gray gnatcatcher nest. (My guardian angel had little time for loafing!)" "Oh," she exclaimed, "one who has never peered into a bird's nest has missed the most delightful thrill of birding!" Once again she recalled those days of driving through a longleaf pine forest in a buggy at dawn. "The stillness was impressive. Then suddenly the luminous air was filled with silvery sound, the voices of the pinewoods sparrows coming from all directions. The exquisite beauty still lives with me."

Carolina wrens, Carolina chickadees, and tufted titmice were her favorite winter birds, Carolina wrens being the "most winsome" of birds. Once, a Carolina wren built a nest in an inaccessible spot under the hood of her car. Whenever she had to go to the store, she started the engine and the female flew out and perched on a dogwood tree branch. When Carrie returned, the wren resumed her care of first the eggs, then the nestlings.

In addition to recording her observations of bird behavior, Carrie also used *Bird Talk* to champion persecuted bird species such as owls and red-tailed hawks. Not all birds were "good"—Cooper's and sharp-shinned hawks, shrikes, and blue jays all destroyed birds and eggs and were therefore "bad" birds. For the most part though, birds were valuable as insect eaters, in Carrie's opinion.

Carrie had always been an ecologist, realizing the importance, for instance, of habitat for bird species. She mourned the disappearance of lark sparrows that had once lived on the now-vanished hill farms and the disappearance of the pinewoods (now Bachman's) sparrows of the open, virgin, longleaf pine forests. The dangers of monoculture were also clear to her; she inveighed against the clearing of hardwood trees, which provided food for the birds, in favor of planting pine trees.

Her concern about pesticidal poisons had been aroused by Rachel Carson's *Silent Spring*, and Carrie's final piece, "When the Last Birds Sing," was a diatribe against the use of DDT and heptachlor. In fact, she spent a good deal of time writing influential people to protest the use of pesticides. She wrote to bird artist Roger Tory Peterson, hoping he would put his considerable influence behind the banning of fire ant control and Dutch elm disease spraying. Her place had once been a "paradise for birds. I used to lie in bed at dawn and count about twenty different notes. Now there are about six. At feeding time, I would go out and call 'Birdies!' and (especially in winter), they would simply rain down. Pine warblers, titmice, kinglets, and even red-breasted nuthatch would eat from my hand. Last year [1965] I had one kinglet and not a single nuthatch!"

Her files are filled with other letters she wrote to politicians about many of the environmental issues of the day—flooding the Alaska Barrens, ruining the Everglades, establishing a National Wildlife Refuge in Alaska, and damming the Red River. Honors came late to Carrie, but they did come. Even though many people found her fussy, they also recognized her contributions to society. In 1960 she received what she called in her diary, "the highest honor that has been accorded me yet. The Garden Club of America has given me the Eloise Paine Luquer Medal for achievement in botany." The following year the American Horticultural Society cited her "for outstanding contributions to horticulture, for valuable information on flowering plants . . . [and] for her writings and extremely accurate drawings of plants."

But it took several years of pressure on the part of influential friends to get Carrie what she wanted most of all. In January of 1965 she received an honorary Doctor of Science degree from Louisiana State

University. Her citation recognized her contributions in three fields—
botany, horticulture and forestry—and praised her for her artistic
achievements as well as her ability to arouse public interest in the
beauties of Louisiana.

The following year the American Horticultural Society recognized
Briarwood as a "sanctuary for the flora of the south." Once again
friends helped her realize a dream—to preserve Briarwood for future generations through the founding of the Caroline Dormon
Foundation.

Her last years were spent as a semi-invalid. She died on November 21, 1971, in a nursing home, not at Briarwood, as she had wished.
However, for the most part she had, in her words, "done what I wanted
all my life. . . . I simply loved nature always and could no more have
stopped studying birds, flowers and trees, and drawing pictures of
them, than I could have stopped breathing!"

# Rachel Carson

PIONEERING ECOLOGIST

SHE WROTE, according to Supreme Court Justice William O. Douglas, "the most important chronicle of this century for the human race." Rachel Carson, the only American woman field naturalist who became a household name, called her book *Silent Spring*, but public reaction to it was anything but silent. Vilified by chemical and agricultural interests, praised by conservationists and a large segment of the scientific community, her conclusions were vindicated by President John F. Kennedy's Science Advisory Committee report. She became, in the two years left to her, a national heroine for daring to speak up about the dangers of pesticides to nature and humanity.

Writing about pesticides was not a job she had undertaken lightly. She preferred to write about her beloved sea or about the beauty of nature in general, and she was happiest when she was poking around in tide pools. She was the kind of person, she asserted, "who wants above all to get out and enjoy the beauty and wonder of the natural world, and who resorts only secondarily to the laboratory and library for explanations." Rachel Carson was at heart a field person even though she had a master's degree in marine biology from the Johns Hopkins University and had spent the requisite number of hours in the laboratory dissecting catfish to get it.

She was not a child of the sea but of the Allegheny hills of western Pennsylvania. Born on May 27, 1907 in Springdale, just north of Pittsburgh, her modest home was tucked amidst sixty-five rural acres of woods and fields. Far younger than her brother and sister, she lived the life of an only child, alone but not unhappy as she explored the natural world her mother helped her appreciate.

Her mother, Maria, was her dearest companion and had the greatest influence not only on what Rachel became but on how she lived the rest of her life. Maria Carson loved books, music, and nature and made certain that Rachel loved them too. Furthermore, she never allowed Rachel to believe that because she was a woman she would have to settle for less in life. Both mother and daughter were small, frail-looking women, but both had indomitable spirits and a sense of their own worth. When there was not enough money to help Rachel through college, her mother sold the family silver and good china to help out.

By then Rachel already had a reputation as a conscientious student who wanted to be a writer. She had been spurred on, as many children were in those days, by her writing debut in *St. Nicholas* magazine at the age of ten. She won a four-year tuition scholarship of one hundred dollars per year at the nearby Pennsylvania College for Women (now Chatham College), where she majored in English. She thought this was the key to becoming a successful writer.

Years later, when powerful forces sought to discredit Rachel as an oddball — unsociable, unathletic, unattractive to men — one friend from her college years, Dorothy Seif, painted an entirely different picture. She portrayed a schoolgirl who was a goalie on the field hockey team and who described herself as "seldom happier than when I am before a glowing campfire, with the open sky above my head. I love all the beautiful things of nature, and the wild creatures are my friends." She did not excel in sports, but she enjoyed swimming, tennis, hiking, riding, and basketball and enthusiastically attended sport events. Like other college girls, she went to proms and had a boyfriend whom she dated throughout her college career.

She had several close female friends and two teachers who greatly influenced her future direction. The first, an English professor named Grace Croff, gave Rachel an eye-opening course in English composition. The second, Mary Scott Skinker, was a young idealist like Rachel herself. Mary came to the Pennsylvania College for Women imbued with the idea that young ladies should work hard in college. Her first-year course in biology terrorized most of the socially adept but not particularly scholarly women who made up the student body.

Rachel took her course and was enthralled by both the subject and the brilliant woman who taught it. For more than a year she agonized over a change of major, frightened of having to take chemistry, physics, and math. Finally, in the middle of her junior year, she took the momentous step of switching from English to zoology, thereby condemning herself to almost unremitting laboratory courses until she graduated magnum cum laude in 1928. To her friend Dorothy Seif she confided that although she had always wanted to write, she didn't have much imagination. "Biology has given me something to write about. I will try in my writing to make animals in the woods or waters, where they live, as alive to others as they are to me." But she had grinding years of school and work ahead of her before she could try.

Miss Skinker continued to encourage Rachel and helped her get a scholarship to the prestigious Johns Hopkins University in Baltimore. Rachel also received a summer-study fellowship from her college to the Marine Biological Laboratory at Woods Hole in Massachusetts. At last Rachel met the sea she had been dreaming and writing about all her landlocked years in Pennsylvania.

She saw her first sea anemones and sea urchins at Woods Hole, and for several summers there she had the field experiences she cherished so much. But back at Johns Hopkins she pursued her master's in marine biology mostly in the laboratory, writing a painstaking study of "The Development of the Pronephros during the Embryonic and Early Larval Life of the Catfish (*Inctalurus punctatus*)."

Once she had her degree in 1932 she emerged straight into the worst of the depression years, desperate to earn enough money to support herself and her parents. They had sold their home in Springdale and moved down to Maryland to pool their resources during such difficult financial times. The best she could do, at first, was to teach zoology at Johns Hopkins summer school and part-time at the University of Maryland in winter.

Teaching was what she had wanted to do, but two half-time appointments did not add up to enough money to live on, especially after her father died of a heart attack in 1935, leaving her the sole support of her mother. So she looked around for other work, and she took the test for the job of junior aquatic biologist, grade P-1, at the U.S. Bureau of Fisheries. Outscoring the other applicants, all of whom were males, she became the second woman ever hired by the bureau for other than clerical positions.

To be closer to her job, she and her mother moved to Silver Spring, Maryland, a Washington suburb, and were almost immediately joined by two grammar-school–age nieces — Virginia and Marjorie — whose mother, Marian, Rachel's older sister, had died prematurely at forty. Rachel was now supporting a family as large as many men at that time did.

Up until that time all of Rachel's mentors had been women, but in 1937 her boss at the bureau, Elmer Higgins, rejected one of her radio broadcasts. Saying it was too literary, he suggested that she send it in to the *Atlantic Monthly*. They published it as "Undersea," where it caught the eye of a literary giant of the times, Hendrik

Willem van Loon, author of *The Story of Mankind,* and of an editor, Quincy Howe at Simon and Shuster. Both men wrote to Rachel and added their urgings to Higgins's that she make a book out of it. A month before Pearl Harbor, *Under the Sea Wind* was published by Simon & Shuster.

The reviewers loved it, but the public, distracted by the war, hardly noticed; it sold less than sixteen hundred copies after six years in print. Rachel had been recognized, though, by important people, including the scientist-writer William Beebe. He not only corresponded with her but included excerpts from *Under the Sea Wind* in his collection of the world's best nature writing, which he called *The Book of Naturalists.* That book was published in 1944, and it must have given Rachel a sense of well-being to see her name at the end of a book beginning with such immortals as Aristotle and Pliny and progressing through the male litany of names, which included Gilbert White and John James Audubon, Henry David Thoreau and Charles Darwin, John Muir and Henri Fabre, Ernest Thompson Seton and Donald Culross Peattie.

*Under the Sea Wind,* which was subtitled *A Naturalist's Picture of Ocean Life,* had been written in the style of Rachel's favorite author, Englishman Henry Williamson, whose classics, *Salar the Salmon* and *Tarka the Otter,* were continually reread by Rachel throughout her life. Instead of one wild creature protagonist, though, Rachel had several to illustrate what she called her "descriptive narratives unfolding successively the life of the shore, the open sea and the sea bottom." Her characters included Rynchops, the black skimmer, Blackfoot and Silverbar, the sanderlings, Scomber, the mackerel, and Aguilla, the female eel. It was the two chapters on Aguilla that Beebe chose to excerpt, calling them "a dramatic presentation of this almost unbelievable aspect of natural history."

She had written the book in the late evening hours after returning home from a day in the office. In 1940 her own Bureau of Fisheries had been merged with the Biological Survey and renamed the Fish and Wildlife Service, under the Department of the Interior. Rachel's new boss was Dr. Ira N. Gabrielson, who later recalled her shyness when she asked him for a writing job. Despite her quiet manner, she moved up the ranks as the years passed — from assistant to associate to aquatic biologist by the end of the war, then information specialist and finally biologist and chief editor — until her resignation in 1952 to become a full-time writer. Always her work was connected with writing, because she not only gave her best when she wrote but demanded it of those who worked for her. Throughout the war she produced pamphlets to encourage people to eat fish dur-

30. Rachel Carson and Robert W. Hines looking for snapping shrimp in a sponge along the Missouri and Ohio Key, Florida. *Photograph by Rex Gary Schmidt, courtesy U.S. Fish and Wildlife Service*

ing meat shortages. After the war she wrote *Conservation in Action* booklets about National Wildlife Refuges; this got her out in the field again, visiting such places as the Florida Everglades, Chincoteague Island off the Maryland coast, and the Parker River Refuge in Massachusetts.

Those who worked for and with Rachel admired her insistence on high quality writing, but both she and they recognized the often inept work that goes on in a government office. Nonetheless, Rachel joked about it with her friends, and during those years she was regarded as a fun-loving, party-going, sociable person with a mischievous sense of humor—the same personality that her friend Dorothy Seif had described back in her college years.

And so she was, despite frustrations with an ever more demanding job that gave her little or no time to do the kind of writing she wanted to do. She also made a new friend, Shirley Briggs, who joined the Fish and Wildlife Service in 1945 and loved hiking and outdoor exploration as much as Rachel did. Together they took many field trips, often with the local Audubon Society, to nearby natural areas.

In July of 1946 she found the place she really wanted to live — the coast of Maine. That summer she rented a cabin on the Sheepscot River near Boothbay and ecstatically watched the seabirds and explored the tide pools. To Shirley she wrote, "the only reason I will ever come back is that I don't have brains enough to figure out a way to stay here the rest of my life. . . . My greatest ambition is to be able to buy a place here and then manage to spend a great deal of time in it. . . ."

But she still had her family to think of, and so back she went to her job by day and a new writing project at night, when she pored over books about the sea. She was also free to use the previously classified wartime research on oceanography, which the government had pushed vigorously and which she had learned about during her own work with the fishing industry during the war. All of this material she labored over in preparation for her classic book *The Sea Around Us*.

After she had amassed her material and written a list of tentative chapters, she went searching for a literary agent. She fortuitously discovered Marie Rodell, who became just the kind of agent she was looking for as well as one of Rachel's closest friends and admirers. A year of work produced a third of the book in draft form — enough for Oxford University Press to bind her to a contract in 1949.

As part of her research, she was persuaded by William Beebe to do some undersea diving in Florida. Although she only went fifteen feet under, it was enough to give her a feeling of "what the surface of the water looks like from underneath and how exquisitely delicate and varied are the colors displayed by the animals of the reef."

She also decided she had better spend some time on the Fish and Wildlife Service's research vessel, the *Albatross III*, which was then studying fish populations off the Georges Bank south of Nova Scotia. Her presence was to be a first for the all-male crew, so her bosses insisted that she bring another woman as a chaperon! Marie Rodell was her choice, and for both of them their ten days on the *Albatross* remained an unforgettable experience. "When I stood," Rachel later wrote, "on the after deck on those dark nights, on a tiny manmade island of wood and steel, dimly seeing the great shapes of waves that rolled about us, I think I was conscious as never before that ours is a water world dominated by the immensity of the sea." This is exactly the impression she tried to create in her grand book about the sea.

Before it was completed, though, both William Beebe and another good friend, naturalist-writer Edwin Way Teale, helped her get a Eugene F. Saxton Memorial Fellowship, which awarded money to creative writers. Also, Marie Rodell tried hard to place prepublication chapters with national magazines. After being turned down by most of the major ones, including the *Atlantic Monthly*, she made the first breakthrough in *Yale Review*, closely followed by the *New Yorker*, whose brilliant editor, William Shawn, recognized the greatness of her work when he read it. So did his readers. They besieged Rachel with letters asking if she was going to make a book of it. To her amazement, the money she received from the *New Yorker* for the half of the book they published was as much as she received all year from her government job.

The rest, of course, is literary history. *The Sea Around Us* was published on July 2, 1951, and by September 9 was number one on the *New York Times* best-seller list, remaining there for eighty-six weeks. The shy woman from the Fish and Wildlife Service had become a literary personage, forced to deliver talks to eager fans and to those who honored her with awards, such as the John Burroughs Medal for the outstanding natural history book of the year and the National Book Award.

In those talks, she revealed a little about herself and how she wrote, delivering her painstakingly prepared speeches in a quiet, uninflected voice. It was what she said that caught people's attention. For instance, when she delivered her acceptance speech for the National Book Award, she commented on how many readers had been glad to escape the human realities and lose themselves in contemplation of larger truths — the vastness of time and of the sea. She wondered if perhaps instead of looking "first at man with his vanities and greed, and at his problems of a day or a year; and then only, and from this biased point of view, . . . [looking] outward at the earth and at the universe of which our earth is so minute a part," we should instead look first at the earth and the universe and would then "find less time and inclination to plan for our own destruction."

Now that she was famous, *Under the Sea Wind*, quickly reissued by Oxford University Press, also made the best-seller list. Other honors, including doctorates from both her alma mater and Oberlin College, were gratifying, but soon she had more invitations than she could handle. She had finally made enough money to retire from her government job and devote her life to writing. She did not intend to spend all her time satisfying the intense curiosity of the public as to who she was, what she looked like, and even, for some, whether or not she really was a woman. One man, in fact, flatly refused to believe she was female. Even though he properly addressed her as Miss Rachel Carson, he amended his salutation to "Dear Sir." Rachel later recalled that his explanation was that he believed only "males possess the supreme intellectual powers of the world, and he could not bring himself to reverse his conviction."

Even while the adulation was at its height, Rachel was already working hard on another book, the book whose writing undoubtedly gave her the greatest joy of her life. *The Edge of the Sea*, by its very nature, was a field book, and she spent many happy days splashing in sea edges from the coral and mangrove coasts of Florida to the rocky shores of Maine. She was often accompanied by her former colleague and good friend, Bob Hines — official Fish and Wildlife Service illustrator — who agreed to illustrate her new book.

She also fulfilled her earlier dream to own a summer home in Maine, which she built on land she bought in 1953 in West Southport overlooking Sheepscot Bay. Only her mother accompanied her there, since her nieces were on their own by then, although Marjorie and her small son Roger were frequent visitors.

These then were her halcyon days — free of a job, free of some of her family cares, free to spend her time "in the low-tide world, when the ebb tide falls very early in the morning, and the world is full of salt smell and the sound of water, and the softness of fog." Morning, noon, and night she was in, next to, and beside the sea observing it in all its moods, looking beneath rocks to find thirty sea anemones under one ledge at low tide, and making new discoveries such as "that there is a large and thriving fauna living in and under the crusts of Lithophyllum." "For the first time," she wrote to Marie Rodell, "I'm writing about something while it is right under my nose, and it gives me a very different feeling about it. . . ."

When at last *The Edge of the Sea* was published in 1955, she collected two more prestigious awards, the Achievement Award of the American Association of University Women and a citation for "the outstanding book of the year" from the National Council of Women of the United States. Following that success, she took a rest from writing full-length books for two years. She concentrated instead, on smaller projects, such as writing a script about clouds for the Omnibus television program, even though she never owned a television or had any interest in watching it. She recognized, however, that television was a way to reach the most people with her message about the wonders of nature. She wrote "Something about the Sky" to accompany the excellent film work of meteorologist Dr. Vincent J. Schaefer.

Her next project became, in the words of literary critic Carol B. Gartner, "an excellent summary of her philosophy." It was first published as a magazine article, and later it appeared, posthumously, in book form as *The Sense of Wonder*. Using her young nephew Roger as a model, she tried to show how parents everywhere could teach their children to love nature.

A year later her niece Marjorie died, and at the age of forty-nine Rachel found herself once again a surrogate mother, this time of her grand nephew, as well as the caretaker of her arthritic, eighty-eight-year-old mother. She did, however, have the joy of building a new winter home in Silver Spring, Maryland, on an untamed plot of ground that she filled with bird feeders and birdhouses. Her windows looked out on a tangle of vines and bushes, gnarled trees and young saplings, all providing refuge for the wild creatures that lived there. So finally she had two naturalist homes — summer at the sea and winter in the woods — where she was to write the book that gave her the most fame and the least pleasure and that had nothing and yet everything to do with the environment surrounding her, the book she felt compelled to write because "there would be no peace for me if I kept silent."

The call to write *Silent Spring* came in a letter from one of Rachel's friends, Olga Owens Huckins. Olga and her husband owned a small place in Duxbury, Massachusetts, where they had created a bird sanctuary. The state began aerial spraying of DDT to control mosquitoes. Immediately their birds started dying, but the state insisted that the spraying was a "harmless shower," so Mrs. Huckins wrote to Rachel to ask for help from the proper federal government authorities. Rachel, in her thorough way, began investigating for herself, and the more she learned about pesticide use, the more horrified she became. Suddenly she realized that humanity was tinkering more destructively than ever with the natural world and that all she loved was at stake.

At first she hoped to write a magazine article about the detrimental effects of DDT, using her scientific knowledge of the subject, but no one was interested. In fact, *Good Housekeeping* said outright that they doubted whether her points could be substantiated. She knew that a book would have to be written on the subject, but did she have to be the one to write it? She tried to persuade essayist-writer E. B. White to do it. He, in turn, suggested that she contact William Shawn at the *New Yorker* about her ideas and then write the book herself. Still not reconciled to what would be an enormous task, she suggested to Shawn that she write a magazine article that would serve as a chapter of a book, which would also have other contributing editors. She also volunteered to do an introduction and some general editorial work, and so by degrees, she talked herself into doing the mammoth and often heart-breaking work of *Silent Spring* by herself.

Of course, with her reputation she was able to solicit help from experts all over the world. One of her best sources was a former boss of hers from Fish and Wildlife Service, Dr. Clarence Cottam, who was a pioneer in studying the effects of DDT for the Service. He was particularly involved in opposing fire ant spraying in the South. Other biologists advised her on such things as biological controls, herbicides, and the effects of pesticides on wildlife so that the book reflected the research and opinions of many qualified scientists. Some critics had been quick to label her a mere "birdwatcher," denying the fact that she too was a qualified scientist and preferring to treat her as a "hysterical woman."

It took her four years to marshal all her facts and to write a literate account of pesticide abuse. During that time her mother died and she became a full-time parent to Roger. Friends said she worried equally about *Silent Spring* and Roger—both monumental tasks for a woman whose health was becoming precarious. First she had arthritis, followed by an ulcer, the flu, iritis, and finally breast cancer. Even as she learned more about the danger of cancer from pesticides, she knew she had it herself. She seemed optimistic about going ahead with her life, writing to her editor Paul Brooks before she finished *Silent Spring*, "Of course, I'm not satisfied—now I want time for the Help Your Child to Wonder book, and for the big Man and Nature book. Then I suppose I'll have others—if I live to be 90 still wanting to say something."

But she had said just about all she would be able to say before her time ran out. Once *Silent Spring* was published, she was again in great demand as a speaker. She accepted only those invitations she felt were most important, preserving her limited strength to address such influential audiences as the members of the National Parks Association, the National Council of Women of the United States, and the Women's National Press Club. She focused her energy where she thought it would do the most good, testifying before the Ribicoff Committee, a Senate committee on environmental hazards. And she continued to gather more data about chemical poisonings to illustrate her talks.

She also joined other conservation efforts—to save Assateague

Island off the Maryland coast from exploiters, to protest "wolf control" in Arkansas and the poisoning of "trash fish" in Utah's Green River. Had she lived longer, there is no doubt that Rachel would have become a leader in the struggle to save the natural environment. But her health steadily deteriorated and most of the honors heaped on her had to be accepted by others. "Now, when there is an opportunity to do so much, my body falters and I know there is little time left."

But the naturalist in her refused to give up, and she still delighted in a wedge of geese flying over, the first cowbirds arriving in the spring, the eleven robins on her lawn at sunset and the "first thin bubble of frog song." And she had one last summer in Maine with Roger and her two beloved cats.

The closing months of her life were filled with honors—a conservation award from the Izaak Walton League of America, the Audubon Medal (the first ever given to a woman), and the Cullum Medal of the American Geographical Society. Best of all, she was elected to the American Academy of Arts and Letters, which cited her as "a scientist in the grand literary style of Galileo and Buffon, [who] used her scientific knowledge and moral feeling to deepen our consciousness of living nature and to alert us to the calamitous possibility that our short-sighted technological conquests might destroy the very sources of our being. Who could better exemplify the humanist tradition of this Academy?"

And who could better exemplify the whole tradition of selfless women field naturalists, mostly unknown and unheralded, who also did their best to increase humanity's knowledge and understanding of the natural world? Rachel Louise Carson died on April 14, 1964, at the age of fifty-six. Her funeral was held in the Washington Cathedral, and her pallbearers included Stewart L. Udall, secretary of the interior, and Sen. Abraham Ribicoff. Prince Philip of England, who had said, "I strongly recommend Rachel Carson's *Silent Spring* if you want to see what is going on," sent a wreath. She died a public figure, mourned throughout the world by those who love the earth. But she left a large body of writing that is still an inspiration to read. In one talk she summed up what it is to be a natural scientist: "There is one quality that characterizes all of us who deal with the sciences of the earth and its life—we are never bored. We can't be. There is always something new to be investigated. Every mystery solved brings us to the threshold of a greater one."

So it was with every woman field naturalist.

# Selected Bibliography

*Preface*

McCullough, David. "A Rothschild Who Is Known as the Queen of the Fleas." *Smithsonian* 16 (June, 1985): 139–54.

Rossiter, Margaret. *Women Scientists in America.* Baltimore, Md.: Johns Hopkins University Press, 1982.

Tracy, Henry Chester. *American Naturalists.* New York: Dutton, 1930.

Part I. *The Pioneers*

Cooper, Susan Fenimore. *Rural Hours.* Rev. ed. Syracuse, N.Y.: Syracuse University Press, 1968.

Cunningham, Anna K. "Susan Fenimore Cooper, Child of Genius." *New York History Magazine* 25 (July, 1944): 339–50.

Pinckney, Elise, ed. *The Letterbook of Eliza Lucas Pinckney.* Chapel Hill: University of North Carolina Press, 1972.

———, ed. "Letters of Eliza Pinckney, 1768–1782." *South Carolina Historical Magazine* 76 (July, 1975): 143–70.

Porter, Charlotte M. *The Eagle's Nest: Natural History and American Ideas, 1812–1842.* University: University of Alabama Press, 1986.

Ravenel, Harriott Horry. *Eliza Pinckney.* New York: Scribners, 1896.

Weiss, Harry B., and Grace M. Ziegler. *Thomas Say.* Springfield, Ill.: Charles C Thomas, 1931.

Wilson, Joan Hoff. "Dancing Dogs of the Colonial Period: Women Scientists." *Early American Literature* 7 (1973): 225–35.

Chapter 1. *Jane Colden*

Britten, James. "Jane Colden and the Flora of New York." *Journal of Botany* 33 (1895): 12–15.

Hollingsworth, Buckner. *Her Garden Was Her Delight.* New York: Mac-Millan, 1962.

Keys, Alice Mapelsden. *Cadwallader Colden.* New York: Columbia University Press, 1906.

Vail, Anna Murray. "Jane Colden, an Early New York Botanist." *Torreya* 7 (Feb., 1907): 21–34.

## Chapter 2. *Maria Martin*

Arnold, Lois Barber. *Four Lives in Science.* New York: Schocken Books, 1984.

Audubon, John James. *Letters of John James Audubon, 1826–1840.* 2 vols. Editor Howard Corning. Boston: Club of Odd Volumes, 1930.

Bachman and Martin Family Papers. Charleston Museum, Charleston, S.C.

Coffin, Annie Roulhac. "Audubon's Friend — Maria Martin." *New York Historical Society Quarterly* 49 (Jan., 1965): 29–51.

## Part II. *The Naturalists*

Austin, Mary Hunter. *Earth Horizon.* Boston and New York: Houghton Mifflin Co., 1903.

———. *The Land of Little Rain.* Boston and New York: Houghton Mifflin Co., 1903.

———. Papers. Huntington Library, San Marino, Calif.

Brooks, Paul. *Speaking for Nature.* Boston: Houghton Mifflin Co., 1980.

Brown, Chip. "Miss Wiley, Grand Birder of Central Park." *Washington Post,* Dec. 26, 1986.

Gaston, Kay Baker. *Emma Bell Miles.* Signal Mountain, Tenn.: Walden Ridge Historical Association, 1983.

Miles, Emma Bell. *The Spirit of the Mountains.* Knoxville: University of Tennessee Press, 1975.

Shaw, Cynthia L. "A Talent That Poverty Couldn't Repress." *Christian Science Monitor,* July 29, 1986.

Smallwood, William Martin, and Mabel Sarah Coon Smallwood. *Natural History and the American Mind.* New York: Columbia University Press, 1941.

## Chapter 3. *Graceanna Lewis*

Baird, Spencer Fullerton. Papers. Smithsonian Institution Archives, Washington, D.C.

Bent, Arthur Cleveland. *Life Histories of North American Wild Fowl,* Part 1. New York: Dover, 1962.

Hanaford, Phebe A. *Daughters of America.* Augusta, Me., 1876.

Lewis, Graceanna. "Birds and Their Friends." *Friends' Intelligencer and Journal* 53 (1896): 762–63, 779–80.

———. "Lectures on Zoology." Academy of Natural Sciences Library, Philadelphia, Pennsylvania.

———. Letters to Friends and Relatives. Lewis Manuscripts. Friends Historical Library of Swarthmore College, Swarthmore, Pa.

———. "At Longport, New Jersey, in September." *Delaware County Institute of Science, Proceedings* 4 (1909): 103–10.

———. "Science for Women." *Papers Read at the Third Congress of Women.* Syracuse, N.Y., Oct. 13, 14, 15, 1875, 63–66.

———. "Urbanista in Spring." *Friends' Intelligencer and Journal* 57 (1901): 523–24.

———. "Urbanista in Winter." *Friends' Intelligencer and Journal* 58 (1901): 193–94.

Warner, Deborah Jean. *Graceanna Lewis, Scientist and Humanitarian.* Washington, D.C.: Smithsonian Institution Press, 1979.

## Chapter 4. *Martha Maxwell*

Benson, Maxine. *Martha Maxwell, Rocky Mountain Naturalist.* Lincoln: University of Nebraska Press, 1986.

Brace, Mabel Maxwell *Thanks to Abigail: A Family Chronicle.* N.p., 1948.

Dartt, Mary. *On the Plains, and Among the Peaks; or, How Mrs. Maxwell Made Her Natural History Collection.* Philadelphia: Claxton, Remsen, and Haffelfinger, 1879.

DeLapp, Mary. "Pioneer Woman Naturalist." *Colorado Quarterly* 13 (Summer, 1964): 91–96.

Henderson, Junius. "A Pioneer Venture in Habitat Grouping." *Proceedings of the American Association of Museums* 9 (1915): 91.

Maxwell, Martha Dartt. Papers. Colorado Historical Society, Denver, Colorado.

## Chapter 5. *Mary Treat*

Gershenowitz, Harry. "The Mrs. Treat of Darwin's Scientific World." *Vineland Historical Magazine* 55 (1979): 3–7.

Harshberger, John W. *The Botanists of Philadelphia and Their Work.* Philadelphia: T. C. Davis & Sons, 1899.

———. *The Vegetation of the New Jersey Pine Barrens: An Ecologic Investigation.* Philadelphia: Christopher Sower Co., 1916.

Scudder, Samuel. Papers. Museum of Science, Boston, Mass.

Smith, Nancy. "Mary Treat." *New Jersey Audubon* 9 (Winter, 1983): 18–20.

Treat, Mary. *Chapters on Ants.* New York: Harper & Brothers, 1877.
———. "Controlling Sex in Butterflies." *American Naturalist* 7 (Mar., 1873): 129–32.
———. "The Habits of a Tarantula." *American Naturalist* 13 (Aug., 1879): 485–89.
———. *Home Studies in Nature.* New York: Harper & Brothers, 1885.
———. "Observations on the Sundew." *American Naturalist* 7 (Dec., 1873): 705–707.
———. Papers. Vineland Historical and Antiquarian Society, Vineland, N.J.
———. "Plants That Eat Animals." *American Naturalist* 9 (1875): 658–60.
Weiss, Harry B. "Mrs. Mary Treat, 1830–1923, Early New Jersey Naturalist." *Proceedings of the New Jersey Historical Society* 73 (1955): 258–73.

## Chapter 6. *Annie Montague Alexander*

Alexander, Annie Montague. Field Notebooks. Museum of Vertebrate Zoology, University of California, Berkeley, Calif.
———. Papers. Bancroft Library, University of California, Berkeley, Calif.
Grinnell, Hilda W. *Annie Montague Alexander.* Berkeley, Calif.: Grinnell Naturalists Society, 1958.
Kellogg, Louise. Field Notebooks. Museum of Vertebrate Zoology, University of California, Berkeley, Calif.
Merriam, C. Hart. "The Museum of Vertebrate Zoology of the University of California." *Science* 40 (Nov. 13, 1914): 703–704.
Pfaff, Timothy. "The Evolution of a Giant, Berkeley's Museum of Vertebrate Zoology." *California Monthly* (Oct., 1983): 15–16, 21–22.
Reifschneider, Olga. *Biographies of Nevada Botanists.* Reno: University of Nevada Press, 1964.
Rho, Marguerite, ed. *Alexander and Baldwin, Inc. Eighty Years a Corporation 1900–1980.* Honolulu: Alexander & Baldwin, 1980.
Zullo, Janet Lewis. "Annie Montague Alexander: Her Work in Paleontology." *Journal of the West* 8 (Apr., 1969): 183–99.

## Chapter 7. *Ellen Quillin*

Long, Charles J. Interview with author. San Antonio, Tex., Jan., 1983.
Pisano, Marina. "San Antonio's Founding Mothers." *San Antonio Press,* Nov. 4, 1980.
Quillin, Ellen Schulz. Papers. Library of the Daughters of the Republic of Texas at the Alamo, San Antonio, Tex.

Schulz, Ellen D. *Texas Wild Flowers, A Popular Account of the Common Wild Flowers of Texas.* Chicago: Laidlaw Publishing Co., 1928.
———. *500 Wild Flowers of San Antonio and Vicinity.* San Antonio: Ellen D. Schulz, 1922.
Woolford, Bess Carroll, and Ellen Schulz Quillin. *The Story of the Witte Memorial Museum, 1922–1960.* San Antonio: San Antonio Museum Association, 1966.

## Part III. *The Botanists*

Canby, William M. Papers. Library of the Academy of Natural Sciences of Philadelphia. Philadelphia, Pa.
Crosswhite, Frank S. "J. G. Lemmon and Wife, Plant Explorers in Arizona, California, and Nevada." *Desert Plants* 1 (Aug., 1979): 12–21.
Ewan, Joseph. *A Century of Progress in the Natural Sciences 1853–1953.* San Francisco, Calif.: California Academy of Sciences, 1955.
———. *Rocky Mountain Naturalists.* Denver, Colo.: University of Denver Press, 1950.
Jepson, Willis Linn. "The Botanical Explorers of California." *Madroño* 2 (1934): 130–33, 157.
Kibbe, Alice L., ed. *Afield with Plant Lovers and Collectors: Correspondence of Greatest American Botanists of His Day with Harry N. Patterson.* Carthage, Ill.: Alice L. Kibbe, 1953.
Lemmon, J. G. "A Botanical Wedding Trip." *Californian* 4 (1881): 517–25.
Rodgers, Andrew D., III. *"Noble Fellow" William Starling Sullivant.* New York: Putnam, 1940.
Rudolph, Emanuel D. "Women in Nineteenth Century American Botany; A Generally Unrecognized Constituency." *American Journal of Botany* 69 (Sept., 1982): 1346–55.
Sharp, Katharine Dooris. *Summer in a Bog.* Cincinnati: Stewart and Kidd Co., 1913.
Warner, Deborah Jean. "Science Education for Women in Antebellum America." *Isis* 69 (1978): 58–67.

## Chapter 8. *Kate Furbish*

Coburn, Louise H. "Kate Furbish, Botanist, An Appreciation." *Maine Naturalist,* Nov. 15, 1924.
Cole, John. "The Woman behind the Wildflower That Stopped a Dam." *Horticulture* 55 (Dec., 1977): 30–35.
Furbish, Kate. "A Botanist's Trip to the Aroostook." *American Naturalist* 16 (May, 1882): 397–99.
———. Letters. Gray Herbarium, Harvard University, Cambridge, Mass.

————. Papers. Bowdoin College Library, Brunswick, Maine.

Saltonstall, Richard, Jr. "Of Dams and Kate Furbish." *Living Wilderness* 40 (Jan./Mar., 1977): 42–43.

## Chapter 9. *Kate Brandegee*

Brandegee, Katharine. Letters. Field Museum, Chicago, Ill.

————. Letters. Gray Herbarium, Harvard University, Cambridge, Mass.

————. Papers. University and Jepson Herbaria, University of California, Berkeley, Calif.

Crosswhite, Frank S., and Carol D. Crosswhite. "The Plant Collecting Brandegees, with Emphasis on Katharine Brandegee as a Liberated Woman Scientist of Early California." *Desert Plants* 7 (1985): 128–62.

Herre, Albert W. C. T. *Katharine Brandegee: A Reply to a Fantasy by J. Ewan.* Privately printed, 1960.

Jaeger, Edmund C. "Bold Kate Brandegee, Pioneer California Botanist." *Calico Print* 9 (Mar., 1953): 8–9, 33.

Jones, Marcus E. "Katharine Brandegee, a Biography." *Cactus and Succulent Journal* 41 (1969): 266–69.

————. "Mrs. T. S. Brandegee." *Contributions to Western Botany* 18 (Aug., 1933–Apr., 1935): 12–18.

Lindsay, George. "Notes Concerning the Botanical Explorers and Exploration of Lower California, Mexico." A paper prepared for Biology 199, Stanford University, Winter Quarter, 1955.

Setchell, William Albert. "Townshend Stith Brandegee and Mary Katharine (Layne) (Curran) Brandegee." *University of California Publications of Botany* 13, no. 9.

Thomas, John H. "Botanical Explorations in Washington, Oregon, California and Adjacent Regions." *Huntia* 3 (1979): 5–66.

## Chapter 10. *Alice Eastwood*

Dakin, Susanna Bryant. *Perennial Adventure: A Tribute to Alice Eastwood.* San Francisco: California Academy of Sciences, 1954.

Eastwood, Alice. "Letter." *Science* 23 (May 25, 1906): 824–26.

————. Letters. Gray Herbarium, Harvard University, Cambridge, Mass.

————. Letters to Agnes Chase. Smithsonian Institution Archives, Washington, D.C.

————. Papers. California Academy of Sciences, San Francisco.

Howell, John Thomas. "I Remember When I Think." *Leaflets of Western Botany* 7 (Aug., 1954): 153–76.

Munz, Philip A. "A Century of Achievement." *Leaflets of Western Botany* 7 (Aug., 1953): 69–78.

Pyne, Stephen J. *Grove Karl Gilbert: A Great Engine of Research.* Austin: University of Texas Press, 1980.

Wilson, Carol Green. *Alice Eastwood's Wonderland: The Adventures of a Botanist.* San Francisco: California Academy of Sciences, 1955.
———. "The Eastwood Era at the California Academy of Sciences." *Leaflets of Western Botany* 7 (Aug., 1953): 58–64.

## Chapter 11. *Ynes Mexia*

Eastwood, Alice. Letters. Gray Herbarium, Harvard University, Cambridge, Mass.
Goodspeed, T. Harper. *Plant Hunters in the Andes.* New York: Farrar and Rinehart, 1941.
Mexia, Ynes. "Botanical Trails in Old Mexico—The Lure of the Unknown." *Mudroño* 1 (1929): 227–38.
———. "Camping on the Equator." *Sierra Club Bulletin* 22 (Feb., 1937): 85–91.
———. Letters. Missouri Botanical Gardens, St. Louis, Mo.
———. Papers. Bancroft Library, University of California, Berkeley, Calif.
———. Papers. University and Jepson Herbaria, University of California, Berkeley, Calif.
———. "Three Thousand Miles up the Amazon." *Sierra Club Bulletin* 18 (Feb., 1933): 88–96.

## Chapter 12. *Mary Sophie Young*

Tharp, B. C., and Chester V. Kielman. "Mary S. Young's Journal of Botanical Explorations in Trans-Pecos, Texas, August–September, 1914." *Southwestern Historical Quarterly* 65 (Jan., 1962): 366–93; 65 (Apr., 1962): 512–38.
Young, Mary Sophie. Papers. Eugene C. Barker Texas History Center, University of Texas, Austin.

## Chapter 13. *Elizabeth Gertrude Knight Britton*

Britton, Elizabeth G. K. "Fern Collecting in Cuba." *American Fern Journal* 1 (1910): 75–76.
———. Letters. Gray Herbarium, Harvard University, Cambridge, Mass.
———. Letters to William Farlow. Farlow Reference Library and Herbarium of Cryptogamic Botany, Harvard University, Cambridge, Mass.
———. "The Mosses of El Yungue." *Bryologist* 38 (Jan.–Feb., 1935): 1–3.
———. Papers. Library of the New York Botanical Garden, Bronx, N.Y.
———. "A Trip to Jamaica in Summer." *Torreya* 8 (1908): 9–12.
Britton, Nathaniel Lord. "Cactus Studies in the West Indies." *Journal of the New York Botanical Garden* 14 (May, 1913): 105.

Grout, A. J. "Elizabeth Gertrude Knight Britton." *Bryologist.* 38 (Jan.–Feb., 1935): 1–3.

Howe, Marshall A. "Elizabeth Gertrude Knight Britton." *Journal of the New York Botanical Garden* 35 (May, 1934): 97–103.

Smith, Annie Morrill. "The Early History of the Bryologist and the Sullivant Moss Society." *Bryologist* 20 (Jan., 1917): 1–8.

Steere, William Campbell. "North American Muscology and Muscologists: A Brief History." *Botanical Review* 43 (Jul.–Sept., 1977): 285–343.

Vail, Anna Murray. "Notes on the Spring Flora of Southwestern Virginia." *Memoirs of the Torrey Botanical Club* 11 (Dec. 23, 1890): 27–53.

## Chapter 14. *Mary Agnes Chase*

Chase, Agnes. "Collecting Grasses in Brazil." *Journal of the New York Botanical Garden* 26 (Sept., 1925): 196–98.

———. "Eastern Brazil through an Agrostologist's Spectacles." *Annual Report of the Smithsonian Institution 1926* (1927): 383–403.

———. *The First Book of Grasses.* 3d. ed. Washington, D.C.: Smithsonian Institution Press, 1959.

———. Papers. Smithsonian Institution Archives, Washington, D.C.

———. "Studying the Grasses of Venezuela." *Explorations and Field-Work of the Smithsonian Institution in 1940.* Washington, D.C.: Smithsonian Institution.

———. "Visit to European Herbaria." *Smithsonian Miscellaneous Collections* 54 (1923): 80–82.

Fosburgh, F. R. and Jason R. Swallen. "Agnes Chase." *Taxon* 8 (June, 1959): 145–51.

Harney, Thomas. *The Magnificent Foragers.* Washington, D.C.: National Museum of Natural History, Smithsonian Institution, 1978.

## Part IV. *The Entomologists*

Abbott, Mabel. *Life of William T. Davis.* Ithaca, N.Y.: Cornell University Press, 1949.

Cushman, R. A., and Louise M. Russell. "Grace A. Sandhouse." *Proceedings of the Entomological Society of Washington* 42 (Dec., 1940): 188.

Eckhardt, George H. "A Woman in a Garden." *Frontiers* 25 (Dec., 1950): 57–58.

Evans, Howard Ensign, and Mary Alice Evans. *William Morton Wheeler, Biologist.* Cambridge, Mass.: Harvard University Press, 1970.

Felt, E. P. "Maria E. Fernald." *Journal of Economic Entomology* 13 (1920): 153.

Fielde, Adele Marion. Letters. Academy of Natural Sciences, Philadelphia, Pa.

Harney, Thomas. *The Magnificent Foragers.* Washington, D.C.: National Museum of Natural History, Smithsonian Institution, 1978.

Lillie, Frank R. *The Woods Hole Marine Biological Laboratory.* Chicago: University of Chicago Press, 1944.

Mallis, Arnold. *American Entomologists.* New Brunswick, N.J.: Rutgers University Press, 1971.

"Mary Esther Murtfeldt." *Journal of Economic Entomology* 6 (April, 1913): 288–89.

Muttkowski, R. A. "George Williams Peckham." *Entomological News* 25 (Apr., 1914): 145–48.

Patch, Edith M. Papers. Raymond H. Fogler Library, University of Maine, Orono, Me.

Peckham, George W., and Elizabeth G. Peckham. *Wasps: Social and Solitary.* Westminster, Eng.: Constable & Co., 1905.

Rau, Phil, and Nellie Rau. *Wasp Studies Afield.* Princeton, N.J.: Princeton University Press, 1918.

## Chapter 15. *Anna B. Comstock*

Comstock, Anna. *The Comstocks of Cornell.* Ithaca, N.Y.: Cornell University Press, 1953.

———— [Marian Lee, pseud.]. *Confessions to a Heathen Idol.* New York: Doubleday & Co., 1906.

————. *Ways of the Six-Footed.* Ithaca, N.Y.: Cornell University Press, 1977.

Comstock, Anna Botsford. *Handbook of Nature Study.* Ithaca, N.Y.: Cornell University Press, 1911.

Comstock, Anna Botsford, and John Henry Comstock.. Papers. Department of Manuscripts and University Archives, Cornell University Library, Ithaca, New York.

Smith, Edward H. "The Comstocks and Cornell: In the People's Service." *Annual Review of Entomology* 21 (1976): 1–25.

## Chapter 16. *Annie Trumbull Slosson*

Davis, William T. "Annie Trumbull Slosson." *Journal of the New York Entomological Society* 34 (Dec., 1926): 361–64.

Edwards, Henry. "New Genera and Species of North American Moths." *Entomologica Americana* 3 (Jan., 1888): 181–85.

Leng, Charles W. "History of the New York Entomological Society." *Journal of the New York Entomological Society* 26 (Sept.–Dec., 1918): 129–33.

Osborn, Herbert. *Fragments of Entomological History.* Columbus, Ohio: Herbert Osborn, 1937.

[Skinner, Henry]. "A Loved and Respected Entomologist." *Entomological News* 30 (Dec., 1919): 300.

Slosson, Annie Trumbull. "Coleoptera of Lake Worth, Florida." *Canadian Entomologist* 27 (1895): 9–10.

———. "Collecting at Lake Worth, Florida." *Entomological News* 6 (May, 1895): 133–36.

———. "Collecting on Biscayne Bay." *Entomological News* 10 (Apr., 1899): 94–96.

———. "Collecting on Biscayne Bay, Part II. *Entomological News* 10 (May, 1899): 124–26.

———. "Collecting on Mt. Washington, Part I." *Entomological News* 4 (Oct., 1893): 249–52.

———. "Collecting on Mt. Washington, Part II." *Entomological News* 4 (Nov., 1893): 287–92.

———. "Experiences of a Collector." *Bulletin of the Brooklyn Entomological Society* 12 (Apr., 1917): 25–29.

———. "A Few Memories." *Journal of the New York Entomological Society* 23 (June, 1915): 85–91.

———. Letters to Philip Powell Calvert and Henry Skinner. Library of the Academy of Natural Sciences, Philadelphia, Pa.

———. Letters to William T. Davis. Staten Island Institute of Arts and Sciences, Staten Island, N.Y.

———. "May Moths in Northern New Hampshire." *Entomological News* 1 (Feb., 1890): 2–19.

———. "Winter Collecting in Florida, Part I." *Entomological News* 1 (June, 1890): 81–83.

———. "Winter Collecting in Florida, Part II." *Entomological News* 1 (Sept., 1890): 101–102.

## Chapter 17. *Edith Patch*

Adams, J. B., and G. W. Simpson. "Edith Marion Patch." *Annals Entomological Society of America* 48 (1955): 313–14.

Brockway, P. J. "Dr. Patch of America." *Maine Alumnus* 18 (Apr., 1937): 5–11.

Gibbes, Elizabeth. Interview with author. Orono, Me., Nov. 18, 1986.

Mallis, Arnold. *American Entomologists.* New Brunswick, N.J.: Rutgers University Press, 1971.

Olson, Cheryl. "Edith Patch: Receiving Credits Long Past Due." *Bangor Daily News*, Sept. 3–4, 1983.

Patch, Edith. Papers. Special Collections Department, Raymond H. Fogler Library, University of Maine, Orono.

————. "Tour to the Entomological Congress." *Journal of Economic Entomology* 31 (Feb. 20, 1939): 775.

## Part V. *The Ornithologists*

Ainley, Marianne Gosztonyi. "The Contribution of the Amateur to North American Ornithology: A Historical Perspective." *Living Bird* 18 (1979–80): 161–71.

————. "Family and/or Field-Work in Science: North American Women Ornithologists, 1900–1950." Simon de Beauvoir Institute, Concordia University, Canada. Photocopy.

————. "Women in North American Ornithology During the Last Century." Paper presented at the First International Congress on the Role of Women in the History of Science, Technology and Medicine, Veszprem, Hungary, Aug. 15–19, 1983.

Brooks, Paul. *Speaking for Nature.* Boston: Houghton Mifflin Co., 1980.

Laskey, Amelia. Papers. Cumberland Science Museum, Nashville, Tenn.

Strom, Deborah, ed. *Birdwatching with American Women.* New York: W. W. Norton and Co., 1986.

## Chapter 18. *Florence Merriam Bailey*

Bailey, Florence Merriam. "Birds of the Humid Coast, Part I." *Condor* 19 (Jan., 1917): 8–54.

————. "Birds of the Humid Coast, Part II." *Condor* 19 (May, 1917): 95–101.

————. "A Drop of Four Thousand Feet." *Auk* 28 (Apr., 1911): 219–25.

————. "Meeting Spring Half Way, Part I." *Condor* 18 (July, 1916): 151–55.

————. "Meeting Spring Half Way, Part II." *Condor* 18 (Sept., 1916): 183–90.

————. "Meeting Spring Half Way, Part III." *Condor* 18 (Nov., 1916): 214–19.

————. "Notable Migrants Not Seen at Our Arizona Bird Table." *Auk* 40 (July, 1923): 393–409.

————. Papers. Smith College Archives. Northampton, Mass.

Horner, Elizabeth B., and Keith B. Sterling. "Feathers and Feminism in the 'Eighties.'" *Smith Alumnae Quarterly* (Apr., 1975): 19–21.

Kofalk, Harriet. *No Woman Tenderfoot: Florence Merriam Bailey, Pioneer Naturalist.* College Station: Texas A&M University Press, 1989.

Merriam, Florence A. *A-Birding on a Bronco.* Boston: Houghton Mifflin, 1896.

————. *Birds of Village and Field.* Boston: Houghton Mifflin, 1898.

————. *Birds through an Opera Glass.* Boston: Houghton Mifflin, 1889.

————. *My Summer in a Mormon Village.* Boston: Houghton Mifflin, 1894.

Oehser, Paul H. "Florence Merriam Bailey: Friend of Birds." *Nature Magazine* 35 (Mar., 1950): 153–54.

————. "In Memoriam: Florence Merriam Bailey." *Auk* 69 (Jan., 1952): 19–26.

Stone, Witmer. Collection. Library of the Academy of Natural Sciences, Philadelphia, Pa.

### Chapter 19. *Althea Sherman*

Brown, Joseph K. "Althea Sherman." *Iowan* 21 (Spring, 1973): 5–9.

Nice, Margaret Morse. Papers. Department of Manuscripts and University Archives, Cornell University Library, Ithaca, N.Y.

————. "Some Letters of Althea Sherman." *Iowa Bird Life* 22 (1952): 51–55.

Palmer, T. S. "Althea Sherman." *Auk* 64 (Apr., 1947): 348–49.

Sherman, Althea R. "Birds by the Wayside in Egypt and Nubia." *Wilson Bulletin* 27 (September, 1915): 369–93.

————. "Birds by the Wayside in Europe, Asia, and Africa." *Wilson Bulletin* 27 (Mar., 1915): 243–271.

————. *Birds of an Iowa Dooryard.* Boston: Christopher Publishing House, 1952.

————. "Nest Life of the Screech Owl." *Auk* 28 (Apr., 1911): 155–68.

————. Papers. Fred Pierce, Winthrop, Iowa.

————. Papers. State Historical Society of Iowa, Manuscripts, Des Moines, Iowa.

————. Papers and Paintings. Garnavillo Historical Society, Garnavillo, Iowa.

————. "Summer Outings of Bats during Fourteen Seasons." *Journal of Mammalogy* 10 (Nov., 1929): 319–26.

Taylor, Mrs. H. J. "Iowa's Woman Ornithologist Althea Rosina Sherman, 1853–1943." *Iowa Bird Life* 13 (June, 1943): 18–36.

Youngworth, William. "T. C. Stephens—The Complete Birdwatcher, Anecdotes from Other Days." *Iowa Bird Life* 24 (June, 1954): 31–33.

### Chapter 20. *Cordelia Stanwood*

Graham, Frank., Jr. "Squire of Birdsacre." *Audubon* 81 (Nov., 1979): 24, 29.

Hutchinson, Gloria. "Birdsacre." *Down East* 27 (Sept., 1980): 52–59.

Labbie, Edith. "The Lady of 'Birdsacre' Sanctuary." *Lewiston Journal*, Nov. 19, 1977.

Richmond, Chandler. *Beyond the Spring: Cordelia Stanwood of Birds-acre.* Lamoine, Me.: Latona Press, 1978.

Stanwood, Cordelia. "The Hermit Thrush: The Voice of the Northern Woods." *Bird Lore* 12 (May–June, 1910): 100–104.

———. Papers. Stanwood Wildlife Sanctuary. Ellsworth, Me.

## Chapter 21. *Margaret Morse Nice*

Laskey, Amelia. Papers. Cumberland Science Museum, Nashville, Tenn.

Nice, Margaret Morse. Papers. Department of Manuscripts and University Archives, Cornell University Library, Ithaca, N.Y.

———. *Research Is a Passion with Me.* Toronto, Can.: Consolidated Amethyst Communications, 1979.

———. "A Study of the Nesting of Mourning Doves." *Auk* 39 (1922): 457–74.

———. *The Watcher at the Nest.* New York: Macmillan, 1939.

Parkes, Kenneth C. "Margaret Morse Nice." *Wilson Bulletin* 86 (Sept., 1974): 301–302.

Trautman, Milton B. "In Memoriam: Margaret Morse Nice." *Auk* 94 (July, 1977): 430–41.

## Chapter 22. *Amelia Laskey*

Goodpasture, Katharine A. "In Memoriam: Amelia Rudolph Laskey." *Auk* 92 (Apr., 1975): 252–59.

———. Interview with the author, Mar. 13, 1987.

Laskey, Amelia. "Breeding Biology of Mockingbirds." *Auk* 79 (Oct., 1962): 596–606.

———. "Cowbird Behavior." *Wilson Bulletin* 62 (Dec., 1950): 157–74.

———. Papers. Cumberland Science Museum, Nashville, Tenn.

———. "Some Nesting Data on the Carolina Wren at Nashville, Tennessee." *Bird-Banding* 19 (July, 1948): 101–21.

———. "Some Tufted Titmouse Life History." *Bird-Banding* 28 (July, 1957): 135–45.

———. "Watching a Carolina Wren's Nest." *Chicago Naturalist* 9 (1946): 59–62.

## Part VI. *The Ecologists*

Peskin, Perry K. "A Walk through Lucy Braun's Prairie." *Explorer* 20 (Winter, 1978): 15–21.

Stuckey, Ronald L. "E. Lucy Braun (1889–1971), Outstanding Botanist and Conservationist: A Biographical Sketch, with Bibliography." *Michigan Botanist* 12 (Mar., 1973): 83–106.

## Chapter 23. *Ann Haven Morgan*

Alexander, Charles P. "Ann Haven Morgan, 1882–1966." *Eatonia* 8 (Feb. 15, 1967): 1–3.

Morgan, Ann Haven. *Field Book of Animals in Winter*. New York: G. P. Putnam Sons, 1939.

———. *Field Book of Ponds and Streams*. New York: G. P. Putnam Sons, 1930.

———. "Mayflies of Fall Creek." *Annals of the Entomological Society of America* 4 (June, 1911): 93–117.

———. Papers. Williston Memorial Library/Archives, Mt. Holyoke College, South Hadley, Mass.

## Chapter 24. *Carrie Dormon*

Crittenden, Bob. "Miss Caroline's Dream Became Louisiana's National Forest." *Forests and People* 30 (1980): 24–29.

Dormon, Caroline. *Bird Talk*. Baton Rouge: Claitor's Publishing Division, 1969.

———. "Botanical Ramblings." *Louisiana Society for Horticultural Research* 3 (1967): 80–84.

———. *Flowers Native to the Deep South*. Harrisburg, Penn.: Mount Pleasant Press, 1958.

———. *Natives Preferred: Native Trees and Flowers for Every Location*. Baton Rouge: Claitor's Book Store, 1965.

———. Papers. Watson Library, Northwestern State University of Louisiana, Natchitoches, La.

———. Papers and Paintings. Briarwood, Saline, La.

———. *Wild Flowers of Louisiana*. Garden City, N.Y.: Doran and Company, 1934.

Moore, Diane M. *The Adventurous Will: Profiles of Memorable Louisiana Women*. Lafayette, La.: Arcadiana Press, 1984.

Rawson, Donald M. "Caroline Dormon: A Renaissance Spirit of Twentieth-Century Louisiana." *Louisiana History* 24 (1983): 121–39.

Snell, David. "The Green World of Carrie Dormon." *Smithsonian* 2 (Feb., 1972): 28.

## Chapter 25. *Rachel Carson*

Anticaglia, Elizabeth. *Twelve American Women*. Chicago: Nelson-Hall Co., 1975.

Briggs, Shirley. "A Decade after Silent Spring." *Friends Journal* 1 (Mar., 1972): 148–49.

Brooks, Paul. *The House of Life: Rachel Carson at Work*. Boston: Houghton Mifflin Co., 1972.

Carson, Rachel. *The Edge of the Sea.* Boston: Houghton Mifflin Co., 1955.

————. Miscellaneous Papers. Rachel Carson Council Library. Chevy Chase, Md.

————. *The Sea Around Us.* New York: Oxford University Press, 1950.

————. *The Sense of Wonder.* New York: Harper & Row, 1956.

————. *Silent Spring.* Boston: Houghton Mifflin Co., 1962.

————. *Under the Sea Wind.* New York: Oxford University Press, 1941.

Christopher, Barbara. "Rachel Carson, American Author-Biologist." *National Business Woman* 53 (May, 1963): 4–5.

Gartner, Carol. *Rachel Carson.* New York: Frederick Ungar, 1983.

Graham, Frank, Jr. *Since Silent Spring.* Boston: Houghton Mifflin Co., 1970.

Moore, Lillian. "Rachel Carson's 'Silent Spring'—Its Truth Goes Marching On." *Smithsonian* 1 (July, 1970): 4–9.

Seif, Dorothy Thompson. "Letters from Rachel Carson, A Young Scientist Sets Her Course." Typescript.

Sterling, Philip. *Sea and Earth: The Life of Rachel Carson.* New York: Thomas Y. Crowell, 1970.

# Index

Audubon, Victor, 13
*Audubon*, 145, 181, 187
Audubon Medal, 272
Audubon Society, 178, 187, 204, 238,
241, 267
*Auk, The*, 182, 192, 193, 195, 204,
224, 230, 236, 239
Austin, Mary Hunter, 16
Austin, Rebecca, 72–74
Austin, Tex., 116–18

Bachman, Eva, 10
Bachman, Harriet Martin, 9, 10, 13
Bachman, John, 9–10, 13
Bachman's sparrow, 11
Bagg, Helen, 187
Bailey, Florence Merriam, 53, 103,
182, 183, 199, 224, 227, 228; as
A.O.U. fellow, 186, 195; childhood
of, 186; death of, 196; education
of, 187; as field ornithologist, 191–
95; marriage of, 186, 191, 196; as
writer, 188–93, 195, 196
Bailey, Henry T., 213–15
Bailey, Liberty Hyde, 160, 166
Bailey, Vernon, 103, 183, 186, 191–
96, 199
Baird, Spencer Fullerton, 21–22, 23,
24, 37
Baja California, 59–60, 89, 91
Baldwin, Henry, 49
Bandeiro, Maria, 138
Baraboo, Wis., 31, 33, 34, 35
Bard, Samuel, 7
Bartram, John, 7
Bechtel, Ellen, 20, 26
Beckwith, Martha, 50, 54
Beebe, William, 246, 265, 267, 268
*Begonia mexiae*, 106
Behr, Hans Herman, 86, 87
*Belonocnema treatae*, 45
Bent, Arthur Cleveland, 182, 199,
201, 208, 217
Bernard, Vincent, 20
Berry, Will, 156
Bevan, W. C., 67
Biddlecome, Hannah, 76
Big Bend National Park, 65, 118
*Bird-Banding*, 228, 238
*Birdcraft* (Wright, M. O.), 181
*Bird-Lore*, 181, 192, 208, 212, 217, 226

*Birds of America, The* (Audubon,
J. J.), 9, 11
*Birds of Amherst and Vicinity* (Clark,
H. L.), 223
*Birds of an Iowa Dooryard* (Sher-
man, A.), 182, 209
*Birds of Massachusetts* (Forbush,
E. H.), 182, 199, 218
*Birds of New Mexico* (Bailey, F. M.),
186, 195, 196
*Birds of Oklahoma, The* (Nice,
M. M., and L. B. Nice), 226
*Birds of Village and Field* (Bailey,
F. M.), 190–91
*Birds through an Opera Glass*
(Bailey, F. M.), 188–89, 190
*Bird Stories* (Patch, E.), 178
*Bird Talk* (Dormon, C.), 259, 260
Blake, Doris Holmes, 152
Blake, Sidney, 152
Blossomdell, 233
Bodley, Rachel, 24
Boiling Spring, 215
*Book of Naturalists, The* (Beebe,
W.), 265
*Botanical Gazette, The*, 125
*Botanical Journal*, 135
Bowdoin College, 78, 82, 84
Boyd, Louise, 101
Bracelin, N. Floy, 103, 106
Brackenridge Park, 65, 67
Braeside (home of Edith Patch), 178
Brandegee, Kate, xii, xiv, 96; as bota-
nist, 87; childhood of, 86; as collec-
tor, 89–92; death of, 91; education
of, 86; marriage of, 87–88, 91;
"Reminiscences" of, 85
Brandegee, T. S., 85, 87–89, 91, 96
Braun, Annette, 242, 243
Braun, E. Lucy, 242–43
Brewer, T. M., 21, 22
Brewster, William, 188, 195, 209
Brewster Medal, 186, 195
Briarwood, 250, 251, 252, 255, 258,
261
Briggs, Shirley, 267
Britton, Elizabeth Gertrude Knight,
47, 88, 241; as botanist, 124–25,
126, 128, 130; as bryologist, 124,
129, 131; childhood of, 125; educa-
tion of, 125; marriage of, 126, 130;

*Index*

*Women in the Field* was composed into type on a Compugraphic digital phototypesetter in ten and one-half point Palatino with one and one-half points of spacing between the lines. Palatino Italic was selected for display. The book was designed by Jim Billingsley, typeset by Metricomp, Inc., printed offset by Thomson-Shore, Inc., and bound by John H. Dekker & Sons, Inc. The paper on which this book is printed carries acid-free characteristics for an effective life of at least three hundred years.

TEXAS A&M UNIVERSITY PRESS : COLLEGE STATION